THE HOLY LAND

A PILGRIM'S GUIDE TO
ISRAEL, JORDAN AND THE SINAI

THE HOLY LAND

A PILGRIM'S GUIDE TO
ISRAEL, JORDAN AND THE SINAI

G.S.P. Freeman-Grenville

CARTA · JERUSALEM

Acknowledgements
Frontispiece and page 139: Zev Radovan
Page 20: Reuben and Edith Hecht Museum, University of Haifa
All other photographs: Garo Nalbandian
Maps, plans and illustrations: Carta, Jerusalem
Cover design: Mike Horton

ISBN 965 220 334 3

Cover: The Church of the Coenaculum and the Dormition Abbey on Mount Zion
Frontispiece: Khirbet Qumran, where the Dead Sea Scrolls were found

PREFACE

This is a guide for pilgrims to the Holy Land. It is principally concerned with the Gospels and the places where the events of the Redemption took place. It includes an excursion to Jordan, where the ancient Israelites wandered, and one to Sinai, to the mountain where the Ten Commandments were revealed. This is the order observed since the fourth century at least by pilgrims landing at the port of Jaffa, near Ben-Gurion Airport.

After general notes and a historical introduction, the eight itineraries start from Jerusalem, the principal communications centre. Bethlehem and other sites easily accessible from Jerusalem follow, and then we move on to Nazareth and Capernaum in the north. Itinerary 8 (Beersheba and the South) is chiefly of archaeological interest, and not always practicable. In these ways the places associated with the life of Jesus Christ, and the final drama of the Passion, Resurrection and Ascension, are brought together with the earlier history of Israel, which the Fathers saw as the preparation for the Gospel. By definition, a guide book must be easy to carry around: a guide which mentioned every site would be far too heavy.

It is fifty years since the writer first visited what was then Palestine, and parts of Jordan and Lebanon. Great changes have taken place, particularly in population movements. New buildings have sprung up, and a modern road system in Israel and Jordan has replaced what were at best tracks. What was simply tawdry or dirty fifty years ago has now been cleaned up. The great achievement of 1994 was the recovering of the Dome of the Rock with gold plating: one sees it today as majestic as it was when first completed in 691. At the time of writing the three communities responsible for the Holy Sepulchre have agreed to complete the redecoration of the interior of the great dome above the Tomb of Christ. The disfiguring scaffolding will be removed. These are but two examples. Particularly moving is the restoration of the Herodian Pavement in the Via Dolorosa by the Israel Antiquities Authority; this has given us the privilege of treading where Jesus would have trod.

Very many have helped me while this guide was in preparation. My particular thanks are due to the late Fr José Montalverne de Lancastre, OFM; Father Kenneth Campbell, OFM, until recently commissary for the Holy Land in Great Britain; Brother Fabian Adkins, OFM, for many years the chief Latin sacristan of the Holy Sepulchre; Bishop Kuregh Kapikian, in charge of the Armenian excavations in the Holy Sepulchre; George Hintlian, principal secretary to the Armenian patriarch; Isam Awwad, architect in charge of the Dome of the Rock and the Aqsa Mosque; William Lancaster, late director of the British Institute in Amman of Archaeology and History; and Dr R.L. Chapman III, executive secretary of the Palestine Excavation Fund. Also special thanks go to Mr Garo Nalbandian, who was responsible for most of the photographs. Others, too numerous to name, have not less my deepest gratitude.

G.S.P.F.-G.
Sheriff Hutton, York

CONTENTS

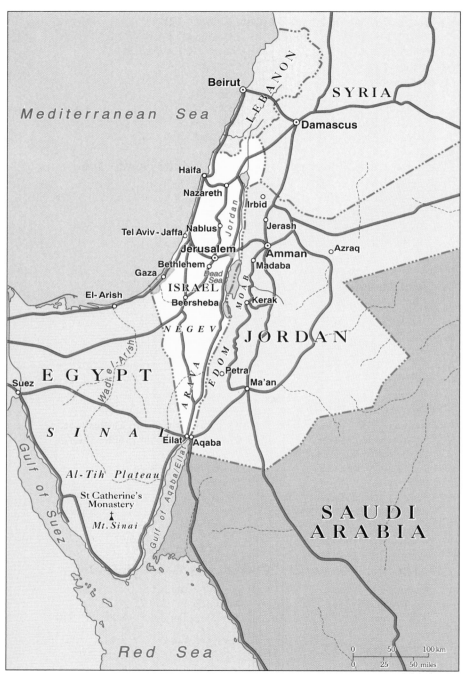

General Introduction

Israel is a land of contrasts, combining both the European traditions of many of its immigrants, and their immemorial national customs, and the culture of both Christian and Muslim Arabs. The prudent visitor will be conscious of the various sensitivities of all. The historical buildings that Christian pilgrims visit are often in Christian or Muslim possession. Generally speaking, churches are open all the hours of daylight, although some open before dawn, and a few close for an afternoon siesta. The Holy Sepulchre is open daily from 5 am to 9 pm (4.30 am to 7 pm in the winter). First Mass is at 5.30 am and High Mass at 7.30 am (4.30 am and 6.30 am respectively in the winter). The Noble Sanctuary, containing the Dome of the Rock and the Aqsa Mosque, as well as other buildings, is open daily from 7.30 am to 11.30 am and from 1.30 pm to 3 pm. All mosques used for public prayers should be avoided between 11.30 am and 12.30 pm, and between 2.45 pm and 3.30 pm. Islamic buildings are closed to non-Muslims on Fridays and festivals.

Synagogues and Yad Vashem (the Holocaust remembrance complex) are closed to visitors at 2 pm on Fridays, and all day on Saturdays and Jewish festivals. Museums and ancient sites under the Israel Antiquities Authority are also shut on Saturdays and Jewish holy days.

Entry to churches is usually free, but it is customary to make a donation. In many cases freewill offerings are the principal support of the church and clergy, and the main source from which to keep buildings in repair. The Dome of the Rock, the Aqsa Mosque, and other public monuments and museums in the care of the Antiquities Authority charge visitors for entry. Tickets are always given as receipts, and any attempt to obtain money without offering a ticket should be discountenanced. Prices and opening times in this guide are correct at the time of writing.

Dress should be fairly conservative. When visiting the Holy Places, men are advised not to wear shorts, and women not to wear trousers, or sleeveless dresses or blouses. It is a courtesy if women cover their heads, as is the local Christian custom. In the Holy Sepulchre Jews will be seen from time to time with their heads covered, an act of religious courtesy as they would do in a synagogue. In the very conservative Jewish quarter of Me'a She'arim public notices request both men and women to wear head coverings and modest dress.

There can be a 40° Fahrenheit (5° Celsius) difference in temperature between Jerusalem and Jericho. In winter it can be wet and windy, but snow is not common, and seldom lies for long. The winters in Jordan are more severe than in Israel. The coastal zone, however, is relatively mild. It is recommended to wear layers of clothing which can be removed or replaced at will.

It is sensible to have a cardigan handy, for the unheated stone buildings can be chilly even in summer. In a few churches overdresses are kept by the doorkeepers for women who are not acceptably dressed, but their provision cannot be relied on. In all mosques used for prayer both men and women must remove their shoes before entering. The reason is not religious, but simply to keep the mats or carpets clean. In any building in Muslim possession it is regarded as offensive for a non-Muslim to display any overt sign of prayer, and it can be dangerous to do so.

The minaret of the Omar Mosque (left) and the Church of the Holy Sepulchre, Jerusalem

Wheeled transport is impossible in most of the Old City, but do watch out for small carts and laden donkeys; it is easy to get hurt. Strong shoes are advisable.

Outside the Old City, opposite Damascus Gate, there are frequent and very cheap bus services to other parts of the country. Jordan also has a highly developed bus and coach service. It is also possible to hire a self-drive car. Information about such a service is easily obtained from hotels and hospices; it is also available at the Christian Information Centre (02-272692) in Jerusalem.

There are numerous taxis for hire: insist the driver uses the meter or agree on the fare beforehand (the latter is essential on a long journey). It is wise to make the arrangement through a hotel or other agency, before a witness in any case of doubt.

Persons visiting desert areas should always carry drinking water with them. Those without desert experience should under no circumstance go out without at least one experienced companion. On such occasions the hotel receptionist, or some other reliable person, should always be told where one is going, and the expected time of return.

Antiquities are defined by law in Israel as any object made before AD 1700. They may only be taken out of Israel with a written export permit from the Israel Antiquities Authority, at the Rockefeller Museum, Jerusalem, on production of a receipt from the vendor. The fee is ten percent of the purchase price. Numerous fakes are on display in the shops, and it is imprudent to buy antiquities, or for that matter carpets, without independent expert advice.

CALENDAR

For civil purposes both Israel and Jordan observe the Gregorian (or western Christian) Calendar. For religious purposes Israel observes the Hebrew Calendar, a lunar calendar which to a great extent is brought into relation with the Gregorian Calendar by leap years. For religious purposes Muslims in Israel and Jordan observe the Islamic Calendar of 354 days, with 355 days known as *kabisa* in irregularly distributed leap years (details of this system are available in G.S.P. Freeman-Grenville, *Islamic and Christian Calendars*, Garnet Press, UK, 1995). For any certainty within these systems consult a local diary. For religious purposes Catholics and Protestants use the Gregorian Calendar; the Greek Orthodox and other Oriental Churches adhere to the unreformed Julian Calendar instituted in 46 BC by Julius Caesar. The Julian Calendar is currently thirteen days behind the Gregorian Calendar.

The Hebrew and Islamic calendars both reckon the day from sundown to sundown, and not from midnight to midnight as in the Gregorian and Julian calendars. Respectively, Saturdays and Fridays are weekly holidays.

CHURCH SERVICES
At the Christian Information Centre (Tel: 02-272692; by Jaffa Gate, the Old City, Jerusalem), lists of church services with times for Catholics, Orthodox, and Protestants are available.

Mass arrangements for the Jerusalem and Bethlehem areas can be made at the Franciscan Pilgrim Office, PO Box 186, Jerusalem 9100. Tel: 02-272697.

Anglicans can celebrate in the Chapel of St Abraham adjacent to Calvary, which is accessible through the Greek monastery, on the recommendation of the Anglican bishop to the Greek Orthodox patriarch.

CURRENCY
In Israel the currency recommended by banks is the US dollar or the British pound, which are easily converted into Israeli shekels. The exchange rate varies from time to time, and it is wise to inquire where the best rate may be obtained. Likewise in Egypt, US dollars are preferred. In Jordan, English travellers' cheques are best changed in a bank. The export of Israeli and Jordanian currencies is forbidden.

PALESTINIAN SELF-RULE AREAS
The areas under Palestinian self-rule around Jericho and the Gaza Strip should not be visited by foreigners without first consulting their consulate, who can advise on the current situation.

MAPS
Carta publishes a wide variety of road maps and guides, as well as detailed city maps of Jerusalem, Haifa and Tel Aviv. Survey of Israel maps are available at most bookshops, and the Egged Bus Company publishes a number of city maps, available at bus stations, of bus routes superimposed on the street plan.

In Jordan, the Royal Geographical Society publishes a wide range of town plans. There is much road building, and these and other maps become rapidly out of date. Bartholemew's *Israel with Jordan: World Travel Map*, 1992, is the most reliable. The Antiquities Maps of Jordan are out-of-print and out-of-date, but use can be made of the antiquities maps in the *New Encyclopedia of Archaeological Excavations in the Holy Land*, Simon & Schuster, New York, and Carta, Jerusalem, 1993.

For Sinai, in Egypt, the Survey of Israel map, *South Sinai: Map of Attractions, 1:250,000*, 1994 (obtainable from branches of Steimatzky, Israel, and from Stanfords, 12–14 Long Acre, London), is invaluable. It gives details of a number of travel agents in Egypt, Tel Aviv and London who organize tours to Sinai, and of numerous hotels, holiday villages and diving clubs in the area.

VISAS

All foreigners require a visa to enter Egypt and Jordan (these may be obtained, for a fee, at the appropriate consulate or embassy), but no visa is needed to enter Israel. There are also border taxes to be paid on leaving both Israel and Egypt.

PLAN OF VISIT

Although Israel is not a big country, and although it is feasible to cover itineraries 1 to 8 in about ten days, to get the most out of the many sites on offer it is best to take it slower and to be selective.

Due to the distances involved and the slowness of movement, Itinerary 9 requires a minimum of three to four days, including a six-hour visit to Petra. Two further days should be allowed for a visit to Sinai, Itinerary 10.

One is often asked how best to spend a few hours, or a single day, in Jerusalem. Enter the Old City by Damascus Gate, and walk to the Via Dolorosa, and then up to the Holy Sepulchre, before proceeding to the Haram al-Sharif, the Noble Sanctuary of both the Dome of the Rock and the Aqsa Mosque. Walk across the courtyard to the far side, from where both Gethsemane and the Mount of Olives can be clearly seen. Leave the Old City by the Jaffa Gate, where there are almost always taxis waiting, and drive round the western part of the city.

Historical Introduction

The Holy Land of the Bible comprised the present state of Israel and the remainder of the former United Nations Trust Territory of Palestine, which has been administered by Israel as occupied territory since 1967, along with present-day Jordan, parts of Syria and the parts of Sinai ruled by Egypt. It now includes areas under Palestinian self-rule. The whole area is a bridge of fertile land between the land masses of Africa and Asia, bounded on the east by steppe and desert and on the west by the Mediterranean. For many thousands of years it has served as a passage: between southern Arabia and Asia, between Egypt and Syria, with land communications that stretch from the Mediterranean to China. It has thus been the theatre of constant human migrations, wars, and conquests. Only the briefest outline of its long and complex history is possible here.

STONE AGE: 1,200,000–4500 BC

The earliest remains of man in Galilee are dated to c.600,000 BC. Until c.17,000 BC man was a hunter of animals and a gatherer of plants, following animals as they sought water, with no tools except hand axes, scrapers and knives of flint and basalt. Between c.17,000 and 8500 BC nomadic hunters and gatherers began to settle, and build tent-like houses. Between c.8500 and 5500 BC cereal agriculture, the domestication of peas and lentils, and goat-herding produced a population explosion; at Jericho stone walls and towers were built for defence, and houses built of stone with plastered floors. From this time also the first signs of the evolution of religion are evident, of statuettes, busts and skulls reshaped with plaster. In the eastern steppe and desert, hunting and gathering continued in family groups. In c.5500 BC the first pottery was made, a storage revolution in replacing stone vessels.

In the fertile oasis town of Jericho, now under Palestinian self-rule

COPPER AND BRONZE AGES: 4500–1200 BC

In c.4500 BC copper smelting was introduced, but the new axes, arrowheads and hooks only slowly ousted flint and basalt. Cultivation became more intensive, now including wheat, barley, dates, lentils, and olives. Tuleilat al-Ghassul, in Jordan, is the prime example of a Chalcolithic town, built of sun-dried mud bricks, often on stone foundations, and with ample courtyards. Some houses were painted in brilliant colours.

The development of religion is evidenced by the growth of necropolises, veritable cities of the dead. At Jawa in Jordan the first known reservoirs were built. For some unknown reason the earliest towns were abandoned or destroyed between

Remains of the City of David, Jerusalem

2700 and 2300 BC, the people reverting to nomadism. Between c.1950 and 1550 BC new fortified sites were built at Irbid, Amman, Pella and Jericho. Tin was now mixed with copper, thus making a more durable metal, and the potter's wheel replaced the making of pottery by hand.

In c.1800 BC a group of nomadic herdsmen, 318 fighting men together with their families, migrated from Ur in Chaldaea (which was situated in the present-day Iraq) to Hebron. Here, as is told in Genesis, begins the history of God's revelation to Abraham, who is regarded by both Jews and Arabs alike as their forefather, and by Christians as their spiritual forefather. In c.1500 BC the descendants of these families migrated to Egypt because of a famine, settling on the eastern side of the Nile Delta.

Pharaoh Thutmose III (1479–1425 BC) conquered Palestine, Jordan and parts of Syria in sixteen campaigns, and held the major towns with Egyptian governors. From this point on until c.1200 BC Egypt dominated the region, fighting off Mitanni and Hittites in the north. There began a period of peaceful international trade throughout the Aegean Sea, the Mediterranean and the east, brought to an end with the advent of the so-called Sea Peoples, of whom the Philistines were one.

In c.1230 BC, coincidental with the arrival of the Philistines in Palestine — to which they gave their name — the Israelites began to move back whence their forefathers had come. The nature of their migration has been much disputed, but most probably followed two general routes. Of these, one seems to have travelled along the coast, while the other followed a circuitous route through the Sinai desert and then northward up through Jordan. Because of limited water supplies it is not likely that they could have moved in large parties.

IRON AGE: 1200–586 BC

The returning Israelites were very loosely organized under tribal leaders. The 'judges', from among whom war leaders emerged, had primarily been settlers of tribal disputes. The Philistines and the native Canaanites had a cultural superiority in their knowledge of the use of iron and of chariots. These factors forced the Israelites to unite under a king, Saul (c.1020–1000 BC), and to learn a new art of war from their enemies. The process was one of infiltration rather than outright conquest, and it was not until the eleventh century BC that Israelite ascendancy was wholly established. The second king, David (c.1000–961 BC), consolidated the new system, first at the historic stronghold of Hebron, then by seizing Jerusalem, which was controlled by the small tribe of the Jebusites and was thus neutral territory. He was able to make it the religious as well as the civil capital by bringing there the Ark of the Covenant with the Tablets of Stone, the Ten Commandments. Political unity now had the sanction of religion.

Under his son Solomon (961–922 BC), trade with neighbouring countries greatly increased. Across the Jordan River, individual city-states gave way to the kingdoms of Ammon, Moab and Edom, the latter rich in copper mines. North of Amman the trade route from Arabia passed through and enriched Damascus. North of Solomon's kingdom Hiram, the king of Tyre, had far-reaching trade connections with the Mediterranean, and provided Solomon with skilled workmen, sailors and shipbuilders, who built his Temple and founded his trading fleet.

The visit of the Queen of Sheba (properly Saba, now Shabwa in Yemen), which controlled the incense routes and the trading ports on the Indian Ocean, together with Solomon's marriage to Pharaoh's daughter, indicate his prestige and standing as a monarch. For this Israel had to pay, and heavy taxation and overstrict control caused his kingdom to break apart after his death. From then on there were two Israelite kingdoms, Israel in the north, with capitals in or near Samaria; and Judah in the south, with Jerusalem as capital. In both kingdoms prophets arose, crying out against injustice to the poor and demanding purity of religion as the guarantee of political good faith. No less than with other monarchies, the history of the kings of Judah and Israel is marred by crimes of ambition and jealousy, and equally adorned by men of prudence and eminent virtue. The moral teachings of the prophets taught standards unique in their contemporary world and are no less valid today after nearly three thousand years.

The wealth of these small kingdoms made them targets for raids and conquests. The rise of Assyria, in northern Mesopotamia, brought them to an end. Damascus was taken in 732 BC, and Samaria in 721. In spite of the prophet Isaiah's warning that alliance with Egypt was political suicide, Hezekiah joined it against Assyria. When Sennacherib of Assyria attacked Judah in 688, Hezekiah escaped only because the invaders were crippled with plague. It seemed like divine intervention, but Manasseh, his son, was forced to make peace, virtually ceding the independence of Judah, which it regained only in 629/8 BC. Similarly, after 721, Ammon, Moab and Edom had bought off the Assyrians with tribute. This was a peak of prosperity for Bozrah, modern Buseirah, beyond the Jordanian border in Syria.

The Assyrian Empire ended when Nineveh fell to the Chaldaean kings of Babylon, in alliance with the Medes of Persia, in 612 BC. Nebuchadnezzar overcame Egypt in 605 BC, and made Jerusalem a tributary in 604. The Jews, however, were not so easily put down. In 597, after a siege, Jerusalem surrendered to Babylon, and 3,000 Jews were deported. There were further revolts in 595/4. In 588 Nebuchadnezzar began his siege of Jerusalem. In 586 the city fell, and was sacked. The prophets cursed Ammon, Moab and Edom for rejoicing, and accused the Edomites of burning the Temple. Many citizens were deported at the time, and yet more in 582.

UNDER PERSIA: 538–332 BC

In a reign of nearly a generation (559–530 BC), Cyrus II the Great of Persia conquered almost all the Middle East from the eastern borders of Afghanistan to Asia Minor, and south from Syria to Egypt. There were frequent conflicts also with the Greek states of Athens and Sparta. It was the largest empire the Middle East had yet seen, and so vast and ramshackle an institution could only be held together by a tolerant and moderate government. It was divided into provinces under satraps, local governors. A decree, issued by Cyrus in 538, enabled the Jews to return to rebuild Jerusalem, and to repopulate their homeland. Not all, however, desired to return, and a major colony was established in Babylonia, later based in Baghdad, which lasted until 1947.

If exile had destroyed the Jewish polities, it nevertheless strengthened Jewish unity in religion. The rebuilt Temple provided a focus for religion and sacrifice, and domestic and synagogue rituals began to emerge slowly in a system separate from the Temple ritual. Exile likewise had a linguistic effect: the Persian administration used Aramaic as its official language, and it is from this period onward that the Hebrew language slowly declined and eventually disappeared as a spoken tongue, other than for liturgical purposes. By slow degrees, the rabbi would replace the priest.

In Ammon the Ammonites enjoyed an equal freedom, with Tobiah as governor. The Book of Nehemiah records that, in accord with ancient enmity, he tried to hinder the rebuilding of the Jerusalem Temple. Moab and Edom, later to be known as Idumaea, likewise had a quasi-independence within the empire. It all fell to Alexander the Great after April 330 BC.

Alexander the Great (from a mosaic found at Pompeii)

ALEXANDER AND HIS SUCCESSORS: 332–63 BC

Alexander the Great's career of world conquest began on the Danube River in 335 BC, and ended with his death at Susa in Persia in June 323. At the time of his death he controlled a vast area from eastern Europe to India, the Levant, Egypt and Libya. His early death, and that his only son was an imbecile, led to the break-up of his empire among his generals.

Ptolemy, the commander in Egypt, seized it and Syria, and founded a dynasty based on Alexandria, Alexander's own foundation. In 315 he lost Syria to Seleucus, the commander at Antioch, except for Palestine. This his successors held until 200 BC, when the Seleucid Antiochus III retook it.

New Hellenistic cities were founded in Jordan, such as Gadara (Umm Qais); Amman became Philadelphia, and Jerash became Antioch. The official language both in Jordan and Palestine was Greek, Aramaic lingering only as a spoken language. In Jordan, the finest surviving monuments are Iraq al-Amir and Qasr al-Abd (see Itinerary 9). In Palestine, centralization of worship at the Temple in Jerusalem and foreign political control in the secular sphere gave the high priest a new importance. Primarily a religious dignitary, he now emerged as the political leader of the nation.

The Seleucid Antiochus IV Epiphanes initiated a policy of Hellenization in Palestine as much as elsewhere, and in 169 BC the Jewish Temple was plundered. Two years later the city of Jerusalem itself was sacked. The actual cause of the struggle was the nomination of a Hellenizing high priest who was not of the traditional Zadokite family. This led to a revolt which was headed by the Maccabee brothers. In 164 they regained control of Jerusalem, and in 161 they made a treaty

Some of the finest remains in Jordan are to be found at Iraq al-Amir

with Rome. Their Hasmonean dynasty controlled all Palestine, the Golan, or Gaulanitis, in Syria, and much of what is now ruled over by Jordan, almost the area of the kingdom of David and Solomon.

UNDER ROME AND BYZANTIUM: 63 BC–AD 636

The Hasmonean kingdom broke up in the first century BC. In 90 BC the Pharisees rebelled against Alexander Jannaeus; in the same year he was defeated by Obidath, the Arab king of Nabataea on the east side of the Jordan.

The Nabataeans were originally Arabian herdsmen who became merchants, controlling the major trade routes from southern Arabia. Their tentacles reached beyond Egypt to Greece and Rome, and even, through Syria, to India and the Far East. They traded in gold and ivory, in spices, sugar and frankincense, as well as in perfumes and medicines, iron and copper, animals and textiles. In addition they were also expert water engineers, and their canals and dams led to an increase in agricultural productivity. In Jordan their most famous cities were Petra, Khirbet et-Tannur, Lehun and Wadi Rum; there were other Nabataean cities in the Negev and at Madain Saleh in the present Saudi Arabia. The peak of their prosperity was under Aretas IV (9 BC–AD 40), coterminous almost with the life of Jesus; in their temples they worshipped a male god, Dushtara, and his female consort Allat, who later emerges spiritually transformed as Allah.

Obidath's successor, al-Harith (Aretas) III (87–62 BC), repeatedly defeated the Jewish army, and besieged Jerusalem. In 64, because of the unrest throughout the Middle East and the consequent interruption of trade, Pompey came to restore order. He besieged Jerusalem in 63, and took it after a three-month siege. A general settlement followed, but in 57–55 there was a further Jewish revolt.

The Romans preferred indirect to direct rule. Tools lay ready in the Idumaean, or Edomite, family of Herod the Great. He and his sons ruled until AD 6 almost as

The superb façade of the Khazneh, the Treasury, at Petra

independent rulers. In that year final authority was given to a procurator, with headquarters at Caesarea. Pontius Pilate held this office from AD 26 to 37, with members of the Herodian dynasty under him. The ministry of Jesus took place during this period, but from a Roman point of view, it was one incident among many of Jewish unrest. A general rebellion broke out in AD 40, when Caligula ordered his statue to be erected in Jerusalem. Matters were made worse under the repressive and corrupt rule of Claudius Felix, governor from 52 to 61. The finale came in 66, when the Gentiles of Caesarea massacred the Jews. The Zealots rose in Jerusalem and murdered the Roman garrison. The rebellion spread throughout Judaea, Galilee, and across the Jordan.

The emperor Vespasian on a gold coin minted in Rome in honour of the Roman victory over Judaea

In 67, Emperor Nero sent Vespasian, and his son Titus, together with 60,000 men and Arab auxiliaries, to put down the rebellion. Having regained Transjordan and encircled Judaea, Vespasian was then proclaimed emperor. His son took Jerusalem after a six-month siege. The Christians had fled across the Jordan, to Pella. All survivors in the city were sold into slavery. The Sanhedrin was abolished and the Temple utterly destroyed, as Jesus had predicted. To re-build it was forbidden. Henceforward Jews were forbidden to proselytize and they were subjected to a special tax. It was at this period that Jewish colonies spread to Arabia and became firmly established in the trading cities. In religion there was an end to the sacrificial rites that were bound up with Temple worship; the priest ceded to the rabbi the leadership of a community that was bound together by the Torah. In 73, Masada, the last Jewish stronghold, fell; its defenders committed suicide rather than surrender to the Romans.

Jewish nationalism was not extinguished. A second revolt in 132–135 was precipitated when the emperor Hadrian determined to erect a statue of Jupiter Capitolinus on the Temple site, together with one of himself. Between 132 and 134, fifty fortresses were razed, 455 villages destroyed, and 585,000 Jews killed. Above the Tomb of Christ a temple was built in honour of Jupiter, with a shrine in honour of Venus on Calvary. In Bethlehem the Cave of the Nativity was covered by a shrine in honour of Venus and Adonis. The *favissae*, or rooms for the disposal of the remains of sacrifices and of incense, still exist underground at all three sites. As for the Jews, they were permitted to visit Jerusalem once each year. The Holy City was, for the time being, nothing but a Roman garrison town.

Across the Jordan the Ten Cities, or Decapolis, flourished in the north. In the south the Nabataeans remained independent until 106, when the emperor Trajan annexed their kingdom, making it part of the Roman Province of Arabia. However, they failed to overcome the desert tribes or to penetrate the south. Jerash (Gerasa) expanded during this period, and became a typical Roman provincial city of the time, with temples, theatres, a gymnasium and colonnaded streets. It developed particularly after Hadrian's visit in 130. In Amman little is left except for the centre, but at Gadara (Umm Qais) and elsewhere much of the imperial splendour remains.

The move of the imperial capital from Rome to Constantinople had no particular significance either for Palestine or across the Jordan. However, Emperor Constantine's decision in 313 to make Christianity a licit religion was of permanent

Remains of the Roman forum at Jerash, on the eastern side of the Jordan River

consequence. Following the Council of Nicaea in 325, at which more than 300 bishops took part, from cities as far apart as York in Britain and Sana'a in Yemen, Jerusalem became a focal point for the Christian world. Already in the second century devout men had come to tread in the steps of Jesus and the prophets who had foretold him. The Holy Places in Jerusalem and Bethlehem, sites long known to local Christians, and authenticated by Hadrian's pagan shrines, now had great basilicas erected at imperial expense. The emperor attended the consecration of the Basilica of the Holy Sepulchre in person, and pilgrims began to flock to the Holy Land. Monasteries sprang up everywhere, having originated in the middle of the third century in Egypt.

In the Holy Places an elaborate commemorative liturgy developed, of which we know from St Cyril of Jerusalem in the mid-fourth century, and in detail from a pilgrim nun, Egeria, c.384, from Galicia in the far west of Spain. Today archaeology is still unfolding the story of the expansion of Christianity. By the fifth century the Christian community in Jordan, and especially that living in the Madaba region, was prosperous enough to afford the most splendid mosaics in churches, monasteries, and even private houses. In this sphere, more is known of the Christians across the Jordan River than in Byzantine Palestine. It was a time of peace, and before the Persian invasion of 614–629, when Chosroes II of Persia carried off the Wood of the Cross to Ctesiphon, the only incident of violence was the Samaritan revolt of 529. It was a halcyon period that was not to last.

UNDER THE ARABS AND TULUNIDS: AD 636–969

Far away to the south a movement was beginning which was to evolve and give a new twist to the tangled skein of human history. Born about 570, the Prophet Muhammad began to teach in Mecca c.610, in response to what he claimed was a direct personal revelation from God. Arab authors claim that the Zamzam Well in Mecca had given water to Hagar and Ishmael, and that the black meteorite, the Black Stone preserved in the Kaaba, had been given to Ishmael by the angel Gabriel, who had instructed him in the ceremonies of pilgrimage. In this sanctuary some 300 deities were worshipped, with Allah as the supreme god. Muhammad proclaimed that there was one God, and one alone, and that this was the true religion revealed to Abraham. This, he claimed, both Jews and Christians had distorted. In sober fact, his teaching had much in common with what both Jews and Christians taught. Here he taught until 622, when his friends in Medina invited him to the city of Yathrib, now henceforward al-Madina, the City of the Prophet. From having been a teacher in Mecca, he now emerged as a ruler and lawgiver. In 630 he made the pilgrimage to Mecca in the form that veritable millions of Muslims have since undertaken; it was the beginning of the unification of the Arabs in the peninsula. He returned again on pilgrimage in 632, and died quite suddenly in the June of that year, three months after his return to Medina.

Under the caliphs (literally, the successors of Muhammad), there began a period of Arab conquest that was to reach from Egypt to the Atlantic, and through Syria to Iraq and Persia. In Syria the Arabs defeated the Byzantines in the Yarmuk Valley in 636, and Palestine and Syria fell into Muslim hands. Jerusalem fell two years later, and Caliph Omar came to visit the city. It was sacred to Muslims because of its connections with Abraham and the Prophets, and because it was from Mount Moriah that Muhammad was believed to have ascended in his mystical night journey to heaven.

Omar respected the Christian Holy Places, only building a mosque that has long since disappeared, probably on the site of the Aqsa Mosque. At the end of the century, when there was a rival caliph in Mecca, Caliph Abd al-Malik ibn Marwan erected on the summit of Mount Moriah the Dome of the Rock. For some authors the object was to replace the pilgrimage to Mecca with one to Jerusalem. The Sakhra (rock) was claimed to be that on which Solomon's Temple had been built; the cave underneath was almost certainly its *favissa*. Not less significant was that the plan of the Dome of the Rock imitated the rotunda round the Tomb of Christ in the Holy Sepulchre, and that the inscriptions within the dome were chosen from the Qur'an because they denied the Sonship and Godhead of Jesus Christ. If not the most beautiful, certainly it is among the greatest artistic achievements of man.

After being subject to a series of Arab governors, Palestine, within the Province of Syria, fell to the usurping Tulunid dynasty of Egypt from 870–905, and was then once again under Arab governors until 969. Jerusalem remained a centre of Muslim pilgrimage, third only to Mecca and Medina. For Christians and Jews the only penalty was the payment of a poll tax from which Muslims were exempt.

During this period, in the reign of Charlemagne in Aachen (771–814), and particularly during the reign of Harun al-Rashid as caliph (786–809), there were active relations between East and West. Embassies came and went between the two rulers. In the vicinity of the Holy Sepulchre a hostel for pilgrims and a church for the Latin rite, St Mary la Latine, were built, evidence of accommodation between West and East, and of Islam with Christianity.

UNDER THE FATIMIDS: 969–1099

In 909 the Aghlabid dynasty in Morocco was overthrown in Kairouan by one Sa'id b. al-Husayn, who claimed descent from Fatima, the daughter of Muhammad, and her husband Ali. Sa'id and his successors established a dynasty which is known as Fatimid, the only major Shi'ite dynasty in Islam. By 969 the Fatimid armies had carved out an empire which stretched from the Atlantic to the Nile, and beyond, in 988, as far as Aleppo in northern Syria. For Christians and Jews this was a peaceful enough change, for the new rulers were tolerant in matters of religion.

In 1009 Caliph al-Hakim (996–1021), a megalomaniac, began a persecution that embraced Christians, Jews, and his fellow-Muslims with impartial venom. Commerce was forbidden except by night, and women forbidden to walk abroad. Even the making of women's shoes was forbidden. In 1009 he ordered the destruction of the Holy Sepulchre, and it was razed to the ground. In 1020 al-Hakim declared himself divine, a claim that gave birth to the Druze sect. In the following year he set out by night, as was his custom, on his donkey on the Moqattam Hill above Cairo. He was never seen again, nor was any trace of him found.

His son and successor, al-Zahir (1021–1035), gave permission for the rebuilding of the Basilica of the Holy Sepulchre, but lack of funds delayed this being carried out until 1042–1048. In 1070 the Seljuq Turks, who had been penetrating steadily from inner Asia, took Jerusalem. The chaos and lack of security that they caused throughout the Middle East halted the long-established custom of pilgrimage to the Holy Places, and this eventually led to the Crusades, preached for the first time by Pope Urban II at the Council of Clermont, 17 November 1095. In doing so, he unleashed the pent-up energy and enthusiasm of Europe. Although in 1099 the Fatimids recovered Jerusalem from the Seljuqs, nothing could stop the Crusaders. On 15 July 1099 the city fell to Geoffrey de Bouillon, and he was installed as 'baron and defender of the Holy Sepulchre', disdaining the royal title.

The Horns of Hittin in the Galilee, where Saladin destroyed the Crusader army in 1187

UNDER THE CRUSADERS: 1099–1291

The Crusader's first act was to massacre all the Muslim inhabitants; by this act of cruelty they drove a wedge of hatred between Islam and Christianity. The Jews of Jerusalem, who had fled to their synagogue, were held to have abetted the Muslims. There, to the horror of many Christians, they were burnt alive. Greek Christians had fled, and although the intent had been to restore Byzantine rule to the territory, what was largely a French dominated state resulted. Crusader rule was efficient, and the country prospered under feudal rule. This did nothing to allay Muslim enmity, and they set about reconquering the land. The turning-point was reached after nearly a century. On 3–4 July 1187 Saladin destroyed the Crusader army at the Horns of Hittin; Guy de Lusignan, the king of Jerusalem, was taken prisoner. Jerusalem surrendered on 2 October. A century of intermittent fighting followed.

In 1250 Saladin's Ayyubid dynasty gave way to the Bahri Mamluks, Turks or Greeks that Saladin himself had originally introduced into Egypt as a slave bodyguard. Much of Syria was taken by the Mongol Hulagu Khan in 1260, but on 3 September the Mamluks under Baybars I, sultan of Egypt 1260–1277, defeated the Mongols decisively at Ain Jalut. He had no respect for Christians or Crusaders, and Nazareth and its churches were destroyed. Fighting continued off and on for a generation, and the last Crusader stronghold of Acre (Akko) was taken in 1291.

THE MAMLUKS AND OTTOMAN TURKS: 1299–1917

Under the Mamluk sultans of Egypt, Syria was a frequent battleground. Jerusalem, off the main route of the armies, became a backwater, although it continued to attract Christian pilgrims, and accounts of their travels are numerous. The pilgrims came not only from the Mediterranean area, but from as far north as Iceland and

Bethlehem in the nineteenth century, during the reign of the Turkish sultan Abdul Hamid

Norway, as well as from Russia. Unlike Cairo, which now became the intellectual centre of the Islamic world, Jerusalem never developed as a centre of culture. Even after the Ottoman Turkish conquest of Jerusalem in 1516 and of Cairo in 1517, Cairo remained the Islamic Athens. In 1333 the Franciscan Order became established in Jerusalem, with the duty of caring for the Holy Places and for pilgrims, duties they have faithfully performed ever since, in spite of opposition and sometimes murder.

As for the Ottoman Turks, the pashas sent to govern the Turkish provinces were political bloodsuckers, capricious and self-seeking. Their administration was largely in Greek hands, or that of Greek converts to Islam. In this way in the eighteenth century the Greek Orthodox gradually regained the hegemony that Greek speakers had enjoyed in the earliest times of Christianity.

Under the Ottomans, the whole empire was sunk in apathy and decline. Many travellers have written accounts of their times. Towards the end of the period refugees began to seek refuge in Palestine, mainly Jews fleeing persecution in Europe, but also Christians from Russia. Small Russian colonies are to be found today in Jordan, mostly Circassian. The Ottomans ruled the area from Salt, which even today preserves the appearance of an old-fashioned Turkish provincial town. In 1912 it had a population of some 15,000. Ordinary market-towns, such as Jerash (1,500 people) and Madaba (2,350), were little more than villages. Jerusalem was an exception, with some 70,000 people, of whom 45,000 were Jews and 15,000 Christians. These last included Armenians, Copts, Ethiopians, Greeks, Latins (Roman Catholics), and 100 Aramaic-speaking Syrians. Outside the city, with its paved streets, the roads were no more than tracks.

Latin Mass in the Basilica of the Nativity at Bethlehem, at Christmas

MODERN TIMES: 1918 TO THE PRESENT DAY

The British received the surrender of Jerusalem on 9 December 1917. Following the Treaty of Versailles, Britain received League of Nations mandates over Palestine, what was to be called Transjordan, and Iraq; France had mandates over Lebanon and Syria. In the latter, the eldest son of the sharif of Mecca, Faysal, was appointed king. It was an uneasy throne, and the politicians side-tracked him to found a dynasty in Iraq. His politic brother Abdallah made himself emir of Jordan under the British, exchanging this title for that of king in 1946, when Jordan became formally independent.

In Palestine, on 2 November 1917, Lord Balfour, as British foreign secretary, promised the Jews 'a national home' without defining with precision what that might mean; under the mandate Britain was entrusted with preparing both the Arabs and the Jews for political independence and self-rule. It was a solution that satisfied neither Arab nor Jewish nationalism, both equally legitimate in their own eyes. It could only lead to strife. The earliest Jewish settlers and immigrants turned towards agriculture. A result of the Jewish persecution in Germany from 1931 onward was to bring in a more sophisticated group of Jewish settlers, professional people of every sort, and with distinguished qualifications.

Hitler's persecution of the Jews in the Holocaust brought about an urgent demand for Jewish settlement in what was to become Israel. Faced at the same time with Arab nationalism, in 1947 the British Labour Government announced that the mandate would be relinquished on 14 May 1948. That same day, David Ben-Gurion proclaimed the establishment of Israel as a state, and the armies of Egypt, Jordan, Lebanon and Syria invaded the former Palestine. In spite of overwhelming military superiority by land and air, they had neither a common command nor a cohesive policy: the Israeli army was able to bring about a military stalemate, and in 1949 an armistice with Egypt (February), Lebanon (March), Jordan (April), and Syria (July). A large number of Arabs had been displaced — about 600,000 according to the British; 800,000 according to the Arabs themselves.

By the end of that year Israel had admitted over 100,000 immigrants, with more than 200,000 arriving the following year, and 170,000 in each of the following two years. No other state has more than doubled its population within four years, or absorbed, housed, and provided for heterogeneous immigrants from so many different nations, and divided by as many tongues. It was an extraordinary feat of national construction.

In two of the wars that were to follow, in 1967 and 1973, Israel won control of East Jerusalem, the former Jordanian territory on the west bank of the Jordan River, and the Gaza Strip from Egypt. Juridically, in international law, all three are technically 'occupied territory'. In 1979 the Camp David Agreement brought about talks between Israel and Egypt; since 1992, there have also been talks with other adjacent countries. Instrumental in this has been diplomatic pressure from the United States on the Palestine Liberation Organization, a blanket organization which covers a wide spectrum of Arab politics, from moderation and conciliation to fanatical pan-Arabism and Islamic fundamentalism. In 1995 it can be said that a majority of both Arabs and Israelis desire peace, but the road to accommodation is fraught with a multitude of difficulties. At the moment of writing (August 1995), Israel has withdrawn from an area centred in Jericho, and from the Gaza Strip, in favour of Palestinian self-rule.

Across the river in Jordan, 60 percent of the population is made up of Palestinian Arabs out of a total of some 4 million: 92 percent of the Palestinians are Muslims, and 6 percent Christians, the latter chiefly Greek Orthodox. Among them, while older people look back with nostalgia to Palestine, the rest have settled to trade and professions, and show little disposition to further movement.

In December 1994 an accord was signed between Israel and Jordan, recognizing one another. King Hussein of Jordan presented Prime Minister Yitzhak Rabin of Israel with a copy of *The Mosaics of Jordan*, written by a Franciscan, Fr Michele Piccirillo, whose Order has served in the Holy Land since 1218. Felicitously, it records the oldest known inscription in the Arabic language: *salama*, peace.

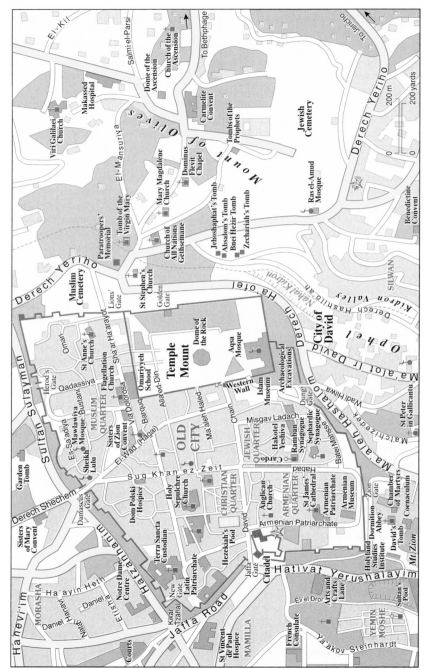

© Carta, Jerusalem

1. Jerusalem, the Holy City

HISTORY OF THE CITY AND ITS WALLS

As the visitor approaches the Old City of Jerusalem, the splendid walls rebuilt in the sixteenth century by the Ottoman sultan Sulayman the Magnificent stretch out proudly before him. They convey an illusion of immemorial antiquity.

The Old City has formed its present shape since AD 135 only; Sulayman's walls follow those laid out for Hadrian's Aelia Capitolina. Part of his Roman northern gate has recently been exposed beneath Sulayman's Damascus Gate. Innumerable pilgrims and tourists have been perplexed by the fact that Golgotha (the site of Jesus' cruxifixion) and the Holy Sepulchre now lie within the city walls, and some explanation of the various changes is necessary. The different stages were finally ascertained in the 1960s by Dame Kathleen Kenyon, of the British School of Archaeology in Jerusalem, and independently by Dr Ute Lux, of the German School of Archaeology in Jerusalem, using the most rigorous archaeological methods. Subsequent discoveries have confirmed their findings. The original city, of the Jebusites and of King David, lay outside these walls to the south-east.

The present Old City, one quarter of a square mile in area, is built on two ridges some 2,723 feet (830 m) above sea level, and traversed by the valley Flavius Josephus called the Tyropoeon, which is partly filled in by the debris of 3,000 years of occupation. Some idea of the depth of this fill can be gained outside Damascus Gate, although it has only been cleared down to the level of AD 135.

On the east the city is bounded by the Silwan (Siloam) Valley, that of the ancient brook Kidron, and, on the west and south, by the Valley of Hinnom, or Gehenna. The Hinnom, the Tyropoeon and the Kidron merge south of Ophel Hill, which was selected as a dwelling site in ancient times because it controlled the Gihon Spring, later the Virgin's Fountain, one of Jerusalem's only two permanent sources of water supply. Here, in c.996 BC, David's forces crept up the water-shaft (2 Sam. 5.8) and took the Jebusite city, making it the capital of Judah.

This city, situated on Ophel Hill, south of the Temple Mount, was built partly on artificial stone terraces. However, no building remains of David's city, to which he brought the sacred Ark that Solomon gave a permanent home in the Temple.

The area of the Temple was first enclosed by Solomon, when an enormous terrace was constructed, the Mountain of the Lord, or Temple Mount, as it is called by the Jews; the Haram al-Sharif (Noble Sanctuary) as it is called in Arabic. Today it includes the Qubbat al-Sakhra (Dome of the Rock), the Aqsa Mosque, and a number of auxiliary buildings and offices, comprising a sixth of the whole area of the Old City, still the dominant feature of Jerusalem today.

Solomon's Temple was destroyed when Nebuchadnezzar captured Jerusalem in 586 BC, but rebuilt on the same plan when the exiles returned from Babylon in 538 BC. It was to make the Temple more glorious that Herod the Great undertook its rebuilding c.20 BC, extending the terrace to its present size. This had the effect of burying all preceding structures, which included Solomon's palace, the palace of Pharaoh's daughter, and other buildings. In the eighth to seventh centuries BC the city itself spilled over westwards as far as what is now the Armenian Quarter. This was probably outside the walls which have been discovered in the present

A panoramic view of the Old City of Jerusalem as seen from the Mount of Olives

Jewish Quarter. During this period elaborate water systems were constructed.

After the return from the Babylonian Exile in 538 BC, the population of the city, which had dwindled during the exilic period, greatly increased. The returned exiles immediately set to work to rebuild the Temple, but the city walls were not repaired until Nehemiah's governorate, 445–433 BC. Some of his roughly built but solid work still survives. First under Persia, and then Alexander the Great, Jerusalem was of little importance. After Alexander's death in 323 BC, it was ruled by the Ptolemies of Egypt; they lost Palestine to the Seleucids of Syria in 198 BC. They inaugurated a vigorous policy of Hellenization, in the course of which Antiochus IV Epiphanes sacked the city and profaned the Temple in 169 BC. To control it he built the Akra Fortress, on a site still disputed, but most probably that of the Citadel.

This may at first have been an isolated building, but shortly afterwards, either under Simon Maccabeus (143–135 BC) or John Hyrcanus (135–105 BC), all of the Upper City (the present Armenian and Jewish quarters) was walled. The next extension of the city, and its walls, belongs to the rebuilding operations of Herod the Great (37–4 BC), whose reign was a grand climacteric in the history of Israel in more ways than one. An Idumaean, a Romanophil, and opposed to the archaism of Jewish orthodoxy, his aim was to make the city rank in grandeur with other great cities of the Roman Empire. The rebuilding of the Temple is to be seen in this context, not that of piety. Although not a vestige of his Temple remains, in accord with Jesus' prediction that not one stone would be left upon another (Matt. 24.2 ff.), the stupendous platform of the Haram al-Sharif is still buttressed on the west, south and east by his retaining walls, at least in the lower courses. Laid like bricks, the huge stones are markedly different from later building, as can be seen clearly.

Likewise dominant over the city is the Citadel, of which one tower, known erroneously as the Tower of David, is certainly Herod's work, as are some of the lower courses elsewhere there. However, most of his palace lies either below the

present police station or to the south of it. North-west of the Temple he built a second fortress, named the Antonia, from which the Temple area could be controlled, approximately on the site of or near the present Omariyyeh College. He also built a theatre in the Greek fashion, and, like other rulers, made special provision for water conservation. Among other reservoirs, his Serpents' Pool, Tower Pool, Sheep Pool and his Strouthion Pool remain today. The last named lay inside the Antonia Fortress.

North of the Temple lay the sheep market, and to the west other markets and storehouses astride the Tyropoeon Valley. This was now included within a second wall, which stopped on the western side immediately east of the little hill of Golgotha. Here, in the area now covered by the Church of the Holy Sepulchre and adjoining properties, was a quarry, outside the city wall. Archaeologically it is certain that this area was unoccupied between the seventh century BC and AD 135, when the Roman city of Aelia Capitolina was laid out by Hadrian with the intention of obliterating all trace of the earlier Jerusalem.

It is thus clear that the sites of Golgotha and the Holy Sepulchre can be authentic; it does not prove, of course, that they are authentic. However, among many other good reasons, it should be added that when the emperor Constantine built the Church of the Holy Sepulchre post-326 the site was within the Roman city, and this must have been as perplexing to him as it has been to later pilgrims. Accordingly, the tradition held by the Church of Jerusalem that this was indeed the site must have seemed to him to be of great strength to persuade him to build here.

After the death of Herod the Great in 4 BC, foreign procurators ruled until AD 66. In AD 40 Herod Agrippa, Herod the Great's grandson, was allowed by Rome to rule over much of his grandfather's kingdom. Herod Agrippa died in AD 44. Those four years were ones of hectic building activity: David's Jerusalem had covered just under 11 acres, Herod the Great's covered 140 acres, and Herod

The Tower of David

Agrippa increased it to 310 acres. Begun under Herod Agrippa, a new wall was now constructed that encompassed the area north of the city. It was in this way that the original quarry area of the Holy Sepulchre and Golgotha came to be surrounded by the walls. Part of this wall is visible below the Roman remains at Damascus Gate, and there is evidence to connect it with the reign of Herod Agrippa. Twenty-two years later the cruelty and misrule of successive procurators culminated in provoking open rebellion. Warfare began in AD 66. First Galilee, and then Judaea, was subdued by the future emperor Vespasian. Soon after he had been proclaimed emperor in AD 69 he left for Rome. In AD 70 it fell to his son Titus to gain control over Jerusalem, and he imposed a siege that lasted from the spring until the autumn. Titus's Arch in Rome records the capture of the city: sacred objects from the Temple are carried in the procession; leading Jews are shown as prisoners; the city is shown as a desolation. Literary evidence witnesses that the walls were destroyed and the Temple burnt. Only three towers of Herod's palace on the Citadel site remained, and part of the southern wall, where Titus left a garrison. The Tenth Legion Fretensis ruled over a ruin: later on some 800 veterans were brought in to repopulate the city. Elsewhere there were several risings in centres of Jewish settlement. In AD 130, Hadrian visited Jerusalem.

What prompted him to determine to rebuild Jerusalem as a Roman city is not clear. It was the announcement that Hadrian's statue would be erected on the Temple Mount (sacred to a religion which forbade graven images) that sparked off Bar Kokhba's revolt (AD 132–135). Only after it had been suppressed could Hadrian's plan go ahead to build Aelia Capitolina: Aelia because his full name was Publius Aelius Hadrianus, Capitolina because the city was dedicated to the triad of Roman deities, Jupiter, Juno and Minerva. Much of the lay-out of this typical Roman city survives in the present grid of streets. Solemn pagan rites inaugurated the boundaries of the city, and were commemorated on coins: these show the emperor, who was represented by the governor, Tinneius Rufus, ceremonially ploughing a furrow along the course of the walls to be built, with a cow and an ox. The northern wall was approximately the present one, as were those on the west and east, where their limits are controlled by the lines of the high ridges. The south wall followed, for the most part, the line of the present one.

Part of the Triumphal Arch built by Hadrian survives as the Ecce Homo Arch, part of which is situated in the Sisters of Zion Convent. Some of the columns of the main street, the *cardo maximus*, are to be seen in the Russian convent commonly known as the Russian excavations, near the Church of the Holy Sepulchre. The top of a column is visible in front of a shop on the eastern side of the Suq Khan ez-Zeit.

Constantine the Great's declaration that Christianity was a licit religion was a turning point in the history of Jerusalem. In 326 the city began to be transformed into what now became the focus — as it had been the epicentre — of the Christian world. Firstly Golgotha and the Holy Sepulchre, and then other churches and monasteries, were raised in succession, in the

The Ecce Homo Arch

Old City, near Gethsemane, on the Mount of Olives, and in Bethlehem and other sites made sacred by traditional memories. Under the empress Eudoxia new churches and pilgrim hospices were built; under Justinian (527–565) the city was again enlarged. Then in 638 Jerusalem fell to the Arabs.

The change of ruler made little immediate difference. Caliph Omar carefully avoided praying in the Holy Sepulchre, lest, he said, his followers should make it a mosque. Where he prayed is now the small Mosque of Omar, close by the courtyard of the Church of the Holy Sepulchre. He cleaned the Temple terrace of dirt and debris, and built a simple mosque at the south end, the origin of the Aqsa Mosque. By 680 it was a large structure capable of accommodating 3,000 people. What was now to give Jerusalem a wholly new character was the construction by Caliph Abd al-Malik b. Marwan (685–705) of the Dome of the Rock, completed 691–692. This, one of the most splendid constructions achieved by mankind, was complemented in 780 by the building of the Aqsa Mosque in stone: none of this first building survives.

It was the end of an era of generally peaceable coexistence when the mad caliph al-Hakim gave the order for the destruction of the Holy Sepulchre and other Christian buildings in 1009. Although there was some reconstruction, for the rest of the century the city was subject to the disturbances and violence brought about by the Seljuq Turks.

On 15 July 1099 the Crusaders took the city by storm from the north, west and south. As in Byzantine times, new churches were built, and the Qubbat al-Sakhra

According to tradition Jesus entered the Temple on Palm Sunday through the Golden Gate

became the Templum Domini, the Temple of the Lord. The Citadel, with the adjacent royal palace, once again dominated the city. The southern wall (which had expanded to the south in the Byzantine period, 326–638) receded to its earlier position, leaving Mount Zion and the former city of David outside. The Crusaders were finally expelled in 1187. Their Ayyubid and Mamluk successors were in general tolerant towards Christians and Jews, but themselves controlled the Holy Sepulchre. Jerusalem had no political importance for them, but Muslim religious learning was encouraged. Commercially there was considerable development. At the end of the fifteenth century the expulsion of the Jews from Spain brought a wave of immigrants whose presence in the city can still be noted.

The defences were unimportant, and so neglected. In December 1517 the Ottoman sultan Selim the Grim took the city, but it was left to his son, Sulayman the Magnificent, to rebuild the walls and gates, and give it the aspect it has today. Nevertheless his successors neglected the city as indeed they neglected much else. By the seventeenth century there were only 10,000 citizens, and by 1800 only

6,000. It was under the British Mandate (1917–1948) and after, firstly under Jordanian rule (1948–1967), and then under the State of Israel, that the city has been restored, repopulated and developed.

THE TEMPLE AREA

From the height of the Mount of Olives a splendid view unfolds of what Arabs call the Haram al-Sharif. No city on earth can boast quite so superb a prospect. Its central building, the Dome of the Rock, rises from the vast terrace which itself is like some proud ship at sea. As Jesus rode down on the first Palm Sunday the actual rock was hidden below the grandiose constructions of Herod, the terrace being surrounded by colonnades on all four sides. Which of the three possible routes from the Mount of Olives he actually took is not known. The steepest route, the central one past the back of the Church of Dominus Flevit, is the most likely, although the Palm Sunday Procession (re-introduced in 1933) follows an easier route to the south.

The Church of Dominus Flevit, commemorating Jesus weeping over Jerusalem, was built in 1955, after excavations had disclosed the ruins of a fifth century monastery and a large cemetery on the site. According to tradition, Jesus rode directly to the Temple on the first Palm Sunday, entering through the Golden Gate; however, according to Josephus the Golden Gate was only used by priests. Careful reading of Matthew 21.10 suggests that he entered the Temple after passing through the city, in which case it would have been more natural if he had entered through St Stephen's Gate. Also known as Lions' Gate, in Arabic it is called Bab Sitti Mariam, the Gate of My Lady Mary.

Entering the Temple area Jesus would have seen double colonnades on the north, west and east. The eastern colonnade was known as Solomon's Porch. The southern colonnade had 162 pillars set in four rows, 81 feet (25 m) high. These colonnades enclosed the Court of the Gentiles. The Temple itself most likely stood somewhat north of where the Dome of the Rock now stands; the precise position of its parts has never been ascertained, and the exact position of the Holy of Holies is not known. From the Court of the Women, on the east side of the Temple complex, stairs and a gate led to the Court of the Men, which contained the Altar of Burnt

An illustration of what the Temple Mount looked like during the Second Temple period

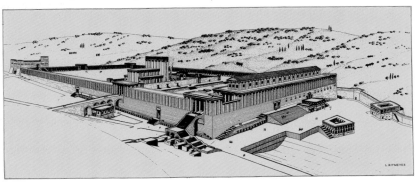

Sacrifice. Behind it to the west lay the Temple proper, and within the Holy of Holies. The Altar of Burnt Sacrifice is thought to have been at what is now the centre of the Dome of the Rock, and on it fire burned day and night. Everything says Josephus to delight eye and heart was presented by the outward appearance of the Temple... It dazzled the eye like sunlight. To strangers approaching Jerusalem it shone out from afar like a snow-clad hill; for, where it was not golden, it radiated a brilliant white.

The Temple is mentioned on numerous occasions in the Gospels. Here (Luke 1.5–22) the angel Gabriel appeared to Zechariah, heralding the birth of St John the Baptist. Here (Luke 2.22) Mary came for the Presentation of the Child Jesus in the Temple; and it was here (Luke 2.41) that Jesus' parents came every year, for the festival of Passover. Jesus' visit at twelve years old was only one such visit (Luke 2.42). It was in Solomon's Porch that Jesus was walking up and down when the Jews tried to draw him into an argument (John 10.23 ff.). Here too the earliest Christians met (Acts 3.12–16). It was in the Temple that Jesus attended the service of the festival of Tabernacles (John 7.1 ff.), with its solemn libations of water, and proclaimed, 'If any man thirst, let him come to me and drink'. Other scenes, too, took place here, and the Cleansing of the Temple, which John 2.14–16 places at the beginning of Jesus' public activity, occurred for the synoptists on the first Palm Sunday, or the day after (Matt. 21.12 ff.; Mark 11.15–17). Finally, it was here, as Jesus died, that the veil in front of the Holy of Holies was rent (Matt. 27.40). Not a single stone of the Temple, he prophesied (Matt. 24.2), would remain upon another. So it is today.

After he had taken Jerusalem in AD 70, Titus destroyed the Temple and burnt it. In AD 135 Hadrian built a temple on this site, with workmen sent from Egypt. A papyrus speaks of it as Kapitol, the Capitol temple in honour of Jupiter, and the goddesses Minerva and Juno. The emperor Julian the Apostate (361–363) encouraged the Jews to rebuild the Temple, but his successor, Jovian, stopped the work. It was not venerated as a sacred site in Byzantine times, and in 638 Caliph Omar found it used as a rubbish dump. He erected a mosque here, probably where the Aqsa Mosque now stands.

THE DOME OF THE ROCK It was Caliph Abd al-Malik b. Marwan (685–705) who, when faced by a rival caliph in Mecca, Ibn al-Zubayr, determined to prevent his influence being spread over Syria by pilgrims returning from Mecca, and to substitute the Sakhra for the Kaaba:

... this Rock, of which it is reported that upon it the Apostle of God set his foot when he ascended into heaven, shall be unto you in the place of the Kaaba. Then Abd al-Malik built above the Rock a dome... and the people took the custom of circumambulating the Rock, even as they had paced round the Kaaba.

Another of his aims, it seems, was to prevent the greatness of the Holy Sepulchre and its magnificence dazzling the minds of Muslims. Other scholars have held that it was to protect his citizens from being attacked on the way to Mecca.

The building he erected (687–691), the earliest surviving Muslim building, and beyond cavil still the most excellent, has a long history of architectural antecedents, both in circular temples in Greece and the mausoleums derived from them in Rome. Similar arrangements exist in churches at Capernaum and on Mount Gerizim. The

An example of the superb mosaics within the Dome of the Rock

rotunda of the Church of the Holy Sepulchre has almost identical measurements, and, as excavated by C. Schick, so had the Church of the Ascension on the Mount of Olives. The Dome of the Rock, however, preserves not only its original ground plan but all its original arches and internal mosaic decorations. Externally the Ottoman Turks substituted tiles for the mosaics in the sixteenth century, and many of these were replaced in 1963 when the gilded wooden dome was replaced by one of aluminium alloyed with gold. In 1994 the roof was replaced with gold plating.

Abd al-Malik b. Marwan not only wished to surpass the Holy Sepulchre in magnificence; he also wished to emphasize the superior truth of Islam as opposed to Christianity. Thus, inside the building, above the octagonal arcade, are two rings of Kufic inscriptions in gold letters. Some of these refer to the Muslim view of Jesus Christ: they are quotations from the Qur'an. For example:

Sura 17.111: Say — Praise be to God who has had no Son or companion in his government, and who requires no helper to save him from dishonour; praise him.

Sura 57.2: ... speak the truth only of God. The Messiah Jesus is only the son of Mary, the ambassador of God, and his Word which he deposited in Mary. Believe then in God and his ambassador, and do not maintain that there are three... God is one, far be it from him that he should have had a son.

Sura 19.34: ... God is not so constituted that he could have a son; be that far from him.

The mosaics are of different periods, but all, most probably, by Syrian Christian artists. At this period Islam had not come to forbid the representation of human and animal forms, for there are examples of both in Jordan from the same period, but the grapes that occur with great frequency are the work of those accustomed to this device as an emblem of the Last Supper. In the drum the gold cubes are set at an angle, tilted forward, so that they appear brighter than the motifs.

The capitals and columns have all been removed from churches, and some bear their original crosses. The windows all belong to Sulayman the Magnificent's restoration of 1552, and the carved ceilings are Mamluk work of the thirteenth century. The reliquary beside the rock itself is believed to contain a hair from the Prophet Muhammad's beard. Below the rock is a cave known in Arabic as Bir al-Arwah, the Well of Souls. Those Muslims who prayed there in former times were given a certificate, to be buried with them, ensuring them admission to heaven.

OTHER BUILDINGS A great number of buildings are contained within the Haram al-Sharif. On the north side the Bab al-Atm, known today as the Bab al-Malik Faysal, is closed to the public. There are nine entrances to the enclosure on the west side, of which three may be used by visitors (the Bab al-Nazir — Nazir Gate; the Bab al-Silsila — Gate of the Chain; and the Bab al-Maghariba — Moors' Gate); the three gates on the south side and those on the north are kept closed. Many of them display fine Mamluk work. There are four minarets: on the north side, at the north-west corner, near the Gate of the Chain, and at the south-west corner. There are also a number of fountains (*sabil*s), raised platforms for prayers (*mastaba*s), independent *mihrab*s (niches indicating the direction to be assumed in prayer) and *qubba*s (small domes of a commemorative nature).

Of especial elegance are the Dome of the Chain, perhaps simply a kiosk (a light, open pavilion); the Qubbat al-Miraj, commemorating the Prophet Muhammad's mystical ascent into heaven; the fountain where ablutions are performed, known as el-Kas (the Cup); and, also on the lower level of the enclosure, on the west side of the Dome of the Rock, the supremely elegant *sabil* of the Egyptian sultan Qayt-Bay, given by him in 1482. It is the only existing example of a carved masonry stone dome outside Cairo.

THE AQSA MOSQUE At the south end of the terrace is the Aqsa Mosque, so called 'the most distant' shrine, the farthest Abrahamic shrine from Mecca. After Caliph Omar's crude mosque, a larger building was constructed 'by setting great beams on some remains of ruins'. Carried out using the ruins of the Royal Porch, and of Hadrian's temple, it was destroyed by an earthquake. Its successor was similarly damaged in 1033, and rebuilt in 1035, by the Fatimid caliph al-Zahir. This gave the mosque its final form, with six aisles, the central nave being double the width of the side aisles, with a wooden dome in front of the *mihrab*.

The plan was almost that of al-Mahdi's in 780, and one still enters through his doorway. About one third of the mosque had to be rebuilt between 1938 and 1942. Then in 1969 it was badly damaged by fire that had been deliberately started in three places. It destroyed much of the marble panelling, some of the mosaics, and the superb pulpit, inlaid with ivory and mother-of-pearl, which was the gift of Saladin in 1168. The initial repairs to the mosaics, some of which have had to be completely reconstructed, were the work of an artist first employed in the mosque in 1927. Further repairs are still being carried out by four of his pupils.

Behind the pulpit is a stone taken from the Church of the Ascension on the Mount of Olives, alleged to bear the footprint of the ascending Christ. To its right a pair of columns close together are said not to permit persons to pass through if they have been born out of lawful wedlock. Beyond, to the right, is a long building with eight bays, known as the Mosque of the Women. To the left of the *mihrab* is another pair of columns similar to those just mentioned, and then a small mosque, known as the Mosque of Omar, with an interesting *mihrab*. Just north of it is a small oratory known as the Mosque of the Forty Witnesses, and, behind it, another oratory known as the Place of Zacharias. In Crusader times the building was used as a church by the Knights Templar, and this gave rise to a myth, wholly without foundation, that the mosque was originally built as a church. The rose window on the east side of this smaller mosque probably marks the site of the Templar chapel, and was a modification of their period. Near the main entrance the graves of St Thomas Becket's murderers are pointed out, but this is mentioned for the first time only in early twentieth century guide-books.

In the courtyard on the extreme south-west a large building, formerly known as the Mosque of the Moors, contains the Islamic Museum, a magpie collection of objects presented to the Aqsa Mosque and the Dome of the Rock from time to time, together with woodwork and sculpture removed from them in the course of necessary repairs. There is a noteworthy collection of Qur'ans of different periods. The elegant metal screen, which the Crusaders placed round the Sakhra in the Dome of the Rock, is exhibited behind a table where two guardians sit. There are fine views from the southern windows. Near the entrance a very elegant mosque lamp of the Mamluk period has a case to itself, near a case of porcelain and twentieth century English china. There is no catalogue or guide available.

To gain some idea of the Temple area in the time of Jesus visit the Holyland Hotel, Jerusalem, where a scale model of the Temple and the city as reconstructed by Herod is displayed. It is on the scale of 1:50, and prepared from details supplied by the distinguished archaeologist, the late Professor Michael Avi-Yonah.

THE LAST SUPPER AND MOUNT ZION
The City of David was on the eastern ridge of the Holy City; at the southern end of the western ridge is Mount Zion. It is reached easily on foot.

THE CITADEL As it stands today the Citadel is largely Mamluk work of the fourteenth century AD. Traditionally the tall tower at the entrance is known as King David's Tower, but it was in fact constructed by Herod the Great, as its huge courses of masonry display. It formed part of a large palace complex built by him, extending beyond the present Citadel into the Armenian Quarter, re-using fortifications of the Maccabean period. This was the principal seat of government in Jerusalem under the Maccabees, the Romans, the Byzantines, the Arabs, the Crusaders, Saladin and the Turks. In the view of some authorities it was the *praetorium* in which Pilate tried Jesus (John 18.28–19.16). Just beyond it to the south is the police station, after which the Armenian Quarter begins. From this point to the complex of buildings on Mount Zion is about 656 yards (600 m).

BENEDICTINE ABBEY OF THE DORMITION Passing through the walls at Zion Gate, on the right up a lane is the site of the House of Caiaphas as claimed

The traditional site of the Last Supper, the Coenaculum

by the Armenians. This is not accessible to the public without permission. A church is being constructed here. There are tombs of the Armenian patriarchs, beside whom are buried the principal secretaries who have served them. A little farther on is the Dormition Abbey, the traditional site of the Falling Asleep of Our Lady. The present church and buildings were erected in 1898–1910. The crypt contains a recumbent statue of Our Lady of great beauty, and, among others, an altar presented by President Houphouët-Boigny of the Ivory Coast. Made of ivory and ebony, it is of distinguished elegance. It is on the site of a Church of Our Lady of Mount Zion built by the Crusaders, and demolished by the Arabs in 1219.

CHURCH OF THE COENACULUM Returning back down the lane in order to turn right, there is an iron door, often locked, which gives access to a charming garden, in which there is the small Franciscan Church of the Coenaculum (the place of the Last Supper). It was built in 1936, with modern decorations. Reached by an outside staircase and across a small room is the traditional coenaculum. The tradition is not recorded before the fifth century AD, when it was associated with an already existing tradition attested by 348, that it was here in an 'upper room' that the Holy Spirit descended on the apostles (Acts 1.13, 2.1). However this may be, the only competing site is the Syrian Orthodox Church of St Mark, which claims to possess the 'upper room', but this is sustained only by oral tradition. For this reason the tradition held by the Franciscans may seem to be the more plausible.

The actual room is divided into two naves by two pillars holding up a vaulted roof of the Crusader period. The elaborate *mihrab*, of deceptively Mamluk appearance, was in fact inserted in 1928 only. To its left a small staircase leads to another small room, of which the door is kept locked. Tradition asserts that the small room is the place of the Descent of the Holy Spirit and the larger the place of the Last

The Church of St Peter in Gallicantu on the eastern slope of Mount Zion

Supper. For these reasons, and for the other events that would have taken place here — the institution of the priesthood, the prayer that all may be one, the giving of the new commandment to love one another, the Washing of the Feet, the appearance of Jesus on Easter Day and the institution of the sacrament of Penance — it is spoken of as the 'Mother of Churches'.

THE TOMB OF DAVID The altar of the Church of the Coenaculum backs on to a medieval building to which access is gained farther down the lane. This contains the Tomb of David, venerated alike by Jews and Muslims, but there is no record of it earlier than the twelfth century AD.

CHAMBER OF MARTYRS Near to the Tomb of David is the Chamber of Martyrs, which commemorates those who died at the hands of the Nazis. It is used for prayer and study.

CEMETERIES To the south-east are Armenian, Catholic and Protestant cemeteries. The Catholic cemetery is Franciscan property, and the keys are held by them. It contains some interesting burials of pilgrims, and modern columbaria. In one of these appears the name of Augustine Lada, who was organist of the Church of the Holy Sepulchre from 1916 until 1989, a record for a church organist.

The Protestant cemetery contains the grave of the eminent English archaeologist, Sir W.M. Flinders Petrie (1853–1942). After his death, as he had requested, his head was removed to be preserved in the Royal College of Surgeons. Also buried here is Leslie Starkey, an English archaeologist who was the first to excavate at Lachish; he was murdered by a servant near Hebron in 1936.

ST PETER IN GALLICANTU On the eastern slope of the ridge, reached by crossing the main road and walking along the steep lane opposite, is the Church of St Peter in Gallicantu (the Cockcrow). The Assumptionist fathers claim this to be the site of the House of Caiaphas (Mark 14.53 ff.). Here Jesus was questioned by him, and here, it is asserted, Peter three times denied his master. The church is built over excavations by the Assumptionists begun in 1887, before the age of modern scientific archaeology. Traces have been found of a monastic church of the seventh century AD, together with structures of the Herodian period, including cellars, stables and cisterns. One of these is claimed to be the dungeon in which Jesus spent the night before his crucifixion. The occupational evidence before the seventh century seems to be wholly domestic, and not to demonstrate any connection with Caiaphas, for whom another house is predicated higher up the hill.

There is a splendid view from the church across the Hinnom Valley. Below is the **Monastery of St Onuphrius**, an Egyptian hermit, whose beard was so luxuriant that it served as his only garment. From the fourth century the burial ground at the bottom has been associated with the **Haceldama**, the Field of Blood of the Gospel (Matt. 27.7–10), bought by the priests with Judas' thirty pieces of silver, or where he hanged himself (Acts 1.18–19).

GETHSEMANE

After celebrating the Last Supper, Jesus went with his disciples across the Kidron Valley to the foot of the Mount of Olives, where there was a garden called Gethsemane (Mark 14.26, 32). It was a place where they went often, for Judas (John 18.2) knew it. Jesus had anticipated Judas' betrayal (Mark 14.17–21), and could quite easily have escaped up the Mount of Olives and beyond into the desert,

The Grotto of Gethsemane

where innumerable caves could have afforded him concealment. Here, therefore, he stopped to decide whether to stand and face his accusers or to run away.

THE CHURCH OF ALL NATIONS Built in 1924, this church encloses a rock in the garden in which Jesus prayed. No one can be certain of the exact spot where he prayed, but this site is very close to the well-worn route that led to the top of the Mount of Olives before the construction of modern roads. The church replaces two earlier ones, one of which was destroyed by an earthquake in c.744–745. A Crusader church was built here c.1170 on a slightly different axis, and preserving some of the mosaic floor of the earlier church, which is still visible through glass panels in the present floor. This church was abandoned in 1345. The present church is richly decorated with mosaics of high excellence, and the dark glass of the windows throws a sombre light which reflects the idea of Jesus' agony.

Outside in the garden are eight ancient olive trees, of which two may be contemporary with the time of Jesus, the others being offshoots of earlier trees. The principal doors of the church on the west side are not in common use, and entry is from a door up the lane on the north side of the church. This leads to a walk round the sides of the garden which, while visible, is not accessible to visitors. The word Gethsemane is a Greek form from the Hebrew *gat shemanim*, meaning oil press, or oil stores.

Leaving by the same door through which one entered, on the opposite side of the lane, an ornamental iron-work door enables a view of another garden, which is not accessible to the public. This garden has a common boundary with the Grotto of Gethsemane, which is visible on the far side. The Franciscans have placed an open-air altar here for the use of Anglicans, as an ecumenical gesture.

CHURCH OF THE TOMB OF THE VIRGIN MARY Walking down the lane and then turning right, very soon one comes across a broad flight of steps that leads down to the Church of the Tomb of the Virgin Mary. Immediately to the right a narrow passage leads to the **Grotto of Gethsemane**, a cave in which the disciples are believed to have slept whilst Jesus prayed in his Agony. Here Jesus is believed to have been betrayed by Judas Iscariot, and arrested. The Franciscans acquired the grotto in 1392; in the twelfth century it was adorned with paintings and mosaics, all of which are now almost completely effaced. At the back there is a Jewish tomb of an early period. Except for the three modern altars and a small amount of unobtrusive furnishing, the cave is no doubt much as it has been for many centuries, and perhaps much as it was when the disciples awaited Jesus. The altar on the right hand side was given by Fr Eugene Hoade, OFM, and by his friends. He was a priest who, over a very long period of time, gave himself to making the Holy Places intelligible to pilgrims.

It is convenient at this point to visit the Church of the Tomb of the Virgin Mary. That she was 'assumed into heaven' was proclaimed as a doctrine of the Church by Pius XII on 1 November 1950, but the belief was in fact far older, and the Feast of the Assumption on 15 August was made a public holiday in England by King Alfred the Great. He believed that she is as we may hope to be.

A church existed here in the time of the patriarch Juvenal (422–458). Geoffrey de Bouillon built an abbey here, of St Mary in the Valley of Jehoshaphat, for the Benedictines of Cluny, and in 1130 Crusaders rebuilt the church in its present form.

The Church of the Tomb of the Virgin Mary

Later that century the abbey and its upper church were destroyed by the Arabs, but the lower church was left because of their veneration for Our Lady, as taught in the Qur'an. The Franciscans obtained it in the fourteenth century, but were expelled in 1757. Since then the Greeks have been in possession with the Armenians. Not only do Abyssinians, Copts and Syrians enjoy minor rights in the church, even Muslims have a special place for their prayers. Because of the expulsion, the Latins hold no services here.

There is a square atrium in front of the church, with steps leading up to a door set in a Crusader arch. On the right, in a chapel dedicated to the saints Anne and Joachim, parents of Our Lady, is the tomb of Queen Mélisande, daughter of Baldwin II and wife of Fulk of Anjou, kings of Jerusalem. Her breviary is on display in the British Museum. Farther down on the left is the chapel of St Joseph. Here Mary, wife of King Baldwin III, Constance, mother of Bohémund III, and Matilda, wife of Eric the Good, are buried. By the steps is a stall for the sale of candles.

One enters what is a perfectly regular cruciform church, with apses at either end to the right and the left. There is a cistern in the left hand apse. Across the crossing, a locked door leads to a corridor which gives access to some tombs. On the right a small edicule (from the Latin *aedicula*, meaning small building) contains the tomb chamber where Our Lady was laid. It has two entrances. An altar slab has been placed over the slab where the body would have lain, and is protected by thick glass. On the right of the edicule is a *mihrab*, indicating the direction of Mecca, where Muslims come to pray from time to time.

THE TRIAL AND THE VIA DOLOROSA

After Jesus' arrest, he was taken first before Annas and then before the high priest Caiaphas (John 18). The site of the dwelling of the first is lost below an Armenian church, while that of the second is disputed. Thereafter, early in the morning he appeared before the Sanhedrin, possibly in a courtroom in the Temple, of which the location is not known. It was only after that he was taken before Pilate.

The normal residence of the Roman procurators in Jerusalem was the Citadel, and overlooking the Temple area there was a secondary palace which had been built by Herod; this was known as the Antonia, in honour of Mark Antony. Like the Citadel, the Antonia was garrisoned in case of riot on great festivals. On the site where it once stood is now a Muslim school, the Omariyyeh College, a former Turkish barracks. Set on a rocky platform that rises sharply above the level of the Via Dolorosa (which means Street of Sorrows), the tactical significance of the Antonia can at once be appreciated if one climbs the stairs in the middle of the terrace. There, a loggia with a window presents a view of the Haram al-Sharif with a suddenness which is breathtaking after the narrow street and mean courtyard. The Stations of the Cross, conducted by the Franciscans with touching simplicity and absence of ceremony, starts from within the school at 3 pm each Friday afternoon. Controversy has long raged as to which of these two sites, the Citadel or the Antonia, was the place where Pilate gave judgement. The Gospels, except in using the word *praetorium*, are not exact in locating the site. For the Jewish philosopher, Philo of Alexandria (d. AD 40), who never refers in any of his works to Jesus Christ, Pilate normally resided at the Citadel when he came up to Jerusalem from his residence at Caesarea for the Jewish festivals. Josephus, equally impartial, says of one of Pilate's successors:

The entrance to the Chapel of the Flagellation

> Florus lodged at the palace. On the next day he had a dais placed in front of the building and took his seat. The chief priests, the notables, and the most eminent citizens then presented themselves before the tribunal.

It is precisely such a scene as this that is described in the Gospels.

The **Franciscan Chapel of the Flagellation** is to the north of the Via Dolorosa. In the courtyard on the right is the Chapel of the

Part of the pavement formerly known as the Lithostrotos in the Sisters of Zion Convent

Scourging; a second chapel on the left commemorates the condemnation to death. Here there begins a large section of stone paving that extends westward under the **Sisters of Zion Convent** and beyond to the Greek Orthodox convent with the Greek words *to praitórion* — the *praetorium* — above the entrance. It was once claimed that this was the pavement called Lithostrotos, in Hebrew Gabbatha, and that it was an integral part of the Antonia Fortress. Across the street stretches the Ecce Homo Arch, above the spot where Pilate was formerly claimed to have brought Jesus before the people, exclaiming: *'Ecce Homo'* (Behold the man). This claim is unhistorical: it is a triple-arched gate which was most likely built when Hadrian had Aelia Capitolina laid out in 135. The northern part of this arch is in the basilica of the Sisters of Zion; the other side has been destroyed. The great stone pavement is most probably from the same time. When Hadrian replanned the city in 135, he built a forum here. This may well be the pavement of that forum.

The devotion known as the Way (or Stations) of the Cross has undergone a long development. In Byzantine times pilgrims went from Gethsemane to Calvary (in the Holy Sepulchre), but without stopping on the way. By the eighth century the procession went round the city to the House of Caiaphas on Mount Zion, then to a *praetorium* said to be that of Pilate somewhere near the Temple, and finally to Calvary. The present route began to evolve only in the thirteenth century, under Franciscan encouragement. Even then there were different views about the correct

Procession along the Via Dolorosa on Good Friday

route, and only eight stations were observed in Jerusalem. The existing route was finalized only in the eighteenth century, but stations I, IV, V and VIII were not localized on their present sites until the nineteenth century. The Way of the Cross is thus to be seen for the most part rather with the eye of faith than scrutinized with the scalpel of history. The present stations, with their locations, are as follows:

First Station: Jesus is condemned to death (Matt. 27 and other Gospels) The First Station is commemorated in the Omariyyeh College. Across the street, on the site of a medieval chapel, is the small Franciscan Chapel of the Flagellation, to the right of the convent of that name. Across the courtyard is the Flagellation Museum. A well-illustrated guide-book is available. The present chapel was built in 1927–1929. To the left of the entrance is the Chapel of the Condemnation, restored in 1903–1904, and used at one time as a mosque. The floor of this chapel is part of the great pavement already mentioned above. Its striations are thought to have been intended to prevent horses slipping. There are also graffiti of Roman soldiers' barrack-room games, probably of the third or fourth century.

Second Station: Jesus receives his Cross This is commemorated in the street outside the Sisters of Zion Convent. Their chapel, known as the Basilica of Ecce Homo, lies down a passage to the left of the entrance; the pavement is striated as before. To the right a staircase leads to the Lithostrotos and an ancient cistern below the pavement, which certainly was still open in June AD 70, because the Romans had to build a ramp across it. An eighth century tradition has it that the Scala Santa (the Holy Stairs) in Rome were removed from here and taken to Italy by the empress Helena. Several of the stone flags have barrack-room graffiti of games similar to hopscotch, mazes, and the game known as Basilicus played with knuckle bones, known to have been popular in the Roman army: the burlesque king was loaded with absurd honours, and put to death at the end of the farce, in a manner which recalls the mockery of Jesus (Matt. 27.27–30).

Farther down the street on the left is the Greek Orthodox convent, where a staircase is exhibited as that of the *praetorium*. One of the grottoes was formerly claimed to have been the prison of Christ, but today is called the Prison of Barabbas.

Third Station: Jesus falls under his Cross for the first time A small Polish chapel, restored in 1947–1948, marks the Third Station outside the entrance to the former Turkish baths of the Hammam al-Sultan. It is not mentioned in the Gospels.

Fourth Station: Jesus meets his afflicted mother This stop is made outside the Armenian Catholic Church of Our Lady of the Spasm. In the crypt, at ancient street level is a large mosaic, belonging probably to the Byzantine Church of St Sophia (Holy Wisdom).

Fifth Station: Simon of Cyrene helps Jesus carry his Cross The route now begins to lead uphill to Calvary. This section of the Via Dolorosa is known in Arabic as Tariq al-Alam (Street of Sorrows). The small chapel was built in 1895; the Franciscans' first convent in Jerusalem was built on this site in c.1229–1244.

Sixth Station: Veronica wipes the face of Jesus Eighty yards (73 m) farther on a column inserted in the walls on the left marks the place where a Jerusalem lady, Veronica, wiped Jesus' face with a handkerchief; the imprint of his face is said to have been left upon it. The incident is not mentioned in the Gospels. There is a Greek Catholic (Melkite) chapel here, and the visible ancient remains are probably of a monastery of the saints Cosmas and Damian, built in 548–563.

On the opposite side of the street is the Benevolent Arts Workshop — vestments are made with exquisite needlework: the proceeds are used to support a number of poor Arab-Christian families, most of the work being done in their homes. It is known as the Veronica Friendship.

Seventh Station: Jesus falls the second time Again, the event is not mentioned in the Gospels. This station is situated where the Via Dolorosa meets the Suq Khan

The Basilica of the Holy Sepulchre in Jerusalem

ez-Zeit. There are two Franciscan chapels here, one above the other. The lower chapel contains a red monolith (a block of stone shaped into a pillar) where a street running from east to west crossed the *cardo maximus*, the main street built by Hadrian in AD 135 that ran from north to south. Here there had been an old gate, and it is probably from here that Jesus left the city for Golgotha.

Eighth Station: Jesus speaks to the women of Jerusalem (Luke 23.27–31) This station is marked by a Latin cross, round which are arranged the Greek letters IC XC NI KA — representing the words Jesus Christ conquers. The cross is in the wall of the Greek church; the altar on the right commemorates the Eighth Station. From this station it is necessary to retrace one's steps back towards the Seventh Station, and then to turn right along the Suq Khan ez-Zeit (Bazaar of the Olive Inn), known to the Crusaders as Malcuisinat (Street of Bad Cooking).

Ninth Station: Jesus falls the third time under the Cross On the right hand side of the street is a stone staircase, at the top of which a winding street leads to the Coptic Patriarchate, adjacent to the Coptic Chapel of St Helena. At the doorway, which is of the Crusader period, the shaft of a column marks the Ninth Station. On the left, as one faces the doorway, another doorway leads to a terrace, with, in its centre, the cupola of the Chapel of St Helena in the Church of the Holy Sepulchre. On this terrace are very small cells inhabited by Ethiopian monks. They have two small chapels, the lower one reached by a staircase from the upper one, and both are elegantly decorated in the Ethiopian manner. From the lower chapel a staircase leads down to a door which gives direct access to the courtyard of the Basilica of the Holy Sepulchre.

Tenth to Fourteenth Stations (all the Gospels) These stations are all commemorated inside the Church of the Holy Sepulchre. The route taken by the Friday procession to the Holy Sepulchre is not through the Ethiopian chapels, but back along the winding lane to the stone staircase and down to the Suq Khan ez-Zeit, continuing along it, before turning right into the Suq ed-Dabbagha. The locations of the following stations are unintelligible without some knowledge of the history and development of the Church of the Holy Sepulchre (see below). Their positions within are:

Tenth Station: Jesus is stripped of his garments In the right hand nave on Calvary.

Eleventh Station: Jesus is nailed to the Cross At the altar in the right hand nave on Calvary.

Twelfth Station: Jesus dies on the Cross At the Greek altar in the left hand nave on Calvary.

Thirteenth Station: Jesus is taken down from the Cross At the altar of Stabat Mater between the two preceding altars.

Fourteenth Station: Jesus is laid in the Sepulchre Below, in the edicule of the Holy Sepulchre.

A detailed history of the stations, together with appropriate meditations and prayers, has been written by Fr J.K. Campbell, OFM, *The Stations of the Cross in Jerusalem*, Cana/Carta.

THE CRUCIFIXION AND THE RESURRECTION

Zalatimo's shop Continuing towards the end of the Suq Khan ez-Zeit, Zalatimo's sweet shop on the right conceals part of the massive fourth century entrance to the Holy Sepulchre. One passes through the outer shop after asking permission, but for a small charge: what remains are tumbled ruins that can only be seen through an ill-lit gap in a recent wall.

The Russian excavations Farther on still the street turns right, and then left. Turning right, almost at once one reaches the Russian Mission in Exile. This contains what are known as the Russian excavations, made in 1883 by the Russian Ecclesiastical Mission in Jerusalem. Passing through a long passage where a small fee must be paid for entry one reaches what are claimed to be the remains of the Judgement Gate built in the first century BC by Herod the Great, the remains of an arch and two columns, built by Hadrian c.135, part of the Basilica of the Holy Sepulchre as begun by Constantine in 326, and the remains of the house of the Augustinian canons, who served the Holy Sepulchre before the Franciscans took the work over.

The arch is certainly of the time of Hadrian; through it, round to the left and reached by a flight of steps, is part of the platform of his temple in honour of Venus placed over Mount Calvary in 135. The sill at the foot of the steps, venerated as the gate through which Jesus went out to Calvary, is misattributed, for it cannot be earlier than 135. The wall once had a veneer of marble, described by Eusebius in c.338, and the pitting made by the dowel pins to hold the marble in place can still be noted. Constantine re-used the wall as the façade for the atrium of his church, cutting out three doors. The south door is visible, and the columns in the recess opposite belonged to the fourth century portico.

It is perhaps best to visit Zalatimo's shop and the Russian excavations first before continuing down the street past a row of shops and through a narrow door, leading into the present courtyard of the Holy Sepulchre on its south side. It gives one some immediate sense of the violence with which time has treated what Constantine the Great intended to be the central shrine of Christendom: the place of the crucifixion and resurrection of Jesus Christ.

Constantine's Basilica of the Holy Sepulchre A first century apocryphal work relates that the empress Protonice, wife of the emperor Claudius (AD 41–54), a secret Christian, visited Jerusalem, and ordered Calvary and the Holy Sepulchre to be handed over to the Christians. At this stage there was no formal cult round either site. After Titus besieged Jerusalem in AD 70, the Jerusalem Christians fled with their bishop, Simeon, a cousin of Jesus, but soon returned to the city. The Jewish revolt of 132 led to the total destruction and rebuilding of the city by Hadrian, and Aelia Capitolina swallowed up the Holy Places: above the Tomb a temple to Jupiter was built, and one to Venus on Calvary. These helped authenticate the position of the Holy Places, and were removed only when the plans of the two architects Zenobius and Eustatius began to be put into effect on the orders of Constantine the Great.

The grand entrance of Constantine's building, as has been seen, survives partly behind Zalatimo's shop, and led into an atrium in front of a basilica with a nave and four aisles. This was built over a cave, now the Chapel of St Helena, with a staircase leading down into the ancient cistern, now the Chapel of the Holy Cross, where St Helena found the True Cross and those of the two thieves. Beyond the basilica lay a colonnaded atrium (*triportico*). In the left hand corner of the atrium as one entered it stood the Rock of Calvary, surmounted by a cross; beyond the atrium lay a rotunda surrounding the Sacred Tomb. The domed rotunda was supported by an internal circle of columns; the outside wall contained three apses.

The Tomb of Jesus, which originally had been dug into a hillside, was freed from surrounding rock, in the way that the Tomb of Absalom in the Hinnom Valley

Plan of the Basilica of the Holy Sepulchre through the ages (sketch plan only)

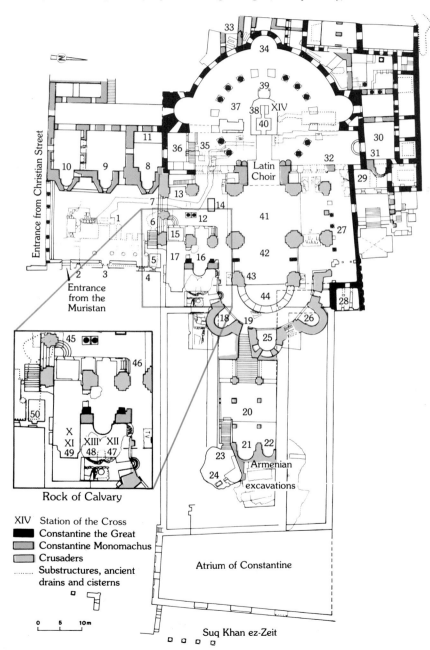

Entrance from Christian Street

Entrance from the Muristan

Latin Choir

XIV

Rock of Calvary

XIV   Station of the Cross
■   Constantine the Great
▓   Constantine Monomachus
□   Crusaders
...... Substructures, ancient drains and cisterns

0   5   10 m

Atrium of Constantine

Armenian excavations

Suq Khan ez-Zeit

had been. The remaining rock, consisting of an octagonal edicule (from the Latin *aedicula*, meaning little house), was left surrounding the tomb chamber. The funeral couch, on which Jesus' body was laid, was left intact. Albeit damaged, it was still intact when it was uncovered last in 1555. Outside the octagon a covered space was built up, the present Chapel of the Angel.

This building was damaged in 614 by the Persians under Chosroes (Khusrau) II, but shortly afterwards restored by Abbot Modestus. A Greek, he had Armenian support. A sixth century representation of the edicule survives in St John Lateran in Rome. It had a conical roof, and above it soared a great dome. Modestus preserved this scheme, as can be seen from a model erected in the Basilica of Aquileia, in North Italy, in the ninth century, where a liturgy special to the city was celebrated at Easter in imitation of that of Jerusalem.

Destruction and rebuilding In 1009 the mad Fatimid caliph al-Hakim destroyed the whole edifice, and it was only in 1048 that a partial restoration was completed by the emperor Monomachus. The atrium and the basilica were not rebuilt. Calvary remained a separate chapel, while an apse with an altar was constructed on the east side of the rotunda. The chapels of St Helena and of the Holy Cross remained, the former being roofed in and lit by a cupola. The reason for the abandonment of so much of the edifice was that the Imperial treasury could afford no more. This church can only have held a very small congregation; thus, the Crusaders undertook a radical reconstruction, and it is this, with but few modifications, that one sees today.

The Crusaders The Crusaders removed Monomachus' eastern apse, replacing it with a splendid triumphal arch. The area of the former *triportico* was used to build a conventional French choir, contained within pillars and piers, with an apse at its eastern end, round which was an ambulatory. From this ambulatory a staircase descended to the chapels of St Helena and the Holy Cross, the same staircase (19) that one descends today. The Chapel of Calvary was now contained within the new church, and the buildings of Modestus on the north side were also incorporated. About this time the Stone of Unction, where by tradition Jesus' body was prepared for burial, first appears in literature. Again on the north side, accommodation was provided for the Augustinian canons who celebrated in the Latin rite.

Legend to plan: 1. Southern atrium; 2. Monastery of Abraham; 3. Armenian Chapel of St James; 4. Coptic Chapel of St Michael the Archangel; 5. Chapel of St Mary of Egypt; 6. Tomb of Philippe d'Aubigny; 7. Main door to church; 8. Chapel of the Forty Martyrs; 9. Chapel of St Mary Magdalen; 10. Greek Chapel of St James; 11. Belfry; 12. Tomb of Godfrey de Bouillon; 13. Bench for Muslim doorkeepers; 14. Stone of Anointing; 15. Greek sacristy; 16. Chapel of Adam; 17. Greek treasury; 18. Chapel of the Derision; 19. Stairway and carved pilgrims' crosses; 20. Crusader Chapel of St Helena (now Armenian Chapel of St Gregory the Illuminator); 21. Altar of St Gregory; 22. Altar of St Dismas; 23. Chapel of the Finding of the Cross; 24. Statue of St Helena; 25. Chapel of the Parting of the Raiment; 26. Chapel of St Longinus; 27. Arches of the Virgin; 28. Prison of Christ; 29. Latin sacristy; 30. Chapel of the Apparition; 31. Column of Flagellation; 32. Chapel of St Mary Magdalen; 33. Tombs of Joseph of Arimathaea and Nicodemus; 34. Chapel of St Nicodemus (Syrian Orthodox); 35. Place of the Three Maries; 36. Armenian divan; 37. Rotunda; 38. Edicule of the Holy Sepulchre; 39. Coptic chapel; 40. Chapel of the Angel; 41. 'Navel' of the World; 42. Greek choir (Katholikon); 43. Throne of the patriarch of Jerusalem; 44. Altar; 45, 46. Stairs up to Calvary; 47. Greek Altar of the Crucifixion; 48. Latin Altar of Stabat Mater; 49. Latin Altar of the Nailing to the Cross; 50. Latin Chapel of the Franks

Rebuilding: 1809–1810 Two major restorations were carried out by the Franciscans in 1555 and in 1718. In 1808 a disastrous fire almost wholly gutted the rotunda of the Holy Sepulchre, and, while the Franciscans vainly appealed to the West for funds, the Greeks obtained a *firman* (decree) from Ottoman Turkey, authorizing them to rebuild it. The present edicule thus replaced that of former times, and high walls were built to enclose the hitherto open Crusader choir, plunging most of the rest of the building into partial darkness. Some idea of the lightness and airiness of the Crusader building can be obtained by climbing the stairs into the Armenian section of the gallery round the rotunda (permission to do so must first be obtained from the Armenians: their sacristy is immediately to the left of the entrance). This enables one to look across the top of the enclosing wall, and at the same time to look down upon the edicule of the Sepulchre itself.

The Status Quo Six communities have the right to celebrate in the Church of the Holy Sepulchre under a decree made in 1757 by Ottoman Turkey, and confirmed at the Treaty of Paris in 1855. The intricate regulations determining their rights in different parts of the building are known as the Status Quo. There are three major communities — in alphabetical order, the Armenians, Greeks and Latins — all sharing certain rights in common, including that to celebrate within the Church of the Holy Sepulchre and on Calvary. There are three minor communities, again in alphabetical order, the Copts, Ethiopians and Syrians. These minor communities only possess the right to celebrate in certain chapels.

Under the Status Quo the communities do not give Holy Communion to each other, nor is it permissible for them to do so to members of any other body. The Latins are represented exclusively by the Franciscans (Order of Friars Minor). The term Roman Catholic is not used lest it should be misleading, because in Jerusalem there are also Christians of Armenian, Coptic, Greek (Melkite) and Syrian rites in communion with the see of Rome.

Repairs and restoration The three principal communities acted together to repair the church after the earthquake of 1927. In 1934 and 1939 the British mandatory government intervened when the building was considered to be in danger of collapse. In 1960 these three communities agreed to repair those parts of the building in their exclusive possession and to contribute to the restoration of those parts shared in common. In this way the rotunda has been almost completely restored, and other parts renovated.

During the restorations, the opportunity was taken to conduct archaeological investigations to throw light on the history of the building. Most notable were the finding of a pagan altar on Golgotha placed there at Hadrian's orders, as reported by Eusebius and St Jerome; the exposure of the rock walls of the Chapel of Adam; and the Armenian excavations at levels below the Chapel of St Helena, which it is wholly impracticable to open to the public because of insufficient space. These show conclusively that the greater part of the church, including Calvary, lies in what was a disused quarry which was not in use for any purpose in the first century AD, other than for burials. On each of the three sides of the Holy Sepulchre itself are three rock tombs. In one of them two compartments of the type known as *kokhim* have been perfectly preserved, and are now referred to as the tombs of Joseph of Arimathea and Nicodemus. The tomb used for Jesus differed from these because

The Edicule (Shrine) of the Holy Sepulchre

it was designed for a single burial only, as stated in the Gospels.

Visit The Church of the Holy Sepulchre is open daily from 5 am to 9 pm (4.30 am to 7 pm in the winter). It is possible to visit it at any time between these hours. Photography is permitted, but flashing lights in the faces of those taking part in the liturgy is understandably regarded as lacking in common courtesy. A sheet showing the times of the celebration of the Orthodox liturgies and services here and in other churches is distributed free on request by the Christian Information Centre at Jaffa Gate. A similar list of Masses is provided for Latin Christians, together with a note of the vernacular in which they are to be celebrated.

The south entrance parvis The present entrance to the church is from the south side, through a courtyard. On its south side a mosque built in 1216, with a minaret added in 1417, stands beside the Greek monastery of Gethsemane. The mosque is said to stand where Caliph Omar prayed in 638. On either side are a number of chapels belonging to the Greeks and Armenians. One enters the courtyard through smallish doorways in the south-west and south-east corners. The Crusader tower is in the north-west corner, and has been truncated, its top having been demolished.

The Holy Tomb of Jesus Christ

In the north-east corner a flight of stairs leads to the Latin Chapel of the Franks (50), which was the entrance to Calvary in Crusader times.

There is a double entrance to the basilica, the right hand side of which has been blocked up. Formerly there was a Crusader *tympanum* over the two doors: the carving between the twin arches and the lintel displayed scenes from the Gospels, of which the best preserved are the Raising of Lazarus and the Last Supper. It has been removed to the Rockefeller Museum, because it was in danger of being destroyed by the weather. The right to open and close the remaining door has been the exclusive privilege of two Muslim families since the thirteenth century. They do so in the presence of the sacristans of the three major communities.

Calvary (or Golgotha) Immediately on the right of the doorway a steep stair leads up to Calvary. It has two naves, with stairs in each. The right hand, or southern, nave, known as the Chapel of the Crucifixion (49), belongs to two periods. The altar area is of the eleventh century, but the part nearer the staircase of the twelfth. This chapel was renovated in 1926, when the marble floor was renewed and the mosaics reconstructed. The altar, of silver on bronze, was given by Ferdinand de Medici (d.1609). The panels in front are the work of Fr Dominico Portigiani, OP, made in 1588. The candlesticks are of gilded bronze. In the mosaic above the altar is a medallion from Crusader times, of Christ ascending into heaven. It is here that the Tenth and Eleventh Stations of the Cross are commemorated.

To the left is the small altar of Our Lady of Sorrows, or Stabat Mater (48), with a wooden bust given in 1778 by Queen Maria de Braganza of Portugal. The heart is pierced by a sword (Luke 2.35). The Thirteenth Station is commemorated here.

In the left hand, or northern, nave of Calvary, the altar of the Greek Orthodox lies across the place where the Cross of Jesus stood (47), marked by a silver circle round a hole. In 1989 the area was excavated, revealing the white limestone Rock of Calvary, which is now displayed covered with bullet-proof plate glass. Behind the altar is a large icon of the Crucifixion, together with lamps and candles in the Greek manner. Here the Twelfth Station of the Cross is commemorated. It is possible to touch the rock where the Cross stood by placing one's hand in the hole. To the right a fissure in the rock is visible, and this fissure can be seen even more plainly in the Chapel of Adam (16) below, which is reached via the staircase on the north side. The fissure is attributed to the earthquake which took place at the moment of Jesus' death (Matt. 27.51–52).

Either side of the entrance were the tombs of Geoffrey de Bouillon and Baldwin I, the king of Jerusalem (1100–1118), but these disappeared in the Greek reconstruction of 1810. Near them were the tombs also of Baldwin II (1118–1131) and Fulk of Anjou (1131–1143); and, beyond, behind the Stone of Unction, those of Baldwin III (1143–1162), Amaury I (1162–1173), Baldwin IV (1173–1185) and Baldwin V (1185–1186). Not a trace of them remains.

The Stone of Unction (or of Anointing) (Matt. 27.57–61) The position of this stone appears to have been fixed by tradition only in the fourteenth century. In the eleventh century there was a small chapel here in honour of Our Lady. Behind the Stone of Unction (14) a new mosaic by an Italian artist in the Greek manner was erected in 1991, depicting the taking down from the Cross, the preparation for burial, and the carrying of the body to the Tomb.

Edicule of the Holy Sepulchre Inside the main entrance, turning left one reaches the rotunda, with the Holy Tomb (38) in the centre. Originally this part of the church was spoken of as the Anastasis or Resurrection, a term now used in Greek and Arabic for the whole church. Between the triumphal arch built by the Crusaders that leads into the Greek choir (42), and the edicule itself, is a raised platform. Two benches flank the front of the edicule, decorated with monumental candlesticks; over the door itself there are four rows of lamps. The bottom row belongs to the Armenians, the top to the Latins, and the two middle rows to the Greeks.

The interior of the edicule is divided into two parts. The outer section is known as the Chapel of the Angel (40). A pilaster in the centre contains a piece of the stone with which the Sepulchre of Jesus was closed; the rest has all disappeared in pious hands. This is used daily as an altar by the Greek Orthodox. Lamps belonging to the three communities hang inside. A very low doorway leads into the tomb chamber itself; on the right is a marble bench, whose top covers the stone on which Jesus was laid. It is this cover, placed there in the sixteenth century, which receives the veneration of the faithful. The split in this marble cover was made on the orders of Fr Boniface of Ragusa, OFM, in 1555, lest the Ottoman Turks should steal so fine a piece of marble. He was *custos*, or father guardian, of the Holy Land, and the last to put the Tomb itself in repair. There are three pictures, each belonging to one of the principal communities, and numerous lamps, among them some belonging to the Copts. Externally the edicule recalls certain features of its pre-1810 predecessors, of which the earliest example known is a fifth century reliquary which survived at Samagher in Italy.

Behind the edicule is a small Coptic chapel (39), and behind it, in the western apse, a Syrian Orthodox altar (34), and two rock tombs. Under the Coptic altar some of the virgin rock of the Tomb is visible, much blackened by candle smoke.

Chapel of the Appearance of Jesus to St Mary Magdalen On the north-east side of the rotunda (in the far right corner as one comes through the arch towards the edicule) there is a chapel of this name (32) belonging to the Franciscans. Originally this event was commemorated in front of the Tomb. The commemoration was transferred here only in 1719 (Matt. 28.1–10; Mark 16). Excavations here in 1968 disclosed an Iron Age quarry of c.900–550 BC, and walls belonging to Hadrian's buildings of AD 135.

Chapel of the Apparition of Jesus to his Holy Mother Two steps lead up into this chapel (30) which commemorates a tradition not found in the Gospels. The magnificent bronze doors, the work of Frank Gatt of Melbourne, were donated by the people of Australia in 1982. The interior was renovated in 1982, when the blue mosaic in the apse was made by two Jewish artists, Mr and Mrs Sabi, of Jerusalem; and a bronze tabernacle erected, the work of Fr Andrea Martini, OFM, of Rome. The chapel dates from the ninth century. In the south-east corner of the chapel a truncated column (31) is said to be part of the column to which Jesus was tied when he was scourged. The Holy Sacrament is reserved behind the altar. This chapel is used by the Franciscans for singing their office. Each day at 4 pm a procession led by the Franciscans visits the principal holy places within the church, and concludes here with Benediction of the Most Holy Sacrament. A processionale, giving the hymns, prayers and music, is available on loan from the sacristy; it is in Latin.

The Latin sacristy Immediately east of this chapel is the sacristy (29) belonging to the Franciscans. In a glass case on the wall the sword and spurs reputed to belong to Geoffrey de Bouillon are kept, for use by the Latin patriarch in giving the accolade to knights of the Holy Sepulchre. This may be seen only after application for permission. A priest is on duty either here or in the vicinity all hours that the church is open. The private quarters of the Franciscans, which occupy the site of the former patriarchal residence, lie behind to the north.

The northern aisles and the apses Behind the Chapel of the Appearance of Jesus to St Mary Magdalen is a gloomy pair of aisles, almost wholly cut off from light by the Greek choir. The right hand aisle belongs to the church of the Crusaders, the left is a relic of the colonnades of Constantine's *triportico*. At the far end is a Greek chapel known as the Prison of Christ (28), for reasons that are obscure. Continuing round the ambulatory are the Greek Chapel of St Longinus (26), the Roman soldier who pierced Jesus' side with his spear, and, immediately behind the altar of the Greek choir (44), the central chapel of the apse, the Armenian Chapel of the Parting of the Raiment (25). Continuing round, a passage leads to a stairway (19), followed immediately by the Greek Chapel of the Derision (18).

The Greek choir This (42) occupies the place of Constantine's colonnaded atrium and the choir built by the Crusaders for the Augustinians. The walls on either side and the iconostasis are wholly modern, built in 1980 in the place of earlier ones. So too are the marble furnishings in the vicinity of the altar, which stands in front of the main apse. At the western end a navel-shaped object (41) represents the legendary centre of the earth. This choir is also spoken of as the Greek Cathedral, or Katholikon. The throne on the north is for the patriarch of Antioch, that on the south for the patriarch of Jerusalem (43).

Chapel of St Helena The stairway mentioned above (19) has twenty-nine very steep steps. In its present form the area at the bottom of the steps (20) is a crypt built by the Crusaders in 1130, together with the vaults and the cupola; its roof, as has already been noted, is occupied by the Ethiopians. It is now in the hands of the Armenian Orthodox, and held by them in honour of their national apostle, St Gregory the Illuminator (257–332). It contains two altars and numerous lamps. Behind the left hand altar a concealed door leads to recent excavations by the Armenians, and a chapel recently consecrated to St Vartan: it is not open to the public, and accessible only by special permission. There is an interesting graffito of a ship in the crypt, with the words '*Domine Ivimus*', words familiar in English from the pilgrim psalm, 'I was glad when they said unto me, we shall go into the house of the Lord.' It is probably c.326.

Chapel of the Finding (or Invention) of the Cross To the right, a narrow and steep staircase leads down to the chapel (23) in which the empress St Helena is believed to have found the Cross of Christ and those of the two thieves. It is quite evidently a former quarry, converted later into a cistern. It is of extreme austerity, particularly as part of the rough quarry walls remain. Behind the plain stone altar a rough-hewn rock pedestal supports a statue of St Helena holding the Cross of Christ (24), the gift of the archduke Maximilian of Austria, later emperor of Mexico (1832–1876). This chapel belongs to the Franciscans, who celebrate Solemn Mass there on the Feast of the Invention (or Finding) of the Holy Cross, which is celebrated in Jerusalem on 7 May.

THE ASCENSION AND THE MOUNT OF OLIVES

Looking across the Kidron Valley from the Old City to the Mount of Olives, the tall tower of the Augusta Victoria Hospital and another of the Russian Church of the Ascension dominate the height. Less noticeable, but at the highest point, is the Greek Chapel of Viri Galilaei, where two columns mark the spot where two men in white are said to have addressed the disciples after the Ascension: 'Ye men of Galilee, why stand ye gazing up into heaven?' (Acts 1.11). The tradition first appears in the thirteenth century, and is not solidly established until the sixteenth.

Before the Church of the Ascension can also be seen the tower of the Church of the Paternoster (see Carmelite Convent, below), and the dome and minaret which mark the former Church of the Ascension (marked on the map as the Dome of the Ascension). A motorable road winds round at the southern side of the hill, and a steep lane leads to the top from the Church of All Nations in Gethsemane. Bethany, at the top, seems to have been Jesus' habitual residence when he visited Jerusalem.

According to Eusebius of Caesarea's *Life of Constantine*, the emperor chose three 'mystic caves' to honour the principal Christian mysteries: that of the Nativity at Bethlehem, that of the Resurrection from the Holy Sepulchre, and that 'of the memory of the Ascension upon the top of the mountain'. For early Christians this latter cave ranked equal to the other two, and here too it was believed that Jesus foretold the end of the world and instructed his disciples on many other occasions. The Pilgrim of Bordeaux (AD 333) associated it with where 'the Lord taught his disciples before his Passion', that is, the last discourses in St John's Gospel.

In 1876 French Carmelite nuns built a convent at the top of the steep lane. They

The Mount of Olives, with the Church of All Nations in the foreground

called their church the Paternoster Church, and inscribed the Lord's Prayer in numerous languages in their cloister. In 1910 excavations revealed the remains of a large basilica 75 yards long and 20 yards broad (69 m x 18½ m): this ruined church behind the convent could be none other than the one the pilgrim Egeria saw in 384. Under it was a crypt, she says, and the cave 'in which our Lord used to teach', an observation made by many later pilgrims. The last known of these was Sophronius (d.638), for it was destroyed by the Persians in 614. It was known as the Church of Eleona, a corruption of the Greek *elaion*, meaning of olives. The cave also contains the remains of a first century tomb. The passages leading to it are somewhat confusing, but well signposted.

THE DOME OF THE ASCENSION This lies about 100 yards (91 m) higher up the hill. The earliest tradition appears to have located the Transfiguration here, and to have associated the Ascension with the Church of Eleona (now within the grounds of the Carmelite Convent). In the fourth century the principal celebrations of the Ascension took place in Bethlehem, but a place called Imbomon (from the Greek *in bommo*, on the hill) was venerated as the 'place where our Lord ascended into heaven'. This was the site of the Dome of the Ascension. By 392 Poimenia, a member of the Imperial family, had built a circular church here, with its centre open to the sky, surrounded by a monastery. Already by 386 there was a 'shining cross on the Mount of Olives where the Redeemer ascended to his Father', and from the beginning there were footprints here that were venerated as those made by Jesus when he ascended. One now remains in the stone; the other is to be seen in the Aqsa Mosque.

An Armenian account of c.660 tells of a beautiful domed building with three concentric circles, modelled on the Church of the Resurrection. The extent to which this is true is demonstrated by the measurements of the remains of the rotunda round the Dome of the Ascension, as shown by L. Vincent based on C. Schick's excavation of 1912, which accord very closely with those of the rotunda of the Holy Sepulchre and, moreover, of the Dome of the Rock as measured by Cresswell. The present building is but a shadow of its former glory, for the Byzantine church had fallen into ruins, and the new building, completed by the Crusaders in 1102, was turned into a mosque by Saladin in 1187.

The arcades of the outer octagon have disappeared, and so too have the bases of the pillars found by Schick. Only part of the present surrounding wall follows the foundations of the inner octagon, the rest being of more modern construction, and visibly out of shape. The open arcade of eight pointed arches which originally stood in the centre was walled in by the Arabs. The sacred stone was moved from the centre to one side, and a *mihrab* installed. Besides this building is a small mosque, for Muslims also believe in the Ascension of Jesus into heaven.

On the Feast of the Ascension different Christian communities are permitted to celebrate Mass in the courtyard, while the Latins celebrate within the octagonal domed building.

At the top of the hill, distinguished by a tall tower, is the Russian Orthodox Church of the Ascension, with a strictly enclosed convent of nuns. No visitors, whether male or female, are admitted.

Below on the hillside are a mass of cemeteries, chiefly Jewish, and some of great antiquity. The French Benedictines, and, lower down, the Russian nuns, have houses here. All these buildings belong to the nineteenth and twentieth centuries. The singing of the Russian nuns is of singular beauty.

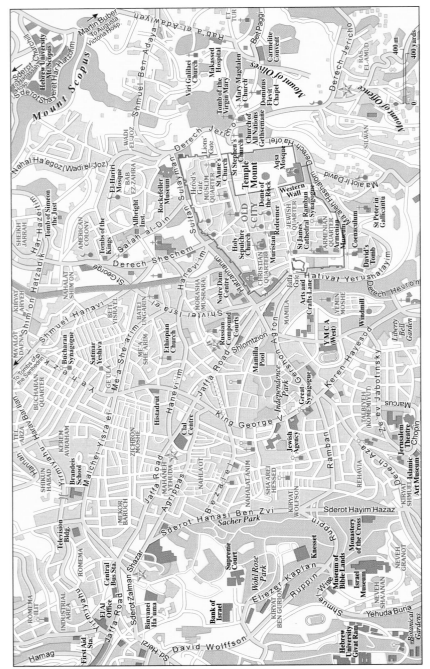

© Carta, Jerusalem

2. Other Places of Interest in Jerusalem

THE ARMENIAN QUARTER

The Armenian Quarter of the Old City lies to the south of the square beyond Jaffa Gate, through which one turns right down the Armenian Patriarchate Road. Passing under an archway after the police station on the site of Herod's Palace, the modern Armenian Seminary and Library, not accessible to visitors, is situated on the right. On the left a low porch gives access to the walled Deir al-Arman, Monastery or Compound of the Armenians, no less than one-sixth of the total area of the Old City, which is wholly surrounded by high stone walls. It contains churches, a convent for women, the Armenian Patriarchate comprising the patriarch's residence and offices, residences for clergy and apartments occupied by a number of laity, a printing press and a museum. Except for the latter, most of this is understandably not open to the public, but permission to visit may be sought in writing from the patriarchate. It is a city within a city, and the centre for some 2,000 Armenians resident in Jerusalem, as well as being a focus for some 6 million Armenians throughout the world.

Armenian Christians are believed to have been present in Jerusalem from the ·fourth century, if not from the third. Armenia, then an independent kingdom, was officially converted to Christianity in AD 301. By 634 there were seventy Armenian churches in Palestine, many of them in Jerusalem. The independent kingdom was partitioned between Rome and Persia in AD 387. The Bible was translated into Armenian in AD 410, and religion as the central focus of Armenian national life was further emphasized when the patriarch refused to accept the decrees of the Council of Chalcedon of 451. This was further fortified by the persecution of Armenian Christians by the Persians. Under the caliphate a number of small dynasties were allowed to arise, one of which survived until it was absorbed by Russia in 1801.

Although the Armenians, under their catholicos, or head, were recognized as a self-governing *millet*, or religious community, under the Ottoman Turks, the partition of Armenia between Ottoman Turkey, Persia and Russia led, with the rise of nationalism in the nineteenth century, to a desire for complete national unity and autonomy. It cost them innumerable lives in the nineteenth century, and culminated in the Turkish massacre of 2 million Armenians in 1920. As a people they have been notable in the arts and architecture; it is to them we owe not only numerous churches, but also the walls of Cairo. They have also produced many administrators of outstanding ability, *wazir*s and military and naval commanders.

VISIT One enters from the road through a large, dog-legged porch. An Arabic inscription records an edict of the Mamluk sultan al-Zahir Sayf al-Din Jaqmaq (1438–1453) abolishing all taxes paid by Armenians, and ordering his successors not to tax or oppress them in any way. The second doorway leads into the parvis of St James' Cathedral. Twenty-two *khatchkars* (excised stone crosses of especial Armenian design) commemorate various events and deaths from 1151 onward. In the porch are two wooden symandra, wooden gongs used before 1840, during a period when the Ottomans had forbidden the use of bells. The cathedral is only open to the public from 3 pm to 3.30 pm.

The rich splendour of St James' Cathedral, in the Armenian Quarter

ST JAMES' CATHEDRAL The door opens on a scene of unimaginable splendour. The floor is richly carpeted in purples, greens and reds. The walls are rich with paintings and tiles. The cruciform church is modelled on the tenth century Church of Haghpad in Armenia. The rib vaulting of the central cupola appears to be a twelfth century restoration of a building originally constructed from the tenth to eleventh centuries. The altar, now on the east side, originally lay on the north, the change having taken place when the church passed from the Georgians to the Armenians in the twelfth century. In the north and south walls there are staircases which give access to the upper chapels.

On the north side is the shrine of St James the Great, with richly inlaid doors of tortoise-shell and mother-of-pearl. The shrine itself is of marble, with a stone under the altar marking the place where his head is buried. On the left is the throne of St James the Less, used only when the patriarch is invested and on the feast day of the saint. Ordinarily he uses the second throne beside it. The principal altar is on a raised dais; both it and the whole church are hung with innumerable lamps. The least noticeable but perhaps most elegant features are the small tiles set among the rich Kutahya wall tiling, depicting incidents from Sacred Scripture and the lives of the saints. Truly one may say with Jacob: 'How awesome is this place! This is none other than the house of God, and this is the gate of heaven.'

THE CHAPEL OF ECHMIADZIN A door on the south side leads into the former narthex, whose arcades were walled up in 1666. It is known as the Chapel of Echmiadzin. Apart from its main altar, a small altar on the right (the Altar of Holy Sinai) has three rocks from Mount Tabor, the Jordan River and Mount Sinai, black and greasy with the kissing of many pilgrims; they are said to have been brought for the consolation of the Virgin Mary because she could not make the pilgrimage to them. Of great beauty are forty-five pictorial tiles of 1719–1727 depicting scenes from the Old and the New Testaments. This chapel is used chiefly for funerals.

OUTSIDE Outside in the courtyard are the Gulbenkian Public Library, with 60,000 books and some 350 periodicals; a theological seminary; the translators' School of St Tarkmanchatz; a library of 4,000 manuscripts; and the St James Printing Press (1839), the first printing press in Jerusalem.

DEIR AL-ZAITUN Farther on through a narrow passage is the Deir al-Zaitun, or Convent of the Olive Tree, known by the Armenians as the Church of the Holy Archangels. It has recently been restored. It is on the traditional site of the house of the high priest Annas. An olive tree in the courtyard is said to be the offspring of a tree to which Our Lord was bound when he was brought here from Gethsemane.

The tradition that it was the House of Annas is not attested before the fourteenth century. The chapel, built c.1300, has an unusually large narthex, and is decorated in the Armenian manner. In the middle of the north side is a recess with an altar, known as the Prison of Christ. Its tiles, of violet and yellow, are of great elegance. Outside the chapel is a stone alleged to be that which cried out with 'a melodious Hosanna' when Christ answered the Pharisees that the stones would cry out.

OTHER CHAPELS Within the Armenian Quarter are several other small chapels. The Yaqubiah Mosque preserves its medieval dedication to St James of Persia, and lies behind the Anglican Christ Church (1849). Another small mosque was formerly the Armenian Church of St Thomas. Farther away is the Syrian Orthodox Patriarchate Cathedral of St Mark, a small chapel of uncertain date. Elegantly decorated, there are claims that a painting on leather of the Virgin and Child was the work of St Luke. Until it is cleaned it is not possible to date it, but it is possibly Byzantine. Above the church is what is claimed to be the house of Mary, mother of St Mark, and the Upper Room of the Last Supper. Our Lady is said to have been baptized in the small baptistery, and St Peter said to have founded the first church here. This church is open daily from 7 am to 12 noon, but is closed on Sundays.

On the north side of the Armenian Quarter was the Church of St Mary of the Germans, founded by German members of the Knights of St John of the Hospital, who in 1190 became an independent order known as the Teutonic Knights, with large territories in northern Europe.

ARMENIAN MUSEUM Farther down the road from the entrance to the Armenian Quarter is a separate entrance to the Armenian Museum, open daily from 10 am to 5 pm except Sundays and holy days. It contains an interesting selection of articles given to the patriarchate at different periods or brought from different churches, and provides a brief conspectus of Armenian art through the centuries. No other Christian community in Jerusalem displays even a selection of its treasures, and a visit here is something that certainly should not be omitted.

THE CHRISTIAN QUARTER

Unlike the Armenian Quarter, the three remaining quarters — the Christian Quarter, the Muslim Quarter, and the Jewish Quarter — are not separated from one another by walls, but by long-standing preferences of habitat.

The principal monuments of the Christian Quarter are the Holy Sepulchre and the buildings nearby, as described in Itinerary 1. These include the Mosque of Omar, south of the Holy Sepulchre. On its north side the Khanqah al-Salahiyyah, a dervish convent, was founded by Saladin (Salah al-Din bin Ayyub, whence Salahiyyah) on the site of the Crusader Patriarchal Palace, between 1187 and 1189. Its minaret was erected in 1417, the same year as that of the Mosque of Omar, their tops being identical in structure. Both contain elements of *ablaq* decoration, in which the use of light and dark stone produces a striped effect. In spite of their being at different ground levels, a line joining their tops is absolutely horizontal, and this can hardly be accidental. The midpoint of this line falls approximately at the very entrance to the Holy Tomb. One can hardly doubt that this was contrived deliberately, but its purpose is not known. The explanation is probably to be discovered among the more arcane doctrines of Sufi (dervish) mystical theology.

THE MURISTAN It is so-called because it was a hospice, later a hospital, first founded by Charlemagne for pilgrims from the West, and later entrusted to the Knights of St John of the Hospital, or the Knights Hospitallers. It was originally a kind of caravanserai, and the headquarters of the merchants of Amalfi. It was only in 1109 that it became a hospital in the modern sense. There were three churches: St Mary la Latine, St Mary la Grande, and St John the Baptist. The first of these churches is occupied by the modern Church of the Redeemer, built in 1898 for the Lutherans, and incorporating a number of Crusader elements in the structure.

Saladin lodged in the Muristan in 1187, and made it a *waqf* (religious endowment) for the Mosque of Omar. In 1216 his nephew Shihab al-Din returned it to its use as a hospital, when it acquired its present Arabic name of Persian origin. The adjacent Greek monastery of Gethsemane was formerly the residence of the Grand Master of the Knights. The north side of the Lutheran church, which, if recent, still faithfully follows the lines of the earlier construction, incorporates a Crusader arch depicting the twelve months of the agricultural year outside.

The Church of St John the Baptist is entered from Christian Quarter Street. It serves a Greek monastery, and the priest, when available, opens the church. The two bell towers are a modern addition. The eleventh century structure rests on the foundations of a fifth century church, and was restored by John Eleemosynarius after its destruction by the Persians in 614. The tradition that it was the House of Zebedee, father of James and John, is not attested before the fourteenth century.

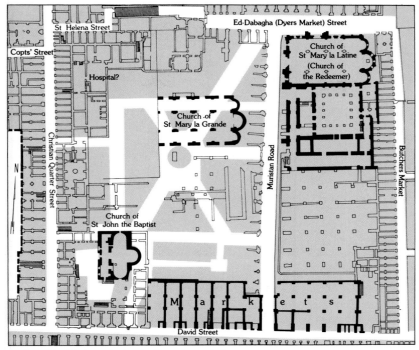

A plan of the Muristan during the Crusader period

The Roman column at the crossing of the four streets of the Muristan serves as a lamppost. Commemorating Marcus Junius Maximus, prefect of Judaea and legate of the Tenth Legion, it was erected in the third century AD by one of his staff, Caius Domitius Sergius Honoratus. The Tenth Legion was stationed in what is now the Armenian Quarter for over 250 years after the capture of Jerusalem in AD 70.

THE MUSLIM QUARTER

The Muslim Quarter comprises 76 acres in the north-eastern part of the Old City. Much of it has been described above, for it includes the Via Dolorosa with the Ecce Homo Arch, the Chapel of the Flagellation, and Sisters of Zion Convent, together with a large number of Mamluk buildings adjacent to the wall of the Temple area. Often these are marked by Mamluk heraldic emblems: a cup for the Cup-bearer, a napkin set between two horizontal lines in a lozenge shape for the Master of the Robes, and two polo sticks for the Master of the Polo Stick.

Another set of blazons is to be seen outside St Stephen's Gate, known by Christians as the Gate of Our Lady Mary, and by others as Lions' Gate, because of the so-called lions (in actuality panthers, the symbol and nickname of Sultan Baybars [1260–1277]) depicted either side of it.

CHURCH OF ST ANNE The only building in this quarter connected with the Holy Places and so far not discussed is that now known as the Church of St Anne.

The Church of St Anne has been beautifully and harmoniously designed

It lies between St Stephen's Gate and the Chapel of the Flagellation, and is used as a Greek (Melkite) Seminary by the White Fathers, who were founded in Algeria by Cardinal Lavigerie in 1868. The modern buildings of the seminary flank the street. Entering the courtyard and passing through it, on the right is the Crusader Church of St Anne, built in 1140. The architecture is of a French church of this period, beautifully conceived. Unfortunately every decoration has been removed, as has the plaster from the walls, so it has a gloomy aspect and a regrettable echo which makes speech — other than conversation in close proximity — difficult.

Below it is a crypt, said to be the home and birthplace of Our Lady. A small cave is shown as her birthplace, and above the altar is a figurine of a babe in swaddling clothes. The tradition, however, appears to have been transferred here from the adjacent ruined buildings and churches of earlier periods.

Leaving the church, and turning right, one reaches an extensive area that has been excavated. St John's Gospel (5.1–13) speaks of Jesus' cure of a man who had been ill for thirty-eight years at the pool of Bethesda, 'a pool with five porches'. Originally there had been a temple here of the god Sarapis (Aesculapius). The White Fathers have erected a painted board which shows the different stages of the buildings disclosed by their excavations. Origen speaks of the five porches c.231: four round the edges and one across the middle. By the mid-fifth century a church in honour of Our Lady had been built here; her home was supposed to be in the vicinity. All this was destroyed by Caliph al-Hakim in 1009, and the Crusaders found nothing but ruins. First they erected a chapel in the middle of the ruins of the Byzantine church, with stairs down to the northern pool so that pilgrims could venerate it. Only in 1140 did they build the Church of St Anne and the shrine of the home of Our Lady. An inscription over the door records that Saladin turned it into a *madrasa*, a college of higher education for teaching Islam. By the

Just inside Dung Gate lie the southern excavations of the Temple area

eighteenth century this was in ruins and buried in rubbish. In 1856 the Ottoman government presented it to France in gratitude for assistance in the Crimean War.

THE JEWISH QUARTER

The Jewish Quarter is in the south-east sector of the Old City, and contains the remains of the terrace on which Herod built the Second Temple. Known as the Western Wall, or Wailing Wall, it was here that the Six-Day War, in which Israeli forces captured the Old City, ended. The area in front, cleared in 1967 (formerly known as the Moroccan Quarter), has become the holiest shrine of the Jewish world. It is said that the drops of dew that form on the stones at night are tears the wall sheds while weeping with all Israel. A number of synagogues were built in the mid-nineteenth century, with other Jewish institutions. The Ramban and Hurva synagogues are on the ruins of the Crusader Church of St Martin. The area is worth a visit because of its splendid vistas of the Temple area. Among the ruins are those of the Nea, Emperor Justinian's church in honour of Our Lady.

NORTH JERUSALEM

Until the nineteenth century the northern and western areas of Jerusalem were almost non-existent. Only after 1870 did small settlements grow up, including the American Colony, originally a charitable mission, the Dominican Convent of St Etienne, and the German Hospice and College. These are all accessible via Derech Shechem — Nablus Road (see Itinerary 5). Immediately north of the Old City a complex of dual carriageways makes foot passage difficult, and covers the remains of an ancient Armenian monastery. Opposite Herod's Gate is the **Rockefeller Museum**. Founded in 1927, it is remarkable not only for its collections but also for the intrinsic beauty of its architecture. With an octagonal tower over the main entrance, the galleries are grouped round a cloistered courtyard with a rectangular pool in the centre. It was conceived by the late E.T. Richmond, the director of Antiquities (1927–1937) under the British Mandate. A typed handlist is available on loan at the entrance barrier. The galleries are divided into the following subjects:

1. Entrance Hall — temporary exhibits; exhibit of the month.
2. South Octagon — exhibits from the Late Canaanite (Bronze) Age.
3. South Gallery — exhibits from the Stone Age, Chalcolithic, and Early, Middle and Late Canaanite (Bronze) Ages.
4. South Room — carved wooden beams and panels from the Aqsa Mosque, eighth century AD.
5. Cabinet of coins of different periods.
6. West Gallery — carved plaster (stucco) and statues from the palace of the caliph al-Walid II (744) at Khirbet el-Mafjar, near Jericho.
7. Jewellery of different periods.
8. North Room — exhibits from the Israelite (Iron) Age, and of the Persian, Hellenistic, Roman, Byzantine, Arab and Crusader periods; reconstructed Middle Canaanite (Bronze) burial-cave from near Jericho.
9. North Octagon — synagogue inscriptions, first to sixth centuries AD; *menorah*s carved in stone, mosaics.
10. Cloisters — various architectural features, sarcophagi, inscriptions on stone, and objects of different periods.

The museum is open daily, except Saturdays and holidays, from 10 am until 5 pm; Fridays 10 am to 2 pm.

TOMBS OF THE KINGS, AND OTHER BURIALS Travelling along Salah al-Din Street one comes to the Tombs of the Kings, cut from the rock in about AD 50, of which the principal burial is of Queen Helena of Adiabene (died AD 65). They have been much robbed, and the sarcophagi used as drinking trough fountains at different times in various parts of the city. Farther on, before the Sheikh Jarrah Mosque and to the right, is the Tomb of Simeon the Just, a high priest of the late fourth century BC. One-and-a-half miles (2.4 km) north-west of Damascus Gate is a huge cemetery known as the Tombs of the Sanhedrin, or Judges. It belongs to the first century AD, and is in a park. Further burials lie beyond.

MOUNT SCOPUS Eastward, one approaches the Hebrew University, north of the Augusta Victoria Hospital. The latter's tower, 195 feet (60 m) high, is one of Jerusalem's major landmarks. Built by Emperor William II of Germany and his wife Empress Augusta Victoria, it opened in 1910. The complex contains a hospice and hospital sponsored by the Lutheran World Foundation and the United Nations. Beyond lies the campus of the Hebrew University. Free tours are available at 11.30 am daily from the Bronfman Family Reception Centre. Of interest are a necropolis, some scattered tombs, and a botanical garden. Beyond the university is Hadassah Hospital (1938). On the north-west side is the British Military Cemetery from World War I, notable for its Australian section, men who played a foremost part in the defeat of the Ottoman Turks in 1917.

WESTERN JERUSALEM

Western Jerusalem, almost entirely a creation of the late nineteenth and twentieth centuries, contains the principal official buildings and many museums. Many of

The Monastery of the Cross, with the Israel Museum in the background

the latter are specialized, and only a selection can be mentioned here. To reach the Monastery of the Cross from the Old City one can go via Independence Park, which contains the Mamilla Pool. The pool may have existed in Herodian times, and was certainly linked to the main Jerusalem water system in the fifteenth century.

MONASTERY OF THE CROSS Isolated in an area of parkland is the Greek Orthodox Monastery of the Cross. It is said to have been founded by King Tatian of Georgia (466–499), a kingdom west of Armenia in the Caucasus. The first monastery was destroyed by the Persians in 514, and rebuilt by the emperor Justinian c.536. It is fortress-like in appearance. Until after the middle ages the Georgians had a number of monasteries in Jerusalem, and rights in the Holy Places. In the seventeenth century the Georgian community fell into debt, and in 1644 the Monastery of the Cross was sold to the Greek Orthodox. It takes its name from a legend that a twig of the Tree of Knowledge of Good and Evil (Gen. 2.16 ff.) was given to Seth, son of Adam, who planted it by his father's grave. It was watered by Lot, and later cut down to provide wood for the building of the first Jewish Temple. Some wood was left over, and this was used for the Cross of Christ. Needless to say, anyone who believes this will wish also to believe in the legend of the Holy Donkey.

The monastic quarters, the library and the refectory are private, and only the church is open to visitors from Monday to Friday. The huge walls and fortifications remind one that the monastery was often attacked by brigands.

While traces of earlier buildings survive, the building as it is belongs to the eleventh century. A narthex leads into a beautiful domed basilican church with a nave and two side aisles. The altar and *pastophoria* (the rooms on either side of the apse) are hidden by a splendid iconostasis. The walls are covered by late medieval frescoes that have been heavily restored. They recount the story of the tree. At different times the tree has been alleged to have been located either behind the altar or in a room which is accessible from the north (left-hand) aisle through a passage, which contains a number of icons. The monastery is now used as a hostel for pilgrims and students.

THE ISRAEL MUSEUM Although the Israel Museum is not far from the Monastery of the Cross as the crow flies, it is necessary to travel over twice as far to reach it by road. The museum is open daily 10 am to 5 pm; except for Tuesdays, 4 pm until 10 pm, and Fridays and Saturdays 10 am to 2 pm. There are varying opening times on public holidays, and it is prudent to telephone for times of opening. Special tours are available. The museum is arranged on three levels: there are elevators, making it easier for the disabled and elderly, although the distances are a consideration. There are a number of pavilions. The ticket office is at the main entrance. The principal sections are the Shrine of the Book, the Archaeological Museum, the Bezalel Art Gallery, the Billy Rose Art Garden (modern art), and the Department of Antiquities. For the Shrine of the Book, and its contents, see Khirbet Qumran (p. 105). There is a special section for children. Other rooms house temporary exhibitions.

To the north of the museum, and within walking distance, is the entrance to the Knesset (Israeli parliament), with a huge bronze *menorah* outside, presented by the British government. For security reasons you must take your passport with you. Inside the building (built in 1966) the superb wall and floor mosaics as well as the tapestries were designed by Marc Chagall. The gallery is open to the public when the Knesset is in session. The building may be visited at other times.

HEBREW UNIVERSITY Between 1947 and 1967, when Mount Scopus was situated in Jordanian territory, the university was transferred to the Givat Ram campus. Although many faculties have returned to Mount Scopus, some remain at Givat Ram. This site also houses the Jewish National and University Library. A sports stadium is situated in the valley nearby, with botanical gardens to the south.

MAYER INSTITUTE FOR ISLAMIC ART At the corner of Hanasi Street and Hapalmach, the Mayer Institute for Islamic Art is one of the richest Islamic museums in the world. There is a small entry charge. Built round a covered courtyard with a central well, elevators enable one to travel downward from the nineteenth century AD to the earliest Islamic centuries. The principal collections include much from India and Iran as well as from historical Syria and Egypt.

OTHER NOTABLE PLACES Travelling back towards Jaffa Gate, Keren Hayesod and its continuation King George V Street are encountered. On the latter are the offices of the Jewish Agency, the head office of the World Zionist Organization, the Great Synagogue, and the Chief Rabbinate. To the east of Keren Hayesod is the YMCA, a non-denominational Protestant charitable organization. It is noteworthy for its tall, elegant tower surmounted by a cupola, and half a century ago was outstanding as the tallest building in Jerusalem. Opposite is the King David Hotel. Nearby is the Sir Moses Montefiore Windmill; he was an Anglo-Jewish philanthropist who provided houses in this vicinity for poor immigrant Jews. The windmill is his memorial. Not far away is a tomb complex known as Herod's Family Tomb, albeit he himself is buried at Herodion. The attribution is uncertain, but it is not impossible that some of his family was buried here.

NORTH OF JAFFA ROAD In this area, with cathedrals, offices, and dwellings, are the Russian and Ethiopian compounds. The Russian buildings are occupied to some extent by government and municipal offices. The cathedrals may be visited. Further north is the Jewish Me'a She'arim quarter, built in 1874, the home of strictly orthodox Jews who retain the dress of the medieval ghettoes. Notices request visitors to wear modest clothes and to be well covered-up.

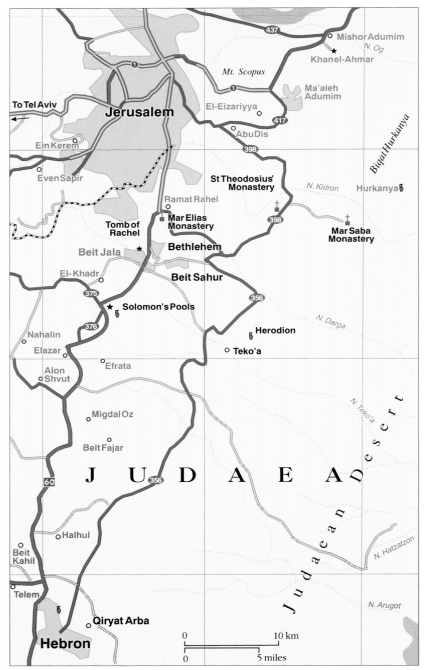

437

Mishor Adumim

N. Og

★ Khan el-Ahmar

Mt. Scopus

Ma'aleh
Adumim

El-Eizariyya

To Tel Aviv

Jerusalem

417

AbuDis

Ein Kerem

398

Biqat Hurkanya

Even Sapir

St Theodosius'
Monastery

N. Kidron

Hurkanya

Ramat Rahel

398

**Tomb of
Rachel**

Mar Elias
Monastery

Mar Saba
Monastery

Bethlehem

★ Beit Jala

El-Khadr

Beit Sahur

375

356

Solomon's Pools

376

N. Darga

Nahalin

Herodion

Elazar

Teko'a

Alon
Shvut

Efrata

Migdal Oz

N. Teko'a

Beit Fajar

J U D A E A

60

356

D e s e r t

Halhul

N. Hatzatzon

Beit
Kahil

J u d a e a n

Telem

N. Arugot

Qiryat Arba

0   10 km

Hebron

0   5 miles

© Carta, Jerusalem

3. Jerusalem to Bethlehem and Hebron

Frequent buses from the main bus station on Jaffa Road reach Bethlehem and Hebron. Taxis are available, and these are necessary, for other than guided coach tours, to visit Herodion and the Judaean monasteries.

Near to Zion Gate is a site believed to be the House of Caiaphas. Across the Hinnom Valley, at the Haceldama Monastery, is the site where Judas Iscariot is said to have hanged himself; there is a tree whose branches all point to the east. However, this tradition has changed from time to time.

The road to Bethlehem, Derech Hevron (Hebron Road), bypasses St Andrew's Scottish Church and the Railway Station. Further along on the left is the fortress-like Mar Elias Monastery (Greek Orthodox), founded in the sixth century, and rebuilt after an earthquake in 1160, in honour of the prophet Elijah. The tradition connecting it with a tale that he fled here to escape the wrath of Jezebel is mythical.

Continuing for another few kilometres, on the right is a small building containing the **Tomb of Rachel** (she has another at Rama). It is especially venerated by Jews, but is sacred also to Christians and Muslims. Its appearance is that of a medieval Islamic tomb. On the right a signpost indicates Tantur, originally a house of the Knights of Malta (1865), which, after passing through the hands of a number of religious orders, has been an Ecumenical House of Studies since 1967. The connection of Rachel with Rama arises from Jeremiah 31.15 and 40.1, and is also mentioned in Matthew 2.17. The tradition placing her tomb near Bethlehem is already found in the fourth century; the Crusaders rebuilt it, and it was rebuilt again in 1788 and 1841.

BETHLEHEM

Manger Square is entered from the north-east side. The courtyard of the Basilica of the Nativity is on the left, and a car park on the right, with shops and offices. Bethlehem has a large Arab population, which has grown since the 1967 war. It has been occupied almost continuously since the Iron Age. One interpretation of the Tell el-Amarna Letters (fourteenth century BC) calls it Bit-ilu-Lakhama, the House of the Goddess Lakhama. The attractive popular explanation that the name means House of Flesh (*lahem* is flesh in Arabic) is not historical.

There are many religious houses scattered about the town, but none of particular historical interest. In and around Manger Square are souvenir shops, which sell religious objects of different kinds, and especially of mother-of-pearl. This is owed to Fr Bernardino Amico, OFM, at one time custodian of Bethlehem and subsequently *custos* (father guardian) of the Holy Land. At the end of the sixteenth century he found the inhabitants of Bethlehem in great poverty, and set them to work making religious objects, particularly those of mother-of-pearl.

HISTORY The history of David is told in the First and Second Books of Samuel (his ancestry is recounted in the Book of Ruth). He was anointed king of Israel here, but made Hebron his first capital. After he had taken Jerusalem and made his capital there, Bethlehem lost all importance. It served simply as a market town for Bedouin. Later, in the fourth century AD, this role became secondary to its position as a place of Christian pilgrimage.

The picturesque town of Bethlehem, the birthplace of Jesus Christ

The Gospels relate divergent accounts of the birth of Jesus Christ, but give no account of the town. According to St Matthew the Child was born to Our Lady of the Holy Spirit in Bethlehem, which was apparently the home of St Joseph (1.18–25). There the Magi, astrologers, came from the East to worship him. They had asked the way from Herod, and presented their gifts of gold, frankincense and myrrh. They returned home by another route, having been warned in a dream not to return to Herod. Joseph was warned in a dream that Herod would search for the child, to destroy him, and told to flee with his family to Egypt. When an angel informed them of Herod's death they returned from Egypt to Israel, but, directed by a dream, settled in Nazareth (Matt. 2.1–23).

St Luke's account begins with the announcement in the Temple of the future birth of St John the Baptist, and, six months later, the Annunciation to Our Lady in Nazareth of the birth of Jesus Christ. Soon after she visited the Baptist's mother, Elizabeth, traditionally in Ein Kerem, in Jerusalem. Later Mary and Joseph went up from Nazareth to Bethlehem, where the Child was born, greeted by angels, and adored in the Manger by shepherds. Eight days later the Child was circumcised, and shortly afterwards presented in the Temple in accordance with Mosaic Law. The family then returned to Nazareth (Luke 2.1–52).

Thus one account has it that Bethlehem was the original home, the other Nazareth. The Presentation in the Temple could, however, have taken place before the visit of the Magi and the subsequent Flight into Egypt.

EARLY HISTORY OF THE SHRINE The early history of the shrine of Bethlehem is very obscure. Writing c.155–160 St Justin Martyr, a native of Nablus, regards the location of the Nativity in Bethlehem as a generally accepted belief. He is the first to say that it took place in a cave, a statement reinforced by Origen, the most distinguished of all the early Fathers, in 248:

In Bethlehem you are shown the cave where he was born, and within the Manger
where he was wrapped in swaddling clothes. These things that they show you
are recognized in the district, even by those who do not share our faith. They
admit, that is, that the Jesus whom Christians adore, was born in this cave.

Yet the evangelists say nothing about a cave. For St Matthew it was a house, while
St Luke says that the Child was laid in a Manger because the inn was full. Perhaps
the most important attestation is that of Origen, that 'those who do not share our
faith', presumably Jews and pagans, accepted the authenticity of the site.

At the end of the fourth century St Jerome says that the emperor Hadrian set up
a shrine of Venus and Adonis to overshadow Bethlehem:

For the space of about 180 years, from Hadrian's time until the reign of
Constantine, the image of Jupiter was venerated on the site of the Resurrection,
and a statue of Venus on Golgotha... Bethlehem, which now belongs to us...
was overshadowed by the grove of Tammuz, that is, Adonis, and the cave where
the Christ-child once cried they wept for Venus's lover... (Ep. 58.3).

Hadrian's order was in line with a similar action in the Holy Sepulchre, and adds
additional confirmation of authenticity.

THE BASILICA OF THE NATIVITY The dull square in front of the Basilica of
the Nativity was once a colonnaded atrium. Some of its columns can be seen in
the garden of the Franciscans on the left. On the right are the walls of the
fortress-like Armenian monastery, dating from Crusader times. A hall, in Crusader
Gothic style, is spoken of as the Lecture Hall of St Jerome; it stands where the
southern colonnade once was. Although he could not have taught in this hall, he
could have taught in the colonnade. The hall is not open to visitors.

The Armenian walls and a huge buttress mask two of the three doorways which
once led into the vestibule. The remaining doorway has been reduced several times,
finally in Mamluk or Ottoman Turkish times. The narthex has been sub-divided,
and part is in use as a police guard-room. Here was a mosaic depicting the visit of
the Magi, in Persian costume. In 614, when the Persians sacked Jerusalem, they
forebore to attack the church because they were misled by the mosaic into believing
that Christians venerated their prophet Zoroaster.

CONSTANTINE'S CHURCH The original church, begun in 326 or 327 on the
orders of Constantine, no longer survives. At the end of the fourth century it began
to be attributed to the empress Helena, but the earlier attributions make no mention
of her, only of Constantine. It was complete by 333, and rich with gold and silver
ornaments, marble, frescoes and mosaics, embroideries, jewelled lamps and vessels. The clay Manger had been covered by one of silver. Excavations revealed the
original plan when the structure was strengthened in 1934. It had a nave and four
aisles, two on each side, like the present church. It ended in an octagonal apse, in
the centre of which it has been thought was an *oculus*, or open space, through which
the faithful could view the place of the Birth. However, this leaves the position of
the altar unresolved, and is contradicted by the fact that there is no trace in the
grotto below of any disturbance to the rock ceiling. Parts of the original mosaic
floor remain, some of which can be viewed through trap doors in the present church.

JUSTINIAN'S CHURCH In 529 the Samaritans revolted. Jerusalem suffered greatly. There is no written record of the destruction at Bethlehem, but a litter of ashes and debris found in 1934 showed that the church had been destroyed by fire. The present building was constructed under the emperor Justinian (527–565), and probably completed in 536. Broadly it followed the earlier pattern, but the octagonal apse was replaced by the present choir and apse, and by apsidal transepts. The excavations showed that the nave and aisle colonnades were entirely rebuilt, and that there were forty-four pillars instead of a previous forty. There was a new narthex, the atrium was removed farther west, and there were now two lateral entrances to the grotto. In all, the church assumed its present shape.

An exception seems to have been the font, which is now to be seen as it were adrift in the south aisle. Its inscription, in Greek, reads:

> For remembrance, and rest, and remission of sins of those whose names the Lord knows.

Similar inscriptions, dated to the sixth century, are found in the Jerusalem area. The dimensions of this font fit precisely the remains of an octagonal structure on the north side of the principal apse, with plumbing arrangements and a cistern for drainage, thus confirming its original position. These remains were found in 1934 in the course of structural repairs. The cistern lies immediately behind the place of the Nativity, and is wholly irrelevant to a series of grottoes which suggest agricultural use. Without straining the meaning of St Jerome's text, this cistern could well have been the *favissa* (the pit for disposing of the remains of sacrifices) in the shrine of Venus and Adonis.

CRUSADER TIMES   This, then, was the church which Tancred and the Crusaders entered in 1099, and where they built a convent for Augustinian canons. In 1101, Baldwin, the first king of Jerusalem, was crowned here by the patriarch, having refused to be crowned in Jerusalem where the Saviour had been crowned with thorns. In 1106–1108 a Russian, Abbot Daniel, visited the Holy Land, and gave us what is the best contemporary description of the church:

> above the holy cave a great church has been built in the form of a cross and its roof is raised in a clerestory, and the church is covered with tin and decorated with mosaic. It has eight [*sic*] round marble columns and is paved with white marble slabs... The cave and the manger where Christ's nativity took place are beneath the great altar like a cavern... As you enter the cave... on the left there is the place down on the ground where Christ our God was born... this cave is decorated with mosaic and beautifully paved.

There may, however, have been some disrepair, for between 1161 and 1169 restorations were carried out by Raoul, bishop of Bethlehem, whom William of Tyre describes as 'a man of letters not without worldly wisdom, an Englishman by race...' The marble panelling and mosaics in the church were relaid or renewed.

THE MOSAICS   When Canon Pietro Casola saw them in 1494 he spoke of 'the most beautiful mosaics that look quite new'; they are since sadly decayed, and only fragments remain. Their destruction was due to the stripping of the roof of its lead covering by the Ottoman Turks, in order to make bullets for one of their interminable wars against the Venetians. The mosaics lasted into the seventeenth century, when we have a complete description given by Fr Franciscus Quaresmius, OFM, in 1626. Much still remained in the nineteenth century, when they were described

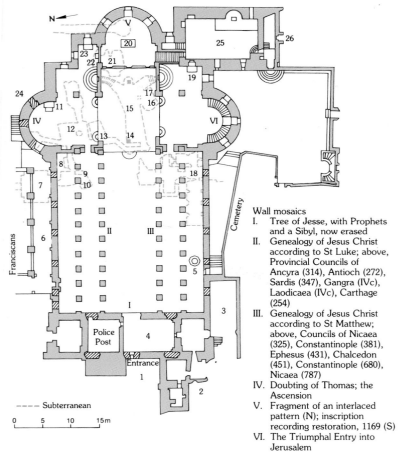

Wall mosaics
I.   Tree of Jesse, with Prophets and a Sibyl, now erased
II. Genealogy of Jesus Christ according to St Luke; above, Provincial Councils of Ancyra (314), Antioch (272), Sardis (347), Gangra (IVc), Laodicaea (IVc), Carthage (254)
III. Genealogy of Jesus Christ according to St Matthew; above, Councils of Nicaea (325), Constantinople (381), Ephesus (431), Chalcedon (451), Constantinople (680), Nicaea (787)
IV. Doubting of Thomas; the Ascension
V.   Fragment of an interlaced pattern (N); inscription recording restoration, 1169 (S)
VI. The Triumphal Entry into Jerusalem

Plan of the Basilica of the Nativity: 1. Courtyard; 2. Armenian monastery; 3. Armenian courtyard; 4. Narthex; 5. Font; 6. Cloister; 7. Chapel of St Jerome; 8. Altar of St Eusebius; 9. Sts Paula and Eustochium; 10. St Jerome; 11. Altar of the Virgin; 12. Tombs of the Holy Innocents; 13. Altar of St Joseph; 14. Cistern; 15. Grotto of the Nativity; 16. Manger; 17. Altar of the Magi; 18. Burial grottoes; 19. Altar of the Circumcision; 20. Main altar; 21. Cistern; 22. Star of the Nativity; 23. Altar of Kings; 24. Church of St Catherine; 25. Sacristy and Chapel of St George; 26. Bell tower

by the Marquis de Vogüé. From these descriptions it would be wholly possible to reconstruct them, and it is to be hoped that one day this may become possible.

All the surviving mosaics are of the twelfth century. The west wall, now quite bare, was decorated with a Tree of Jesse, depicting the ancestry of Jesus Christ, together with figures of prophets bearing scrolls foretelling his coming. Quaresmius counted seven in all, including Balaam and the Roman Sibyl.

The designs on the walls of the nave were arranged in five registers. The lowest register recited the genealogy of Jesus, on the south wall according to St Matthew, the north wall according to St Luke. Then, above a band of fanciful foliage, the

The mosaic depicting Jesus' Triumphal Entry into Jerusalem on Palm Sunday

south wall had representations of the Seven General or Ecumenical Councils, each with an inscription reciting its principal decisions. The north wall records the Six Provincial Councils, with differing artistic emblems, with ornamentation and a dado above. Constantinople II and Nicaea II are missing. All the others are damaged, and only Constantinople I is wholly intact. Quaresmius records the full text of Nicaea I:

> The Holy Synod of 318 holy fathers against Arius, who claimed that the Son and Word of God were created, met under the emperor Constantine the Great. The Holy Synod decreed and confessed that the only Son and Word of God, by whom all things were made, is co-eternal and consubstantial with the Father, begotten and not made. It anathematized Arius.

On the north side St Luke's version of the genealogy of Christ has entirely disappeared. Churches and turrets decorate the inscriptions that depict the Six Provincial Councils, again each with an inscription recording its decisions. On the south side, instead of the conventional representation of councils depicting assemblies of bishops, there are altars, with censers or candlesticks on either side.

The cubes that compose the mosaics were so arranged as to catch the light and throw it down diagonally into the opposite aisles, and it is the destruction of the mosaics that has caused the church to appear so gloomy. A further contributing factor was the removal of the marble lining of the walls; they were originally lined with white marble. This theft was a common Ottoman Turkish practice, not only from churches but even from the once splendid mosques of Cairo, to embellish the mosques of Istanbul. For the best view of the mosaics in the nave stand as far away as possible in the opposite side aisles. Quaresmius also records mosaics in the transepts and in the sanctuary. The Nativity and the Adoration of the Magi are in the south aisle, the Annunciation in the eastern apse, and the Doubting of St Thomas in the northern apse. Fragments of other scenes can be seen, from the Gospels, the Ascension, and the Dormition of Our Lady. In the south transept is the Triumphal Entry into Jerusalem on Palm Sunday: children throw their clothes before the feet of the ass, and Our Lord sits sideways in accordance with oriental convention.

The original dedication inscription, in Latin and in Greek, survives to some extent, and can be reconstructed from Quaresmius and earlier writers. The Greek version reads in translation:

> The present work was completed by the hand of Ephraim the monk, painter and mosaic worker, in the reign of the Great Emperor Manuel Porphyrogenitus Comnenus and in the days of the Great King of Jerusalem our Lord Amaury and the most holy bishop of holy Bethlehem, our Lord Raoul, in the year 6677, second indiction.

According to the Greek reckoning of Creation in 5508 BC, 6677 is equivalent to AD 1169. The Latin version can be translated:

> The King Amalric, guardian of virtue, generous friend, comrade of honour and impiety's foe, patron of justice and piety, avenger of wrong, was fifth on the throne. Over the Greeks there also ruled Emmanuel, the generous giver and pious ruler. Here too there lived as prelate and governor of the church Raoul the kindly, worthy of the bishop's throne, when the hand of Ephraim, they say, made for them the gracious...

It is worth noticing that the order of the two rulers is reversed in the Latin inscription: the Greek text implies that the emperor takes precedence over the king. However this may be, we are fortunate in having a firm date for the composition as a whole, 1169, that is to say more than a century after the schism of 1054, when Rome and Constantinople excommunicated each other. Here in Bethlehem the Orthodox emperor, the Latin king of Jerusalem, and a Latin bishop had evidently joined together, to display dogmatic unity in spite of the formal excommunication.

On the north wall, by the feet of the third angel from the east, are the words 'Basilius Pictor' (Basil the Painter), in gold on a green background. Who he was, and what his relationship to the monk Ephraim may have been, is not known. It need not be more than a coincidence that in the British Museum is a psalter, illustrated by a series of miniatures for Queen Mélisande, the wife of Fulk of Anjou, third king of Jerusalem, and signed by one Basilius. It can be dated to about 1140.

THE PILLAR PAINTINGS A most striking feature of the basilica is the collection of pillar paintings, the largest assembly of Crusader painting in existence. Such paintings are by no means unique, and one such survives in the Basilica of the Holy Sepulchre, which once would have been decorated in a similar fashion. Like those of the rotunda of the Holy Sepulchre, the Bethlehem pillars are all of a local pink limestone which can take a high polish, which has deceived some into believing them to be of marble. If this had been so, they would have been seized either by the Mamluks or the Ottomans for the decoration of mosques. The poor light and the curved surface make them difficult to see. Most pillars depict a single saint; occasionally there are two. Their condition has not been improved by the practice recorded by Fr Felix Faber, OP, who made pilgrimages in 1480 and again in 1483, of rubbing the pillars down with oil. The object was not to improve the paintings, but to make of the oil a kind of secondary relic.

Of the thirty paintings, twenty have their subjects identified in both Greek and Latin; one is in Greek only, and five in Latin only, suggesting a mixed congregation (the last four have no inscription). From other parallel decorations in Eastern churches one might have expected that some sort of hierarchical order would have been observed in their arrangement: the Heavenly Hierarchy, the Earthly Hierarchy, and the laity, soldiers, monks, nuns and kings.

As well as depictions of Our Lady and Child, the Crucifixion, St Anne and Our Lady, there are two each of prophets, apostles, and St Margaret, or Marina (this is not St Margaret, queen of Scotland, for she was not canonized until about a century after these paintings). The most numerous class is that of monks: the saints Sabas, Euthymius and Theodosius were famous Palestinian monastic founders; Antony, Macarius and Onuphrius distinguished Egyptian monastic founders. St Fosca was popular on Torcello Island as well as in Venice, as was St Margaret; Bartholemew, Catald (an Irishman who became a Sicilian bishop), and Leonard were popular among the Normans in Sicily and southern Italy; King Olaf and King Canute were Scandinavians, reminding us that we possess accounts of pilgrimages from as far away as Iceland; Blaise, Leo and Vincent were of more general Western interest.

There is no apparent link that binds them all together into some coherent artistic theme or order. The arrangement appears to be wholly random. Both Byzantine and Western influences are traceable in the composition. Almost every pillar has graffiti below the painting: these have never been deciphered or studied. Including coats-of-arms that can only be of the Crusader period or after, these might tell us something of the pilgrims, of who admired what, if not of the paintings themselves.

As to dating, there are inscriptions of 1130 and 1169 which provide a useful bracket; the bishops depicted are all from after 1150 because of a known change in the pattern of mitres after that date.

THE ROOF   The roof has undergone many changes. Attempts to repair it in 1435 and 1448 failed to secure permission from the Mamluks. Only in 1480 did the Franciscans obtain permission: wood was sent from Venice; Edward IV of England supplied wood; and Philip of Burgundy provided craftsmen. Thus the main structure was preserved, but even in 1483 Fr Felix Faber described it as 'a barn without hay, an apothecary's without aromatic pots, a library without books'. The upper church today is much as it was after the repairs carried out in 1934 by W.E. Harvey, under the Mandatory Department of Antiquities. It is shared between the Greek Orthodox and the Armenians, the latter possessing only the north transept. Further repairs to the roof were necessitated in 1992, and the Israeli government had to intervene because of disagreements between Armenians, Greeks and Latins.

THE ALTAR OF THE NATIVITY   The Cave of the Nativity can be entered from both transepts. A third entrance, from the west, is kept locked, as it was in medieval times. The two entrances from the transepts have stairs that date from the emperor Justinian's rebuilding. Their bronze doors are possibly from that time also. The interior, partly rock and partly masonry, has been altered by man.

Entering from the north, the place of the Nativity is immediately on the left,

The Grotto of the Nativity

where there is a small apse containing an altar belonging to the Greeks, and which can also be used by the Armenians. Under it is a silver star inscribed:

Hic De Virgine Maria Jesus Christus Natus Est — 1717

(Here Jesus Christ was born of the Virgin Mary — 1717)

When permission was granted to the Greeks to repair the roof in 1670 they seized the Grotto of the Nativity. In 1690 the Latins retook it, and in 1717 placed a new silver star in the grotto under the altar in place of an old one which had worn away. Latin control lasted until 1757, when the Greeks succeeded in ousting the Latins. On 12 October 1847 the silver star disappeared. After five years of negotiations between the French, as protectors of Catholics in the Holy Land, and the Ottomans, the sultan ordered the Greeks to allow a new star to be put in place. At the same time the sultan's decree confirmed the Status Quo in the Holy Places. The new star was installed in 1852, but with the former inscription.

The long story of contention between Greeks and Latins cannot be told here. On 25 April 1873 a band of Greeks, monks and laity, broke into the grotto. They wounded eight Franciscans, pillaged the grotto, and carried off everything of value. They even took the marble covering of the Manger. Once again, it was necessary for the Ottomans to restore order, placing a janissary there by day and night. To this day a police officer discreetly keeps guard within the narthex.

The semi-dome of the apse is the only remaining twelfth century mosaic in the Grotto of the Nativity. A pilgrim, Johannes Phocas, describes it as it was then:

In the apse is figured the Virgin reclining upon her bed... as she looks at her infant. Beyond her are the ox and the ass, the manger and the Babe, and the company of the shepherds in whose ears the voice of heaven rang.

Phocas also mentions that the mosaic included the Magi arriving with their gifts, but omits another scene, perhaps because it is not recorded in the Gospels, of the

The silver Star of Bethlehem commemorates the spot where Jesus was born

Washing of the Child. It is still partly visible. The words '*Pax hominibus*' (Peace towards men), from the Angels' song, can also be read.

THE MANGER On the south side of the cave is the Grotto of the Manger, a rock shelf covered with marble slabs. The altar here, of the Adoration of the Magi, is in exclusive Latin possession. The Manger itself is on the west side of the altar. Its dimensions (studied both by a Protestant, Gustav Dalman, and a Catholic, Fr Clement Kopp) accorded with evidence that it corresponded with feeding troughs, one at least of medieval date, cut out of rock by Bedouin. In Constantine's church the Manger had been covered with silver. St Jerome wrote:

> Oh that I might see the Manger where the Lord lay! Now we, as honouring Christ, have taken away that clay Manger and set in its place a silver one; but I prize more that which was taken away.

St Jerome's 'clay Manger' should perhaps be taken with a pinch of salt, for a clay manger would soon have been knocked to bits by cattle. Not impossibly the very authentic dimensions indicate that a rock manger remains underneath the present-day covering of marble. The relic of a wooden manger, carried in procession on the Feast of the Nativity in Santa Maria Maggiore, Rome, cannot be authentic, for there were certainly no wooden mangers in Palestine in the first century.

THE CHURCH OF ST CATHERINE OF ALEXANDRIA On the north side of the basilica is the Latin Church of St Catherine of Alexandria, built by the Franciscans in 1882 to replace a Crusader one built by the Augustinians. A plan of it was published by Fr Bernardino Amico in his *Holy Land Plans*, 1609, and shows a very long, narrow chapel. Its very narrow dimensions were suited to the singing of the Divine Office by a very few canons, who would have been lost in the basilica. It is reminiscent of the very narrow nave of the Abbey Church of

Solesmes, of which only the choir has been enlarged to accommodate a greater number of monks. It might be that the original architect came from Maine.

THE CLOISTER West of the Church of St Catherine is the medieval cloister of the Augustinian canons. This was reconstructed, partly using the original materials, by the distinguished Italian architect Antonio Barluzzi, in 1948–1949.

GROTTOES A staircase on the south side of the Church of St Catherine leads down to the grottoes, which contain a number of chapels. These were all cleared by Fr Farina, OFM, in 1962–1964. He found that the grottoes were occupied between 787 and 700 BC. After being abandoned at the beginning of the seventh century BC, they were reoccupied in the time of Christ and used until AD 333, when the basilica was completed.

There were thirty-five tombs in all, in accord with the early Christian practice to be buried near the tombs of saints and martyrs, and other holy places. The first chapel is dedicated to St Joseph, the next to the Holy Innocents, adjacent to a cave where their remains were believed to have been deposited. This latter is opened only on their feast day. To the left is the tomb of St Eusebius of Cremona, St Jerome's successor as superior of the monastery that he founded. The next tomb on the left contained the remains of the saints Paula and Eustochium, but all the remains have long since been taken away as relics. St Jerome himself describes the construction of these three tombs.

The last chapel is dedicated to St Jerome: it is reputedly where he wrote his translation of the Bible known as the Vulgate, the first official vernacular version of Sacred Scripture. In the great heat of summer, such a cell would have been a pleasant solace, but chilly indeed in winter. This Latin version of Scripture, if only now recently obsolete, has assuredly been heard by more Christians than any other.

THE MILK GROTTO Leaving Manger Square, we reach the Franciscan Chapel of the Milk Grotto. It is venerated by Christians of all rites, as well as by Muslims. It takes its name from the white stone, which is said to have been whitened by some drops of Our Lady's milk. It was first recognized by a bull of Pope Gregory XI in 1375. The building dates from 1872.

HOUSE OF ST JOSEPH This is a chapel built by the Franciscans in 1892, possibly on the site of a small Byzantine church.

BEIT SAHUR AND THE SHEPHERDS' FIELD

A road leads out of Bethlehem to Beit Sahur, a village with a number of Christian institutions and churches. Beyond it is the Field of Boaz, the husband of Ruth. She is remembered chiefly for her filial devotion to her mother-in-law. Here, a thousand paces from Bethlehem, Eusebius determined as the area where the shepherds heard the voices of the angels singing '*Gloria in Excelsis*', bidding them to hasten to Bethlehem to adore the Child. A succession of pilgrims attests the tradition before the Crusades. A Greek Orthodox church covers a cave with a fourth century mosaic floor: it was opened quite recently. To the north is a Franciscan church consecrated in 1954, again on the site of a fourth century monastery. A notice outside proclaims it Campo Dei Pastori, the Shepherds' Field.

Arab shepherds with their flocks in the region of Bethlehem

HERODION

As one drives from Jerusalem to Bethlehem, what appears to be an extinct volcano becomes visible on the left. The resemblance to a volcano arises from a natural hillock which has been surmounted by a stone fortress. This is Herod the Great's palace-citadel, built near the site where, in 40 BC, he achieved an important victory over the Hasmoneans. South-east of Bethlehem, it is accessible via Beit Sahur. There is no bus service, but taxis can be hired in Bethlehem. Josephus gives a very exact description of it:

> This fortress... is naturally strong... a hill raised to a [greater] height by the hand of man and rounded off in the shape of a breast. At intervals it has round towers, and a steep ascent formed by 200 steps of hewn stone. Within it are costly royal apartments made for security and for ornament at the same time. At the base of the hill there are pleasure grounds built in such a manner as to be worth seeing, among other things because of the way in which water, which is lacking in that place, is brought from a distance and at great expense. The surrounding plain was built up as a city second to none, with the hill serving as an acropolis for the other dwellings...

The construction belongs to between 24 and 15 BC, and emphasizes Herod's preoccupation with security. The stone staircase still survives to some extent, forty-one steps remaining. A road leads up to a car park, where entrance tickets are sold. The whole site is run by the Israel Antiquities Authority.

There are two main areas. At the top of the hill is the royal fortress with two parallel circular walls. On the east side there is a circular tower, and three

The fortress at Herodion closely resembles an extinct volcano

semi-circular towers exactly due west, north and south. An earth and stone rampart ran round the top. Within, the eastern half was occupied by a garden surrounded by a portico; the western half contains dwellings, and a Roman bath-house, subsequently modified as a Byzantine chapel. Not all of it has been cleared. There may have been three storeys of buildings. An elaborate system of cisterns was fed with water brought by pack animals from the aqueduct lower down. Both Greek and Hebrew masons' marks can be seen on the stones.

At the base of the hill on the north side was a town covering 35 acres (15 hectares). Here was a large palace, a pool complex with an extensive garden, government offices and private dwellings. There was a central bath-house, a hippodrome for horse and chariot racing, a nymphaeum (temple in honour of the nymphs), and three Byzantine churches.

Josephus describes the burial of Herod here in 4 BC with most elaborate pomp, but his tomb has never been identified. It may seem odd that a Jewish tomb should be situated in a dwelling area, contrary to Jewish laws, but Herod, an Idumaean, was ready to compromise with the 'established church' of Roman paganism.

The site was occupied at different times from the reign of Herod into Byzantine times. There is evidence that iron was smelted here to make weapons for the rebels

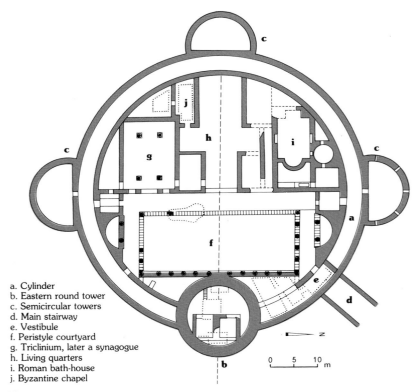

a. Cylinder
b. Eastern round tower
c. Semicircular towers
d. Main stairway
e. Vestibule
f. Peristyle courtyard
g. Triclinium, later a synagogue
h. Living quarters
i. Roman bath-house
j. Byzantine chapel

Plan of the palace fortress at Herodion

in the Bar Kokhba Revolt, when an elaborate underground defence system of tunnels, cisterns, a water shaft, and a guard-room were organized. Apart from the Byzantine churches, it appears that at one time the bath-house was used as a monastery. Apart from the historical interest, the views from the summit are spectacular, and a visit to Herodion is worthwhile for these alone.

MONASTERIES OF THE JUDAEAN DESERT

South of Bethlehem are the remains of the earliest monasteries in the Holy Land. The first monk in Palestine was St Hilarion, who settled near Gaza in 329. Near Bethlehem St Chariton founded the first laura, that is, an association of anchorites, c.330. The first monastery in the commonly understood sense of the word (monks under the authority of an abbot) was founded by Euthymius and Theoctistus in 411. Both in Egypt and in Palestine the monastic movement spread like wildfire at this period, attracting thousands. Far from fleeing from life, the desert monks sought the challenge of life in wild places; from the monasteries there came theologians, historians and poets — some of whose hymns are still common currency in the twentieth century. By the sixth century there were in Palestine 137 lauras and monasteries, and others in Sinai and across the Jordan.

In the lauras each monk lived in solitude during the week, only coming together on Saturday and Sunday for Mass and a common meal. The *coenobium*, on the other hand, was an enclosed monastery, surrounded by a wall, with a gate, a two- or three-storied tower or keep as a refuge in case of danger from marauders. There were one or more churches according to the different vernaculars to be accommodated, a refectory, kitchen, bakery and storerooms. For each monk there was a private cell, sometimes of two rooms. Outside was often a hostel for pilgrims and visitors, or relatives; and sometimes a hospital for the sick.

Some monasteries developed as monastic estates, supporting themselves by agriculture, or by producing oil and wine. There were great variations in practice and occupation, depending upon the character and talents of the men in them. By the sixth century the lauras received only those who had proved themselves in a monastery. Scriptoria, in which manuscripts were copied or written, and painting, whether on the walls of churches and refectories, or as icons, now provided a new outlet for intellectual life inspired by spiritual reflection. A few monasteries, like those on the Mount of Olives, or the foundations made by St Jerome and others in Bethlehem, provided for a developing pilgrim traffic.

However, almost all of some fifty monasteries near Jerusalem and Bethlehem for men and for women were swept away in the Persian invasion of 614. A few were revived, but the over-all numbers declined after the Arab invasion of 638.

ST THEODOSIUS' MONASTERY Between Bethlehem and Mar Saba is the cave-church of St Theodosius' Monastery, with its wall paintings. The main church is a cave, with four adjoining spaces. The whole of the main cave was originally painted. A natural recess which serves as an apse has a painting of Jesus and saints. On the west side of the north wall is Mary with the Child Jesus. All the paintings have been vandalized. There are also paintings of the Ascension, of Jesus with the

The Monastery of Mar Saba

archangels Michael and Gabriel and the saints Sabas and Gerasimus. There are niches containing a Crucifixion, St John of Damascus, Our Lady and Child, Christ as Emmanuel, and St Euthymius. The persons represented in four sepia drawings are unidentified. All the paintings appear to belong to the late twelfth century.

MAR SABA The Great Laura of St Sabas, known as Mar Saba, was founded in 483. From it he founded three other lauras and six monasteries; his disciples founded three lauras and two monasteries. Women are not permitted to enter. The rich library of the monastery has now been transferred to the Greek Orthodox Patriarchate in Jerusalem. The pride of the monastery is the cell and chapel of St John the Damascene, Doctor of the Church, and heroic defender of orthodoxy, against heresy and against Islam. In his early life he was the financial administrator of Damascus, before becoming a monk. He wrote in the first half of the seventh century. Other buildings nearby are the Church of St Sophia, mother of St Sabas, the Monastery of St John Silentiarius, the Cave of St Arcadius, with a tower, the Small Monastery and the Monastery of Zannos.

BETHLEHEM TO HEBRON

Hebron, the site of the mausoleum of the patriarchs Abraham, Isaac, and Jacob, is sacred to Christians, Jews and Muslims. Since 1948 it has been the scene of friction between Arabs and Jews. Although it is easily reached either by bus or by taxi, it is imprudent to visit Hebron without making inquiry about the security situation. No advantage is gained by becoming involved in an affray or riot.

About 2½ miles (4 km) south of Bethlehem, **Qal'at el-Burak**, the Castle of the Pools, is reached. A fortress built by the Ottoman Turks in the seventeenth century to protect **Solomon's Pools**, it can be seen today near the upper pool. South-east is a small but fertile valley, said to be the *Hortus conclusus*, the enclosed garden of the Song of Songs: 'My sister, my spouse, thou art a garden enclosed, a fountain sealed up. Thy plantations make a paradise of delights' (4.12). The large pools are attributed to Solomon following a passage in Ecclesiastes (2.4): 'I undertook great works... I made me ponds to water a fertile wood of plants.' However, they were actually built during the Second Temple period. The three large pools once brought water to Jerusalem, but now this water only goes as far as Bethlehem.

ELON MAMRE (THE OAK OF MAMRE)

At the entrance to Hebron from the north are the ruins of an ancient settlement. It is believed to be the site of ancient Mamre, where Abraham offered hospitality to three strangers (Gen. 14.13), whom Christian thought later held to symbolize the Three Persons of the Trinity. (This is especially a popular subject in Ethiopian Christian art, and a large wall painting of the three strangers is to be seen in the Ethiopian Chapel adjacent to the Holy Sepulchre.) Archaeological investigations by the Catholic Görresgesellschaft found pottery contemporary with Abraham.

HEBRON

Hebron is a large Arab town, with about 60,000 residents. A large Jewish community was slaughtered here in riots in 1929. A new Jewish settlement was built north-east of Hebron in 1970; called Qiryat Arba, it has about 4,900 residents. The central monument is that of the **Cave of the Machpelah**, bought by Abraham

Solomon's Pools actually date from the Second Temple period

from Ephron the Hittite (Gen. 23.7 ff.), in which are buried Sarah and Abraham, Isaac and Rebecca, Leah and Jacob, the latter whose body was brought back from Egypt. The Sacred Enclosure, 211 feet long and 114 feet wide (64 x 35 m), was built as it is today by Herod the Great.

The same drafted ashlars that can be seen best in the Western Wall of the Temple Mount make the identification certain. The crenellation at the top of the walls is of Mamluk origin. Formerly there were four square minarets, but today only those on the north-east and north-west remain. The stone ashlars are so huge that legend has it that they were laid by King Solomon aided by a number of *jinn* (in Mohammedan demonology, spirits with supernatural power over men). However this may be, each course is set back by about half an inch (1¼ cm), thus creating a visual deception that avoids the appearance of heaviness.

The walls are articulated with delicate artistry, broken by pilasters, of stone which has acquired a lustrous patina. Within the floor slopes from east to west, ending with a gutter, showing that originally the building was unroofed. A Byzantine church was constructed, post-570; further alterations were made by the Crusaders c.1115. The cenotaph of Joseph is housed in a room external to the enclosure wall, and the other cenotaphs constructed in the eighth century.

It is no longer possible to view the burial cave of the patriarchs that lies beneath the floor and the cenotaphs. In 1119 Augustinian canons were able to enter, as did a clandestine Israeli exploration in 1970. Possibly some modifications took place in the Ayyubid period, when Saladin added the two existing minarets. A small mosque was built outside the wall in 1318–1320, and a synagogue installed in 1967. Traces of many periods are visible, but a Gothic redolence pervades. The magnificent *minbar*, or pulpit, was made in 1091 for a mosque in Ashkelon, and given by Saladin in 1191.

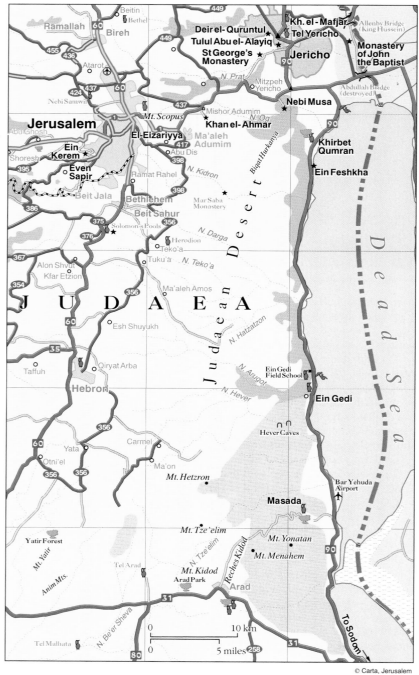

Beitin
Bethel
Ramallah
Bireh
449
449
Kh. el- Mafjar
Deir el- Quruntul
Tel Yericho
Allenby Bridge
(King Hussein)
60
Tulul Abu el- Alayiq
455
436
St George's
Monastery
90
Jericho
Monastery
of John
the Baptist
Atarot
Khan el- Ahmar
Abdullah Bridge
(destroyed)
424
437
60
N. Prat
Mitzpeh
Yericho
Nebi Samwil
437
Mishor Adumim
Nebi Musa
90
Jerusalem
Mt. Scopus
Khan el- Ahmar
N. Og
Abu Ghosh
El- Eizariyya
Ma'aleh
Adumim
Khirbet
Qumran
417
Ein
Kerem
Abu Dis
Shoresh
398
Ein Feshkha
395
Even
Sapir
N. Kidron
386
Ramat Rahel
398
Beit Jala
Bethlehem
Mar Saba
Monastery
Biqat Hurkanya
375
Beit Sahur
356
376
Solomon's Pools
N. Darga
Herodion
367
Teko'a
Tuku'a
N. Teko'a
Alon Shvut
Kfar Etzion
354
Ma'aleh Amos
J U D A E A
356
60
Esh Shuyukh
N. Hatzatzon
35
Taffuh
N. Arugot
Ein Gedi
Field School
Qiryat Arba
Hebron
N. Hever
Ein Gedi
356
Carmel
Hever Caves
60
Yata
Ma'on
Otni'el
356
356
Mt. Hetzron
Bar Yehuda
Airport
Masada
Mt. Tze'elim
Yatir Forest
Mt. Yonatan
Mt. Yatir
N. Tze'elim
Mt. Menahem
Anim Mts.
Tel Arad
Reches Kidod
90
Mt. Kidod
Arad Park
Arad
31
0   10 km
N. Be'er Sheva
0   5 miles
258
31
80
Tel Malhata
To Sodom

D
e
a
d

S
e
a

J
u
d
a
e
a
n

D
e
s
e
r
t

© Carta, Jerusalem

4. Jerusalem to Jericho, Qumran and Masada

This itinerary begins with the birth of St John the Baptist, and continues to his ministry in the Jordan Valley. The route passes through Bethphage and near the Monastery of St George of Koziba, to Jericho, not far from where the Israelites crossed the Jordan, where Jesus was baptized. Near Jericho is Tell es-Sultan (Tel Yericho), reputed to be the oldest city site inhabited by man, and Herodian and Umayyad palaces. To the south is the Islamic site of Nebi Musa with a mosque and cenotaph commemorating the burial of Moses; it is an empty mausoleum. Beyond is the Dead Sea, and the fortress of Masada, scene of the heroic defence of the Jewish Zealots in AD 73, when the last survivors committed suicide rather than fall into Roman hands. From this side Masada is accessible by cable car. On the way to Masada is Qumran, a settlement of the Essenes, whose scrolls have given a new turn to biblical studies, and Ein Gedi. Further on is Sodom.

THE BIRTHPLACE OF ST JOHN THE BAPTIST
Ein Kerem is a village-neighbourhood in West Jerusalem, accessible by bus from the main bus station. Ein Kerem is the traditional site of the Visitation of Our Lady to St Elizabeth (Luke 1.39) and the birth of St John, and is close to one of the sites commemorating his sojourn in the wilderness. Until 1948 it was largely a Muslim village with only 300 Christians, but since then it has undergone a complete change, and is mostly inhabited by Jews. There are a number of Latin and Russian Orthodox establishments, but the only ones of antiquity are as below.

CHURCH OF ST JOHN THE BAPTIST The Franciscan Church of St John the Baptist is at the bottom of the valley as one enters, up a lane on the right. It is built over the remains of a fifth century church which the Crusaders reconstructed, and which was destroyed after their departure. The present building was completed in 1674. On the left a staircase leads to the Grotto of the Nativity of St John. To the right of the church a door leads to the remains of the Crusader buildings. During excavations in 1885 while building the present porch on the west side two rock tombs were found, which have been thought to hold the remains of the Holy Innocents, as described by Epiphanius. South of this, another chapel was discovered in 1941–1942, with a mosaic floor, over a press of the Roman period.

CHURCH OF THE VISITATION Crossing the valley to this Franciscan church one passes what has been known as the Virgin's Fountain since the fourteenth century. The church itself is of two storeys, completed only in 1955, and is reached up a steep path. Archaeological investigation has disclosed pre-Roman and Roman remains, a Hellenistic tomb, a Byzantine reservoir, and a grotto with a cistern, round which the Crusaders erected a church. The existence of two sites in honour of St John is unexplained. The veneration of the site where the Magnificat and the Benedictus were first uttered suggests a secondary site in honour of Our Lady and of the priest Zacharias. The church has a superbly kept garden, and is a wonderful place of peace and quiet.

DESERT OF ST JOHN
From the centre of Ein Kerem, turn down Route 386. At Kerem Junction the road on the left leads to Even Sapir. By the first house on the right a track leads to the

The Baptism of Jesus, as depicted in the Church of St John the Baptist, Ein Kerem

Greek Melkite monastery. Leave cars, taxis and buses at the top: although the track can be driven along, it is never broad enough for a vehicle to turn round.

GREEK MELKITE MONASTERY A chapel and convent here were erected by the Franciscans in 1922, as commemorated by a Latin inscription at the entrance gate. The church is decorated in the Greek manner, but the monks are French, and in communion with Rome. There are vestiges of a twelfth century monastic building, all over a grotto with a spring known as Ein al-Habis (Spring of the Hermit), where St John is believed to have lived in seclusion. Higher up the hill is a building belonging to Huguenot sisters. A small chapel contains a tomb, now empty, under an apse, said to have been that of St Elizabeth. It is possibly of Byzantine origin. This is a retreat house, and permission is needed for entry.

An alternative site for the seclusion of St John in the desert has been proposed by Fr Clemens Kopp, 5 miles (8 km) west of Hebron at Taffuh, where, in a deep narrow valley to the south-west, are the ruins of a well still known as Ein al-Ma'mudiyyah, the Well of Baptism. Buildings belonging to a church and a monastery have been identified as belonging to the reign of Justinian (527–565).

HADASSAH HOSPITAL
One mile south-west of Ein Kerem is Hadassah Hospital, built when the original hospital on Mount Scopus was inaccessible between 1948 and 1967. It is famous not only for medicine, but also for the Marc Chagall windows in the synagogue.

BETHPHAGE
Driving back across Jerusalem to reach the road to Jericho, it is convenient to visit Bethphage and Bethany (believed to be at El-Eizariyya) on the way. Bethphage was the village from which Jesus sent two of his disciples to fetch the donkey on which he was to ride to Jerusalem on Palm Sunday (Mark 11). Its precise location is not known, but there was a church here in the 380s, when the pilgrim Egeria took part in the procession. It commemorated the meeting of Martha and Mary with Jesus when he came from Jericho and raised Lazarus from the dead. Mark 11.4 records that the donkey was found tied at the meeting of two ways, and it is from the road junction near et-Tur that the procession starts today.

In 1883 the Franciscans built a shrine here: it preserves the stone mounting-block Jesus used to mount the donkey. The chapel also conserves a carved stone of the Crusader period, that was discovered here in 1876: on the north side is a castle, with a group of men with an ass and its foal; on the east people are carrying palms; on the south is the Resurrection of Lazarus; an inscription on the west gives the name Bethphage. The paintings were restored by C. Vagarini in 1950; he also painted the frescoes on the walls of the chapel. There are a number of Jewish tombs in the Franciscan property.

PALM SUNDAY PROCESSION
In the fourth century the procession started from the Church of Eleona on the Mount of Olives. After prayers and readings, interspersed with hymns and antiphons, the account of the first Palm Sunday was read, and the people went before the bishop:
> carrying branches, either palm or olive, and they accompany the bishop in the very way the people did once when they went down with the Lord. They go on foot all, down the Mount to the City, and all through the city to the Anastasis [Church of the Resurrection], but they have to go pretty gently on account of the older men and women who might get tired.

In the eighth century the procession entered by St Stephen's Gate and went up to Calvary. In 1008 Caliph al-Hakim forebade the procession. In Crusader times the patriarch came from Bethany and met the people outside the Temple area; they then all entered by the Golden Gate. After them the Armenians carried on the tradition, until it was taken over by the Franciscans c.1345. The Ottoman Turks forebade the procession in 1648, and it was not revived until 1933. In the present century it has been interrupted several times by wars.

The hymn associated with the procession in the Latin liturgy, '*Gloria, laus et honor sit/Tibi, Christe Redemptor*' (All glory, laud and honour/To thee, Redeemer

King), was composed by St Theodulph of Orleans in 821, but with a moving final verse now omitted:

> Be thou, O Lord, the rider, / And we thy humble ass,
> That to the Holy City / Together we may pass.

BETHANY

A path leads down from the Franciscan property in Bethphage to Bethany, which is today known in Arabic as El-Eizariyya, by confusion with the name Lazarus, whose tomb was already venerated here in the fourth century. In a field to the west was the traditional site of the House of Simon the Leper, but Franciscan excavations in 1952–1953 failed to find anything but pits, caves, cisterns and graves.

In this village took place the supper, in the House of Simon the Leper, during which Mary anointed Jesus' head and feet with spikenard, wiping them with her own hair, imitating the woman penitent in the Pharisee's house in Galilee (Luke 7.38). Lazarus' tomb, from which he was resurrected, was here. It was already known to Eusebius, and to St Jerome, at the end of the fourth century. In the sixteenth century the Ottomans made the ruins of the church into a mosque, making it inaccessible to Christians. In 1613 Fr Angelo da Messina, OFM, *custos* of the Holy Land, obtained permission to excavate a new entrance to the tomb. In 1949 the Franciscans cleared the site. A new church was erected in 1952–1953, preserving as far as possible the remains of the earlier churches. A bust of Pope Paul VI records his visit here on 4 January 1964.

Lazarus is believed to have died at Citium in Cyprus, but his relics — according to legend — were taken to Vézelay, in France, in the eleventh or twelfth century. Various legends have gathered here. One is that the Holy Donkey was so disgusted by the Crucifixion that he walked on the water to Sicily. Thence he made his way

Bethany, with the modern Church of Lazarus in the foreground

to Verona, where, instead of saying '*Ite, Missa est*' (Go, Mass is ended), the deacon of the Mass brayed three times in his honour on each Palm Sunday.

ST JOHN THE BAPTIST IN THE JORDAN VALLEY

The evangelists place St John the Baptist's mission in the wilderness near the Jordan River. One road down to Jericho was constructed in Roman times, and is still walkable (down Wadi Kelt). There are buses from Jerusalem to Jericho, the Dead Sea, Qumran, Ein Gedi, and Masada. Visitors should be warned: it can be 40° F (5° C) hotter in Jericho than in Jerusalem. The Dead Sea is 398 m below sea level, making it the lowest point on earth. Hats and sunglasses are advisable.

ST EUTHYMIUS' MONASTERY

About 9 miles (14 km) from Jerusalem a track to the right leads to Khan el-Ahmar. Here are the remains of St Euthymius' Monastery. There are fifth century remains.

THE GOOD SAMARITAN

On the drive down to Jericho, look out on the left (about 11 miles [18 km] from Jerusalem) for some ancient walls known as the Inn of the Good Samaritan. There are fragments of a Byzantine monastery which also served as a caravanserai, reconstructed as a Turkish Police Post in 1903.

THE MONASTERY OF ST GEORGE OF KOZIBA

Coming from Jerusalem, and to the south-west of Jericho, a road on the left leads to Ein Kelt and into Wadi Kelt (Nahal Prat). Negotiable by car, this turn-off is also accessible from Jericho. The *wadi* (ravine) is highly picturesque. After a few miles there are two groups of caves, which St John of Thebes, an Egyptian, transformed into a monastery c.480 out of a laura originated by a number of hermits c.420–430. Just before the monastery are the remains of two aqueducts of Roman origin, restored by the Byzantines and then by the Crusaders. The monastery is reached by a flight of 300 steps.

St George of Koziba was born in Cyprus c.550. For a time he lived in the Laura of Calamon, in Jordan, but later an intense longing for a more ascetic life brought him to live in one of the caves in Wadi Kelt. It was he who gave the monastery its greatest renown. He died c.620, unharmed by the Persians who had virtually destroyed the monastery in 614. Manuel I Comnenus restored it in 1179. It was at this time that a number of legends began to grow up, and to be repeated to attract pilgrims. So the prophet Elijah was said to have stayed here on his way to Sinai; St Joachim wept here because his wife Anna was sterile; and an angel announced the conception of the Virgin Mary to him here. In 1483 Fr Felix Faber saw the monastery in ruins.

The present monastery is a restoration by a Greek monk, Callinicos. Begun in 1878, the buildings were completed in 1901, except for the bell tower, which was finished in 1952. It is open daily from 9 am to 4 pm (9 am to 3 pm in the winter); on Saturdays 9 am until 12 noon. It is closed on holy days.

The cave-church of St Elijah is reached by stairs from the inner court of the monastery, from which there is a picturesque view over the Jordan Valley. It is here that Elijah is said to have lived for three and a half years, 'fed by ravens' (1 Kings 17.3). At the level of the inner court is the principal church, of the Holy

The Monastery of St George of Koziba overlooks the steep ravine of Wadi Kelt

Virgin, with many nineteenth to twentieth century paintings. Here too the Church of St John and St George of Koziba contains many reliquaries, and a mosaic floor of the sixth and seventh centuries. The Church of the Holy Virgin has a Byzantine double-headed eagle in black, white and red mosaic. The royal doors in the relatively modern iconostasis are attributed to Alexius II Comnenus (1180–1183).

There are vaults with the tombs of the five founding Syrian monks near an old entrance, and a reliquary containing the skulls of fourteen monks martyred by the Persians. In the necropolis are some 250 skulls arranged in rows. Farther on was the Laura of St Anne, rebuilt in 1897, and destroyed by the Ottoman Turks in 1917. There are still hermits living in caves in the vicinity.

CENOTAPH OF MOSES
Just south of the Jerusalem-Jericho road (about 17 miles [27 km] from Jerusalem), a road to the right leads to Nebi Musa, where in 1269 Sultan Baybars of Egypt built a mosque and tomb chamber in honour of Moses. This site has no historical authenticity, but is a place of Islamic pilgrimage.

JERICHO
Jericho has been under Palestinian administration since 1993. It is famous as the place where the Israelites entered the Promised Land. Here twelve stones from the riverbed were erected as a memorial that the Jordan stood still to allow the passage of the Ark of the Covenant, and here also the first Passover was celebrated in the

Promised Land, after the rite of circumcision had been renewed. Here also the manna ceased to fall.

Jericho, with some 36 square miles (58 sq km) of land, has been handed over by the State of Israel to the Palestinians in an act of irenic generosity of which the consequences cannot yet be foreseen.

TEL YERICHO (TELL ES-SULTAN) North of the present city is Tell es-Sultan. A number of excavations preceded those of Dame Kathleen Kenyon, 1952–1958, which showed remains of the Epipalaeolithic period, the earliest Stone Age, nearly 10,000 years old. Joshua 6, therefore, recounts the destruction of a city that had already existed for 8,000 years and more; strangely, archaeology has not revealed the existence of any walls that might have fallen down to the trumpets of the Israelites: it does not seem to have been a walled city in the Iron Age. Perhaps a true comparison might be made with the oasis town of Shibam in Yemen, where, as one approaches the town, the closely packed houses give the impression of a walled city. They were packed together so as not to waste the agricultural land of the oasis. In the Neolithic period the walls of Jericho were rebuilt three times, and no less than sixteen times in the Bronze Age. Only a few stumps of wall have been found datable to the Iron Age.

Joshua ordered the destruction of the entire city and all in it, with the exception of Rahab the Harlot and all who were with her, because she had sheltered the spies while they were checking out the city (Josh. 6.17, 22–23). Her family settled among the Israelites, and Joshua pronounced (6.26):

> May the Lord's curse light on anyone who comes forward to rebuild this city
> of Jericho; the laying of its foundations shall cost him his eldest son, the setting
> up of the gates shall cost him his youngest.

Nevertheless, it was settled by Benjaminites, and about 870 BC by Hiel of Bethel (1 Kings 16.34), with the result that Joshua's curse was fulfilled. Elijah and Elisha visited the town, and found a flourishing school of sons of the prophets. The town was rebuilt after the captivity, and flourished under the Maccabees. Mark Antony gave it to Cleopatra, who leased it to Herod. Its gardens, palm groves and balsam trees brought great profit. He built a hippodrome, an amphitheatre, a castle, and splendid gardens watered by aqueducts, and a palatial residence where he died in 4 BC. Jericho as it was then was probably destroyed by Vespasian in AD 68.

Later a new city grew up, with a synagogue on Tell es-Sultan, and several Byzantine churches in the vicinity. The rich soil made it an important agricultural centre, from which the whole locality, with numerous monasteries and lauras, could be supplied. Modern Jericho lies south of Tell es-Sultan, its houses scattered among the groves and gardens, among which remains of several Byzantine churches have been found. The tel has been filled in. Tell es-Samarat is 600 m south-west of Tell es-Sultan. There was a racecourse and a theatre there, of which only traces remain.

TELL EL-HASSAN At Tell el-Hassan, in the present inhabited area of the town of Jericho, are Byzantine and Arab remains.

DEIR EL-QURUNTUL

About 2 miles (3 km) north-west of Jericho a track leads towards the mountains, passing the remains of a Roman villa and a medieval sugar mill. At the foot of the

A tower, c.8000 BC, at Tell es-Sultan, Jericho

mountain are rough stone steps leading to the Mount of Quarantine, the name coming from the Latin word *quarentena*, meaning forty days. It is a common Christian tradition that Jesus spent the forty days of his temptation in the wilderness in a cave near here. In Arabic the name has become Deir el-Quruntul. In 1895 the Greek Orthodox built a convent in front of the traditional grotto. Here the first

The monastery at Deir el-Quruntul

temptation, 'If thou be the Son of God, command that these stones be made bread', would have been uttered by Satan.

The second temptation took place on the pinnacle of the Temple in Jerusalem. The site of the third temptation is in Greek Orthodox possession, and lies half an hour's climb up the Mount of Quarantine. Permission is required from the convent to go up, to where the devil showed Jesus all the kingdoms of the world and their splendour, and was rebuked: 'Be off, Satan! For scripture says: You must worship the Lord your God, and serve him alone.'

Jesus would have passed through Jericho many times, for it was the normal route for pilgrims from Galilee to Jerusalem. His last visit is recorded. Here he spoke the chilling words:

Now we are going up to Jerusalem, and the Son of Man is about to be handed over to the chief priests and scribes. They will condemn him to death, and will hand him over to the pagans to be mocked and scourged and crucified; and on the third day he will rise again (Matt. 20.17–19).

Here too he cured a blind man, and, seeing Zacchaeus climb a tree to get a glimpse of him, commanded him to come down so that he might entertain Jesus in his home.

KHIRBET EL-MAFJAR

About 2½ miles (4 km) north of Jericho is a group of ruins commonly, but wrongly, known as Hisham's Palace. The baths were built during his reign (724–743), but the palace itself, never completed, was still under construction during the one year reign of al-Walid II ibn al-Yazid (744). It is worth a visit from Jericho, not only on account of its beautiful mosaics and carvings, but also because it shows that even in the mid-eighth century Muslim artistic taste had not yet become austere: it luxuriated still in the splendour shared by Christian and Jewish Syrian art.

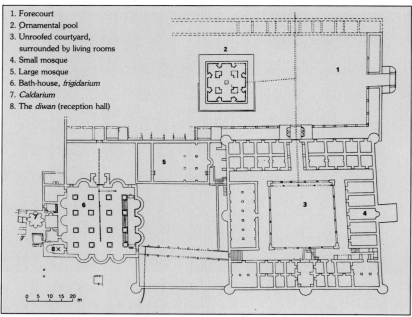

1. Forecourt
2. Ornamental pool
3. Unroofed courtyard,
    surrounded by living rooms
4. Small mosque
5. Large mosque
6. Bath-house, *frigidarium*
7. *Caldarium*
8. The *diwan* (reception hall)

A plan of the sites at Khirbet el-Mafjar

AL-WALID'S PALACE Spoken of as a palace, it is rather a large country-house, like the contemporary 'desert castles' across the river in Jordan, east of Amman. It was the principal dwelling of an extensive landed estate, which, like Qusayr Amra (see Itinerary 9), began with the building of baths, other buildings being elaborated afterwards. A mosque, and later the palace, followed.

It was enclosed by a boundary wall of a park that extended for c.1 mile (1.5 km) along the north bank of Wadi al-Nu'eima. This could have been a game park, or simply a means of protecting cultivated ground against the destructive wild pig.

The entrance is from a car park; there is a kiosk at the gate where tickets are sold. Within the forecourt is an ornamental pool, which was perhaps sheltered at one time by a canopy. The entry into the buildings lies on the left, with a porter's lodge. The buildings were of two storeys. Through a passage two blocks, each of four rooms of approximately equal size, are entered. These would have provided accommodation for each of four wives, in accordance with the precept of the Qur'an that ordains that wives be treated in all ways equally. In front is a colonnaded court open to the sky. On its south side is a small mosque flanked by rooms on either side. This was balanced on the north side of the colonnaded court by a long narrow reception hall, with a roof supported by a central row of pillars. On the west side was a main chamber probably intended for the caliph, with suites of six rooms and a larger chamber on either side.

To the north of this complex was a second courtyard with a large mosque on the east side. The forepart only of the mosque was roofed, the rest being open. On the north side of the courtyard was the original bath-house, with elaborate apsidal

Remains of Hisham's Palace, Khirbet el-Mafjar

walls on three sides, its roof supported by sixteen pillars. It was entered from the east side. A small *caldarium*, or hot room, with eight apses arranged as it were in an octagon lay outside the main structure on the north, and a small *diwan*, or reception room, at the north-west corner. The delight in geometry of a most elegant kind is very evident, and this is also apparent from the rich variation of patterns in the floor mosaics. Among these it is notable that the cross appears in one pattern on the floor of the bath-house, a fashion forbidden in Christian churches in 395. If the majority of the rooms seem somewhat small, it must be remembered that life among Arabs is lived as much in sheltered courtyards as indoors.

A second storey was reached by two staircases from the forecourt. Here there was a reception room, which would have caught the prevailing wind. There is also evidence for privies at this level. The walls were covered in paintings, of which fragments have been found in the ruins, but never in sufficient quantities to enable reconstruction. Some walls also had elaborate stucco decoration. Workmen's graffiti show that the artisans spoke both Greek and Arabic, and included Christians, Jews and Muslims. One graffito has the Hebrew alphabet transliterated into Arabic. There is a medley of styles, Syrian, Mesopotamian and Persian, with some

Sassanian motifs predominating. Of these there is a wide range. The statuary, including an elegant Sassanian horse, warriors, and even a woman, is remarkable. Most spectacular is a statue taken to be the caliph, in ceremonial dress, and carrying a sword; the figure is coloured and painted, with golden brown hair and blackened eyelids, a fashion still in vogue among old-fashioned Arab men. A popular theory is that this magnificent palace was intended for the heir to the throne, if not the caliph himself. The site was possibly abandoned when al-Walid himself was assassinated in 744. Horsemanship, poetry, song and wine were the passions of al-Walid, and the *décor* was certainly in keeping with his tastes.

TULUL ABU EL-ALAYIQ

About 1 mile (2 km) west of Jericho are two mounds known as Tulul Abu el-Alayiq, in an area which was highly cultivated, particularly during the Hellenistic and Early Arab periods. Two Hellenistic towers remain. Herod the Great and many notables had houses and gardens here, with ponds; five aqueducts have been excavated. There remains a Hasmonean palace, with a central building, a series of pools, a southern wing with twin palaces, and a fortified palace on an artificial mound surrounded by a fosse. Herod built three further palaces here; the first was to the south of the present site. The second was an addition to the Hasmonean complex. The third was the most elaborate, with pools, a sunken garden, residential quarters, and a service wing. The earliest finds at the site were of the Chalcolithic period.

The pools were for swimming and bathing. The different complexes show the high degree of sophistication in the time of the Hasmoneans and Herod, and show the extent to which Graeco-Roman culture had penetrated. Most striking of all is the round room in Herod's third palace, 26 feet (8 m) in diameter. It probably had a domed roof and served as a laconicum, or sweating room. All the floors were covered with magnificent mosaics.

THE DEAD SEA

To the north of the Dead Sea is the Plain of Jericho and the Jordan River. It is part of the Great Rift Valley which extends from Lake Hula in the north down through to Kenya and Tanzania. Although round Jericho is a well-watered region, south of it is a desolation of scrub where the Jordan River flows through often grotesquely shaped hills down into the Dead Sea. In former times there were fords across the river at King Hussein Bridge, so named by the Jordanians for King Abdallah's father. It is also known as Allenby Bridge, and is today the principal crossing into Jordan. About 4½ miles (7 km) south of the bridge is the **Greek Monastery of St John the Baptist**, regarded by some as the place of Christ's Baptism by St John. On the opposite side of the road is the Franciscan enclosure, with a small building known as the Little Temple at the Place of the Baptism. A church existed here in the fifth century, and was succeeded by others, most of them destroyed by earthquakes, the last in 1956. The most recent structure dates from that year.

Six-tenths of a mile (1 km) farther on, near the springs of Wadi Kharar remains of Byzantine buildings are said to mark the site of **Bethany beyond Jordan**, where John preached and baptized (John 1.28). The Gospels give abrupt information about his preaching and baptism, to which 'there went out to him Jerusalem and all Judaea, and all the country about Jordan'. His baptism by immersion was for those determined to produce 'fruits worthy of penance' in order to face the forthcoming Last Judgement (Luke 3.8). In this way it differed from the initiation into Judaism of proselytes by immersion, and the frequent purifications of the Essenes and other Jewish sects. At Jesus' baptism, John the Baptist proclaimed him as the Lamb of God who takes away the sin of the world. The next day at Bethany, a group of disciples formed round Jesus (John 1.35–42). This Bethany is not to be confused with the Bethany of Lazarus (see p. 96).

These sites, and the site of Herod's castle-palace at Machaerus, where Herod Antipas had the Baptist put to death, lie in the frontier region between Israeli occupied territory on the West Bank and Jordan, Machaerus itself being on the east bank. They can only be approached with the permission of the authorities.

KHIRBET QUMRAN AND THE DEAD SEA SCROLLS

In the spring of 1947 two Bedouin shepherds accidentally discovered nine jars, one of which contained scrolls. These were in a cave about a mile (1.5 km) north of the site known as Khirbet Qumran. Subsequently, in 1949 and 1951 further scrolls were found in caves by the Jordanian Department of Antiquities; in 1952 Bedouin discovered a great quantity of scrolls in what is known as Cave 4, only 100 metres from Qumran. These, and the excavation of the site of Qumran, completed in 1956, showed that the scrolls and the site had been the property of the Essene sect.

This sect originated in Babylon during the Jewish Exile (586–538 BC). The members of the New Covenant believed that the exile had been brought about deservedly because of religious laxity and failure to observe the Law perfectly. About 164 BC some returned to Judaea and immediately found themselves in opposition to the Temple establishment, which was far from being able to accept that the Essenes alone had the truth. Accordingly they moved into the desert.

By 150 BC one party had moved into Qumran, into a fortress that had been begun in the Iron Age, and which had soon been abandoned. This it would seem was a schism in the Essene movement, for the leader is described in their writings as the 'teacher of righteousness' as opposed to the 'man of lies'. In 159–152 BC the teacher acted as high priest during an interregnum. He was dismissed in 152 BC by Jonathan, who is called the 'wicked priest' in the scrolls. Some of the teacher's hymns have been preserved, and clearly he was a powerful ecclesiastical personality. He introduced Sadducean ideas.

Fundamentally these Essenes were dualists, that is, like the later Manichees, they believed that the Spirit of Truth and the Spirit of Falsehood were both created by God. Thus the object of religion was to free oneself from Satan, who, nevertheless, was equal with God. There were other kinds of Essenes besides those living at Qumran; there were also those of Damascus, of other Palestinian towns, and the Therapeutai (or healers).

The Qumran Essenes abandoned the site, probably in 31 BC, when an earthquake is recorded by Josephus. There have been numerous coin finds, with a gap in the sequence until 4 BC, when they would have returned. The buildings were then restored. In AD 68–69 the Romans sacked the place, and probably massacred the inhabitants. On the Roman approach the Essenes had hidden their most valuable possession, their library, first placing the scrolls into jars. Until the end of the

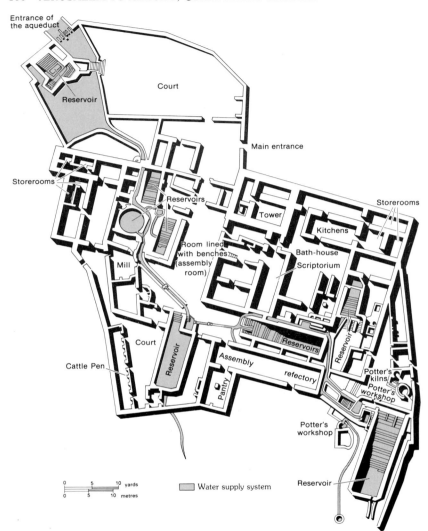

A plan of the site of Khirbet Qumran, showing its elaborate water system

century the Romans maintained a garrison here, and then withdrew. It was a rebel hide-out during the second Jewish revolt (132–135).

The Qumran Essenes lived a life of extreme monastic austerity, dwelling in cliff caves, tents and underground chambers. They gathered only for ritual purifications and ritual meals, and copying the Scriptures and devotional and religious works. For so far unexplained reasons, during the reign of John Hyrcanus (134–103 BC) the community increased to 200, when extensive building took place. Some idea of the size of the community can be gathered from the cemeteries, one with more

The caves where the Dead Sea Scrolls were found, Khirbet Qumran

than a thousand graves, and two others with 100 graves altogether. In the large cemetery only the skeletons of adult males were found, but the two small cemeteries also contained the skeletons of women and children, at first sight strange for a monastic community. Some of these show signs of having been brought from a distance, and possibly they were related by kin or ideology.

Ritual purification with water was an essential part of Essene life. The elaborate system of dams and aqueducts, decantation pools and cisterns, so confusing to the visitor, can best be seen from the tower. The dams contained no less than 880,000 imperial gallons of water. Together with the water that would have been held in the cisterns, something like 1,000,000 gallons of water could be stored.

The central tower was the salient feature of the main building, primarily intended as a watch-tower. The main building, with a central courtyard, had a refectory and/or assembly hall with a pantry, a kitchen, common room, scriptorium, potter's workshop and cattle byres. In the latter were kept the cattle required for ritual meals, unique in character so far as is known, for the remains of animal bones, chiefly sheep and goats, and less commonly cows and calves, were carefully buried. The scriptorium has been reconstructed in the Rockefeller Museum in Jerusalem.

More than 400,000 manuscripts and fragments copied here have been recovered from the caves, all in scroll form. These are still being studied: more than 40,000 documents have now been identified, but only a small number have been published. There has been criticism of what might seem to be undue delay in their publication. The main collection is housed in the Shrine of the Book next to the Israel Museum, Jerusalem, in a building of dramatic appearance. The contents include not only the earliest known manuscripts of the Hebrew Scriptures, but also of orthodox Jewish and Essene devotional works. There is an almost complete manuscript of the Book of the Prophet Isaiah, and several fragments. The twelve Minor Prophets are usually included on a single scroll. Most popular are the Five Books of Moses and the Psalter. It was discovered with some astonishment that these and other works correspond quite remarkably to the Massoretic text of the Hebrew Scriptures, which was provided with vowel points in the eighth and ninth centuries AD, nearly a millennium later. It is an extraordinary example of the strength and dependability of the Jewish tradition.

So far as Christianity is concerned, the Dead Sea Scrolls are important as part of the background to the first century AD. There is no connection between Essene teaching and Christian doctrine, nor between Essene monasticism and the monastic movement that arose in Christianity in the mid-third century AD, whose roots are indicated in the Gospels. The resemblances are superficial, not fundamental.

Two miles (3 km) to the south are ruins at **Ein Feshkha**, the remains of a centre of a religious community, almost certainly of Qumran Essenes. It was probably formed during the reign of Alexander Jannaeus (103–76 BC), and, like Qumran, abandoned in 68 BC. There is a similar system of canals and reservoirs and other buildings; there are also what have been supposed to be a fish pond and a tannery. A passage in Pliny's *Natural History* (V.73) tells that the Essenes lived among palm trees in isolation west of the Dead Sea, at a safe distance from the pestilence-bearing water. To the south is Ein Gedi. At only one site is it certain that palm trees grew in ancient times, and that is between Khirbet Qumran and Ein Feshkha.

EIN GEDI

An oasis on the western shore of the Dead Sea, approximately halfway between Jericho and Sodom, is Ein Gedi, one of the most important and interesting ancient sites in Israel. There are numerous references to it in Joshua, 1 Samuel, 2 Chronicles, Ezekiel, and in the Song of Songs (1.14) with reference to its vineyards. It was the headquarters of a Roman toparchy, and had a Roman garrison. It was renowned for its dates and for its balsam, an oil of culinary, medicinal and religious use in the ancient world, as well as a perfume. This was made possible by an abundant water supply in a tropical climate. It was a shrub that Pliny describes as being the size of a myrtle tree. In Alexander the Great's time the harvest of balsam in the Royal Gardens would only fill a shell; the price was twice its weight in silver.

Ein Gedi was first settled in the Iron Age c.630–582 BC, and was occupied until the Arab invasion. On a hill-terrace above the Ein Gedi spring was found a Chalcolithic enclosure, which appears to have been a cultic place resembling a similar Chalcolithic sanctuary at Megiddo. Later, a synagogue was built in the lower part of the site, but the finds were insufficient to date. By comparison with other synagogues in the vicinity it was austere, and the mosaics refrain, for example, from depicting the signs of the Zodiac commonplace in other synagogues, although the names are listed. It was probably built in the middle or late fifth century. Eusebius mentions Ein Gedi as a large Jewish village. It and its synagogue were destroyed by fire, possibly at the time of the Arab invasion. It is possible that the austerity of the synagogue arises from the adjacent Essenes of Qumran.

MASADA

From Ein Gedi it is 10½ miles (17 km) south to Masada. Built on the summit of a steep cliff 1,480 feet (450 m) above the level of the Dead Sea, from this approach

One of the waterfalls at Ein Gedi

the top can be reached either by cable car or by climbing up the winding snake path — it is a steep climb. On the north-west side is one of the most famous works of antiquity, the Roman siege ramp. It has been shown (1993) that the greatest part of the ramp is a natural feature, an elongated funnel-shaped spur. This reached 243 feet (74 m) above its base and within 43 feet (13 m) of the cliff top. That the greatest

Masada as seen from the north-west, with the Roman siege ramp on the right

part is a natural formation has been confirmed by systematic excavations. Thus all the Romans had to do in the final siege of AD 73 was to fill the gap. Josephus' account that the Romans were responsible for the whole ramp is, like much in his works, exaggeration.

The Jewish revolt against Rome began in AD 66. Jerusalem was taken in 70, and some Zealots, with a number of Essenes, retired to Masada, which they held until 73. A detailed study of the fortress and the heroic stand is to be found in Yigal Yadin's masterpiece, *Masada: Herod's Fortress and the Zealots' Last Stand*, 1966.

Masada was already occupied in the Chalcolithic period, tenth to eighth centuries BC. It was first fortified by the high priest Jonathan Maccabaeus (other scholars believe this Jonathan to be Alexander Jannaeus [103–76 BC]). However this may be, in 40 BC Herod the Great, in flight from the pretender Antigonus, and threatened also by Cleopatra of Egypt, fled with his family to Masada. He then left his brother Joseph to defend the site with 800 men, who had to stand siege by Antigonus. The defenders nearly died of thirst, until a sudden storm filled the water cisterns. In 39 BC, on his return from Rome, Herod succeeded in relieving them.

The principal buildings on the site were erected between 37 and 31 BC, and

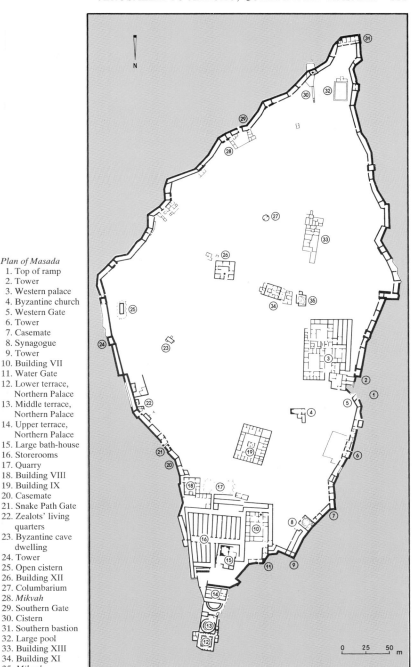

Plan of Masada
1. Top of ramp
2. Tower
3. Western palace
4. Byzantine church
5. Western Gate
6. Tower
7. Casemate
8. Synagogue
9. Tower
10. Building VII
11. Water Gate
12. Lower terrace, Northern Palace
13. Middle terrace, Northern Palace
14. Upper terrace, Northern Palace
15. Large bath-house
16. Storerooms
17. Quarry
18. Building VIII
19. Building IX
20. Casemate
21. Snake Path Gate
22. Zealots' living quarters
23. Byzantine cave dwelling
24. Tower
25. Open cistern
26. Building XII
27. Columbarium
28. *Mikvah*
29. Southern Gate
30. Cistern
31. Southern bastion
32. Large pool
33. Building XIII
34. Building XI
35. *Mikvah*

remained a residence of Herod's family until AD 66. During this period it seems probable that a Roman garrison was stationed here. In 66, at the beginning of the Jewish revolt, the Zealots seized the fortress 'by strategem', and, as will be described, they held out against the Romans until 73. The sole source for these events is Josephus. There is a long history of the excavation and exploration of the site, but the conclusive excavation was that under Yadin in 1963–1965, when most of the site was cleared.

Masada has no permanent water supply. An elaborate system of dams and aqueducts, and cisterns for storage, was constructed to contain 1,400,000 cubic feet of water. Water was also brought up by men and beasts of burden. In addition to the main system, there were smaller cisterns in various buildings, and particularly the palaces, with arrangements for the catchment of rain-water.

The whole site is enclosed by a casemate wall, corresponding with Josephus' seven *stadia* (c.1 mile or 1.6 km). In the walls there were seventy rooms and four gates, with thirty towers. The Serpent, or Snake Path, Gate is on the north-east; the West Gate is of similar plan; on the south-east is Cistern Gate, leading to the main cisterns, and Water Gate was on the north-west corner of the wall. North of Water Gate was the original entry gate of the fortress, subsequently closed. The site was divided, and thus had three internal gates. There were public storehouses, and also smaller storehouses serving particular buildings.

There were four groups of palaces: a palace-villa, or northern palace; a ceremonial and administrative palace (western palace); three small palaces near the latter, probably for the royal family; and a number of palaces or houses of the better sort, perhaps residences for high officials. In addition to the bath-houses in the palaces, there was a principal bath-house in the Roman fashion. Near the western palace was a swimming pool. There was also a columbarium, which was presumably for the cremation urns of the Gentile garrison. This is but the briefest description of the buildings, which, needless to say, underwent repairs and modifications from time to time.

Pottery, and amphorae for storing wine, some with Latin inscriptions, are evidence of the Roman occupation up to 66. The three major palaces were not very suitable for the Zealots and their families. The smaller palaces were preferred, and rooms and courtyards divided to make small dwellings. They built a 'transit camp', of stones and mud, and religious buildings, a synagogue, a *beth midrash* (study hall), and two *mikva'ot* (ritual baths). These were built in accordance with halakhic law, part of the water supplied directly by rain-water collected from roofs. By one *mikvah* archaeologists found a dressing room, with niches for the bathers' clothes.

Among the many objects found, including coins and inscribed ostraca, were biblical scrolls, of the Psalms, as well as Genesis, Leviticus, Deuteronomy and Ezekiel, together with various sectarian scrolls, including part of the lost Hebrew original of Ben-Sira, the Book of Jubilees, and Songs of the Sabbath Service. This latter is identical in contents, style and the calendar mentioned in it, to one found at Qumran, thus providing evidence for dating, and also indicating that Essenes as well as Zealots took part in the revolt against Rome.

When the Romans had subdued the rest of Palestine, Flavius Silvas was sent with the Tenth Legion. He built a huge siege wall round the mountain, with twelve towers. The troops were disposed in eight camps, to prevent anyone escaping. This done, he began to build the ramp, on which he placed catapults and battering rams. Using the rams, a breach soon opened the walls. The Zealots, under Eleazar, hastily built temporary walls, determined not to give way. Made of wood, Silvas ordered them to be set on fire, but the wind changed, and blew down smoke on to the Romans. Even so, Eleazar realised the end was in sight. Josephus reports his words:

It is very plain that we shall be taken within a day's time; but it is still possible to die in a glorious manner, together with our dearest friends. This is what our enemies cannot by any means hinder, although they be very desirous to take us alive.

And, in a long speech, he urged them first to kill their wives and children, then to destroy the fortress by fire and to kill themselves. Many of the garrison demurred, whereupon Eleazar made another impassioned speech, which at last moved them. The women and children were slain; the men divided themselves into groups of ten, electing one man to kill the rest until all were dead.

One 'ancient woman', and another, who was related to Eleazar, hid with five children in a cave, and were the only survivors. There were 960 dead in all.

Next morning the Romans prepared for the assault, but saw no enemy. There was 'a terrible solitude on every side... as well as a perfect silence'. The two women came out from their cave, and told the incredulous Romans what had been done.

Nor could they do other than wonder at the courage of their resolution, and at the immovable contempt of death which so great a number of them had shown, when they went through with such an action as that was (Josephus, *Wars*, Bk VII, ch.viii and ix, trans. W. Whiston).

During the fifth and sixth centuries Masada was occupied by monks. A church was built north-east of the western palace, with a narthex and a diaconicon. It was decorated with colourful mosaics. Adjacent was a service wing and kitchen, and dwellings for the monks, some of whom inhabited caves outside. The site then seems to have been abandoned, perhaps following the Persian invasion of 614.

SODOM AND GOMORRAH

An ancient city, Sodom was perhaps the capital of a group of five cities (Pentapolis). The name means Red Fields, from an organism that grows in the nearby salt pans. It was the dwelling-place of Lot (Gen. 14). Sodom and the nearby city of Gomorrah are chiefly remembered for the story of their sinfulness, and Abraham's prayers and negotiations with God for their forgiveness. Abraham's kinsman Lot and his wife were spared the destruction of the city but, because she looked back at the city, despite having been forbidden to do so, she turned into a pillar of salt. Just over 1 mile (2 km) on are the Caves of Sedom; a pillar of salt nearby is pointed out as the remains of the lady (Gen. 19).

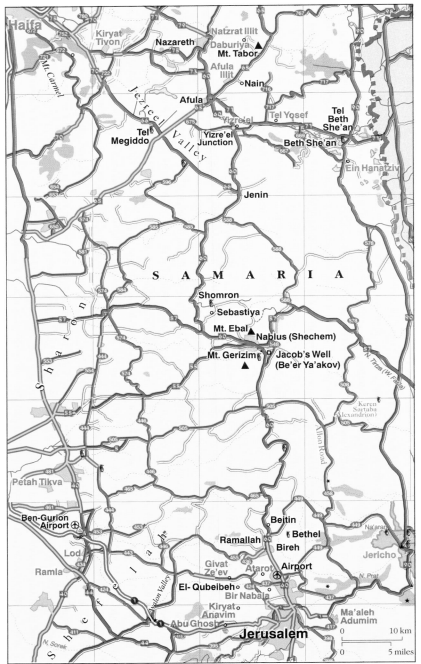

© Carta, Jerusalem

5. Jerusalem to Nazareth via Nablus

There are a number of routes from Jerusalem to Nazareth. The shortest, via Ramallah, Nablus, and passing near the ancient Sebaste (Samaria), is the most picturesque and interesting (85 miles/136 km). A longer route is via Jericho and up the Jordan Valley: much of this is through desert country. Both routes should be avoided in times of unrest, but generally can be traversed by Arab taxis.

There are no direct buses to Nazareth from Jerusalem: take a direct bus from the Egged Central Bus Station to Haifa, from where you can catch a bus to Nazareth.

THE GARDEN TOMB Leaving from Damascus Gate and travelling up Nablus Road (Derech Shechem), the Garden Tomb, otherwise called Gordon's Calvary, is passed on the right. Although in popular belief this can be an alternative to the Tomb in the Holy Sepulchre, it is clear that this cannot be so. The pick marks in its excavation show that the type of pick used was one that was in vogue in the ninth to seventh centuries BC, and that it is an ordinary Jewish double tomb of that period. It has been shown that it belongs to a cemetery containing a number of tombs typical of that period. It cannot thus be the single, 'new tomb', not yet used for burial, that had been prepared for Joseph of Arimathea.

ST ETIENNE Farther on, again on the right, the road passes the Dominican Convent and Church of St Etienne (St Stephen), belonging to French Dominicans. It was from here that the distinguished fathers Vincent, Abel and de Vaux worked, laying the groundwork for much of our present archaeological knowledge of biblical Palestine. The original church was built in 439, but little remains of the original buildings, although the present church (1900) does follow the original ground plan. Some original mosaics survive in it, covered with rugs.

ST GEORGE'S CATHEDRAL Yet farther on, and still on the right, is St George's Cathedral, belonging to the Protestant Episcopal Church of the Middle East, part of the Anglican community. It has a tower that resembles that of Merton College, Oxford. Shortly after is the **American Colony Hotel**, originally a Turkish khan, and still preserving a magnificent reception room on the first floor. Behind is the small **Sheikh Jarrah Mosque**, with a raucous Call to Prayer five times daily.

EL-QUBEIBEH

Continuing away from Jerusalem, somewhat to the left of Bir Nabala is El-Qubeibeh, which Fr Bagatti and others believe to have been the Emmaus of the Gospel (Luke 24.13–35). *Qubeibeh* means little dome in Arabic, and possibly got its name from a domed Crusader building. Fr Bagatti's attribution has been much disputed. In Crusader and Byzantine times the Emmaus of the Gospels was held to be Amwas, near Latrun, on the road from Jerusalem to the coast (see p. 130), albeit it was too far for the two disciples to have gone there and returned to Jerusalem in a single day. El-Qubeibeh was not venerated until the Franciscans decided upon it in 1335. They began a pilgrimage there which was suspended in 1689 because of insecurity, and renewed only in 1852. During the Second World War the British used the monastery as an internment camp for German and Italian residents of Palestine (including Italian Franciscans). It was excavated between 1940 and 1944, the findings being published by Fr Bagatti in 1947.

Remains were found of a village of the Hellenistic period which continued into Roman and Byzantine times, as well as those of a Crusader village. There was a church and a castle. Regrettably, there was nothing diagnostic that might have indicated that this was truly the Emmaus of the Gospel. Nevertheless, this Emmaus corresponds better to the distance indicated in the Gospel than the one near Latrun.

BIREH

Returning now to the main road, the road passes Jerusalem Airport. Further on, the road forks right to Bireh, where it is believed Jesus' parents noticed he was missing from their caravan as they were returning from keeping the Passover in Jerusalem; he had stayed behind to listen and put questions to the teachers in the Temple (Luke 2.41–52). The main road passes through the town of Ramallah.

Two-and-a-half miles (4 km) past Ramallah a road on the right leads to Beitin, the biblical **Bethel**, where Abraham pitched his tent, and where Jacob dreamed of a ladder that stretched from earth to heaven, and was promised the land where he was resting. Among the legends that have gathered round this dream is that the Stone of Tara, in Ireland, was Jacob's pillow. From Tara it was taken to Scone in Scotland, and used as the seat for the coronation of Scottish kings. Edward I of England captured it from the Scots, and it now rests in a compartment under the Coronation Chair used for English monarchs in Westminster Abbey. However, its shape does not suggest that it would have been particularly comfortable as a pillow.

SAMARIA REGION

The road passes through a string of Arab villages, many of them with names recalling minor incidents in the Old Testament, until eventually Samaria is reached. This being the name for the central plateau of Israel, it is bounded on the west by the Plain of Sharon, on the east by the Jordan River, and on the north by the Jezreel Valley (the Plain of Esdraelon).

JACOB'S WELL

Just over a mile (2 km) before Nablus a road on the right leads to Jacob's Well (Be'er Ya'aqov), which the patriarch bequeathed to his descendants (John 4.12), and where Jesus asked the Samaritan woman for a drink, and promised her living water (John 4.5–47), telling her that he was the promised Messiah.

The existing church, the property of the Greek Orthodox, has never been completed. It stands on the site of a Byzantine church built c.340–390 in the form of a Latin cross. The four sides are orientated to the four points of the compass. Restored under the emperor Justinian, the Crusaders rebuilt it on the same plan. The crypt, with the well, was immediately below the high altar. The church was destroyed in 1187. By the sixteenth century the Franciscans said Mass here annually; in the seventeenth century the Greeks from Sebaste celebrated intermittently. They acquired it in 1860, and restored the crypt in 1863. Restoration of the church was begun, but suspended in 1914, and has never been resumed.

The sacristan will let down a pail to show the depth of the well, about 114 feet (35 m). It has been cleaned out from time to time, and some objects are exhibited in a small museum.

North of the well is the white-domed tomb of the patriarch Joseph. In Muslim possession, it is venerated by Christians, Jews, Muslims and Samaritans alike.

Modern Nablus (Shechem) nestles between Mount Ebal and Mount Gerizim

NABLUS

About 39 miles (63 km) from Jerusalem is the village of Balata, beyond which is the site of ancient Shechem; the modern town of Shechem, or Nablus as it is also called, is a little farther on. Shechem existed as a city in the nineteenth century BC, and is often mentioned in the Bible from Genesis on. It had an important sanctuary, and it was here that Rehoboam went to be recognized king in place of his deceased father, Solomon. It was on this occasion that the ten northern tribes of Israel separated from the tribes of Benjamin and Judah, constituting now the two kingdoms of Israel and Judah. There have been extensive excavations in Shechem, revealing a city of c.2000 BC, with walls and gates, a temple, a palace, and a grain store, as well as domestic buildings. It was the principal city of the Samaritans.

Here, between Mount Gerizim and Mount Ebal, is the Valley of Blessing and Cursing (Josh. 8.30–35). On Mount Ebal Joshua built an altar on which he engraved the Law of Moses; and then, with half of the People of Israel in front of Mount Gerizim and half in front of Mount Ebal, 'all Israel, native-born and resident alien alike, with the elders, officers and judges', he read the words of the Law, the blessings and the curses, as Moses had commanded.

MOUNT GERIZIM — THE SAMARITANS For the Samaritans Mount Gerizim is the Holy Mountain. The Samaritans are not counted as true Jews in the sense of descendants of Abraham. They are the descendants of Assyrian colonists who intermarried with Israelites who had escaped deportation and captivity in Babylon. They had adopted the Mosaic Law without abandoning their previous pagan practices. For this reason, on their return from exile, the Jews declined to allow them to share in the rebuilding of the Temple. The schism gave rise to implacable hatred, and on Mount Gerizim the Samaritans built a temple of their own to rival that of Jerusalem. Hence the surprise of the Samaritan woman mentioned above, when Jesus asked her to draw some water for him from Jacob's Well.

In AD 36 Pontius Pilate put to death many Samaritans who had gathered here; more were killed by Cerealis in AD 66 on the command of Vespasian. In 135 the emperor Hadrian built a temple in honour of Jupiter on the top of the mountain.

A remarkable church was built here by the emperor Zeno c.484, and restored by Justinian after the Samaritan revolt of 529. It was dedicated to Our Lady. Within a precinct of walls and seven towers is an octagonal church with an eastern apse. Procopius describes how it was fortified in case of Samaritan attack. The ground plan of the church to some extent resembles the ground plan of the church of the House of St Peter at Capernaum, and there are reminiscences of the rotunda of the Basilica of the Holy Sepulchre. Within there was a portico, also octagonal, formed by columns and pillars, with a narthex to the west, and three entrance doors.

The present-day Samaritans assemble on the top of the mountain three times a year, for the festivals of Passover, Pentecost and Tabernacles. On Passover they sacrifice the paschal lamb, and the people stay in tents for thirty days. On the west side are twelve stones, imitating Joshua's camp. The dignified ceremonies are somewhat marred by tourists.

HISTORY The modern town of Nablus took its name from Flavia Neapolis, a colony for Roman veterans built by the emperor Titus in 72. A temple of Zeus was built and a theatre which, it is calculated, could seat between 6,000 and 7,000 persons. Queen Mélisande lived here from 1152 until 1161, but there are no Crusader remains, for the city was virtually wiped out by an earthquake on 11 July 1927. The somewhat volatile character of the inhabitants and the absence of anything of interest make it a place to avoid. Even the two mosques are converted from Byzantine churches.

The ancient colonnaded street from Roman times at Sebaste

SEBASTE

From Nablus, continue along the main Jerusalem-Nazareth road (Route 60). After 7½ miles (12 km) a road on the right leads to Sebaste (Shomron or Samaria in Hebrew), next to the Arab village of Sebastiya. It was founded in 876 BC by Omri as capital of an Israel that now looked north to the kingdom of Tyre and Mediterranean trade. The marriage of his son Ahab to Jezebel, princess of Tyre, emphasized the new alignment. It was not simply a commercial alignment, but one too of culture and religious synthesis which aroused the anger of the prophet Elijah (1 Kings 16.29–34). Success in trade enabled the rise of a new aristocracy, whose life of luxury, with their couches of ivory, was regarded with disdain by the prophet Amos (3.15; 6.4). Some of the ivories found here are on display in the Rockefeller Museum, Jerusalem. After the Assyrian invasion (724–722 BC) 30,000 citizens were deported and replaced by foreigners, contributing to the foreign element among the Samaritans.

The heyday of Sebaste was during the reign of Herod the Great, to whom it was granted by the emperor Augustus in 30 BC. Herod named it Sebaste, because it was the Greek name for Augustus, erecting a typical Hellenistic city in which little deference was paid to Judaism.

ANCIENT SEBASTE The site is open daily. The excavated areas include a West Gate, which serves as the main entrance, a colonnaded street with shops, a forum, basilica (or law courts), stadium and theatre, and even, in defiance of Jewish sensitivities, a temple in honour of Augustus.

It was here that John the Baptist was executed at the scandalous birthday party of Herod Antipas (Mark 6.17–29) according to Christian tradition, but Josephus places the incident at Machaerus on the other side of the Jordan River. There are two churches in honour of St John, and one also where his head is alleged to have been found. The head is exhibited in the Church of S. Silvestro in Capite in Rome with gory verisimilitude. The Crusaders built a great cathedral here round a reputed tomb in 1165, of which the tomb-chamber can still be entered. An Israelite wall of early date is still visible.

SEBASTE CATHEDRAL The Cathedral of St John the Baptist at Sebaste was on a plan similar to the Church of St Anne in Jerusalem. There survive the capitals of some pillars recounting the story of his decollation, but no paintings or mosaics. The second church belonged to a monastery, and had twenty-five monks according to the *Commemoratorium de casis Dei* of 808. In the east wall of the crypt a niche is divided into two parts by a stone shelf. The upper part depicts the martyrdom of St John the Baptist. The lower part shows scenes illustrating homilies of St Gregory Nazianzus, the Homily to Julian the Tax Collector, and the Homily on St Basil. On the same wall there are also paintings of two angels.

JENIN

Returning to the main road to Nazareth, after about 19 miles (31 km) Jenin, or En-gannim (the Garden Spring), is reached at the southern edge of the Jezreel Valley. It is well named, for it is rich in carob, fig and palm trees, and in gardens. According to tradition it was here that Jesus cured the ten lepers, of whom only one returned to thank him (Luke 17.11–19). It was probably a Samaritan village.

JEZREEL

From Jenin the road continues towards Afula and Nazareth. At Yizre'el Junction a road turns right to Beth She'an, or Beisan, meaning the House of Rest. Near this crossing is the site of the biblical Jezreel (Hebrew Yizre'el), which King Ahab made the second capital of Israel, building a palace near the vineyard of Naboth, who was put to death for opposing Ahab's confiscation of his land (1 Kings 21). It was here too that King Jehu took revenge for the family of Naboth, and, in a dramatic scene, had Ahab's widow thrown down from a window to her death. The site is currently being excavated by the British School of Archaeology in Jerusalem in a ten-year project. A large rectangular fortification has been identified, and was possibly a barracks for chariot cavalry.

BETH SHE'AN

About 15 miles (26 km) east, Beth She'an is the only ancient site of consequence north of Jericho in the Jordan Valley. It lies at a major road junction between the north-south road of the Jordan Valley and the roads from west to east from the coast to Gilead in Jordan. Apart from its strategic importance, it is rich in soil and water. Before excavation the tel was 28 feet (8½ m) high, and revealed evidence of occupation from Neolithic and Chalcolithic times until the seventh century under the Arabs. The latter lived nearby until 1948, when the population fled.

Beth She'an is today the largest Jewish centre in the Jordan Valley. Many of the principal finds from the excavations are in the Rockefeller Museum. Its commercial importance in early times is demonstrated by numerous finds and inscriptions of Egyptian provenance, and Egyptian occupation from the fourteenth to the twelfth centuries BC. It served as an administrative centre.

Under Joshua it was allocated to the tribe of Manasseh, but remained in Canaanite hands (17.11–2). Saul and his sons were impaled on the walls here (1 Sam. 31.10). Solomon made it one of his administrative centres (1 Kings 4.12), and so it continued during the Hellenistic, Roman and Byzantine periods. Under the latter it was known as Nysa or Scythopolis, but its connection with the Scythians is not known. Nomads, covering a territory from China to the Danube, they disappeared from history in the fourth century AD. They were ignorant of writing and had no coinage. They erected no cities, temples or statuary, and their only remains are gold ornaments.

Pompey took it for the Romans in 67, and thereafter a secondary town developed at the foot of the tel. In Christian times it had a number of saints and martyrs, and was the seat of the metropolitan see of Palestina Seconda. It degenerated under the Arabs to a mere village.

VISIT TO TEL BETH SHE'AN There are remains of a Roman theatre, civic centre and colonnaded street, with rows of shops. On the tel some early temples can be seen, and a gate-house; south of the town is an Ottoman caravanserai and fort. To the north are the remains of a monastery of Our Lady Mary. It has a spectacular mosaic of the signs of the zodiac in a circle surrounding a medallion of the sun and the moon, of wholly pagan conception. Nearby there is a synagogue, with a mosaic depicting two *menorahs* flanking the Ark. From Tel Beth She'an take the main road back to Afula to rejoin the road to Nazareth.

Remains of a colonnaded street at the foot of Tel Beth She'an

TEL MEGIDDO

About 7 miles (11 km) south-west of Afula Tel Megiddo rises above the plain. It was strategically situated along the Via Maris, the Way of the Sea, as it crossed from the Plain of Sharon into the Jezreel Valley.

Excavation has shown that it was a fortified city of importance in the Middle Bronze Age, but it is not mentioned in historical sources until the fifteenth century BC, when it led a rebellion of Canaanite cities. This the Egyptian army routed, taking a rich booty, including 924 Canaanite chariots. Megiddo then became the major Egyptian base in the Jezreel Valley. How it came into Israelite hands is not known, but 1 Kings 9.15 mentions it as a city fortified by Solomon, and the head of one of his twelve administrative districts (1 Kings 4.12). Thereafter it fell to Assyria in 733–732 BC. Its strategic importance continued to be recognized, and it is the Armageddon mentioned in the Apocalypse of John (Rev. 16.12 ff.). In 1917 it was the base of British operations against the Ottoman Turks in Palestine, and its name was taken by the victor: he became Viscount Allenby of Megiddo.

In the small museum a plan may be obtained: much has been excavated, for example, temples and a high place, walls and gates, a palace and private houses.

Above: The Basilica of the Transfiguration

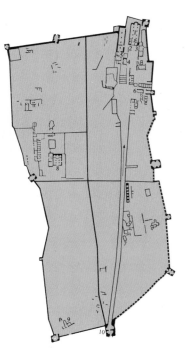

Right: *The buildings on Mount Tabor*
1. Basilica; 2. Chapel of Moses; 3. Chapel of
Elijah; 4. Chapel of Benedictine monastery;
5. Former chapel; 6. Chapel of Franciscan
monastery; 7. Chapel 'Descendentibus';
8. Church of St Elijah and monastery;
9. Greek Orthodox Grotto of Melchizedek;
10. Fortification (1212)

In Canaanite times it was a place of wealth, treasures of jewelry, ivory, lapis lazuli and gold having been found. Canaanite power depended greatly on a highly developed chariotry, and there are remains of stables so large that they could only have been state property. These and human activity demanded a steady water supply, and elaborate precautions, including the use of underground tunnels, were taken to ensure that this supply was safe-guarded in war as well as in peace. There is a large literature on this site, which demonstrates the sophisticated character of the resistance the Israelites met as they entered the Promised Land.

Returning now to Afula, a road to the north-east leads to Mount Tabor, and thence to the southern end of the Sea of Galilee.

MOUNT TABOR

This is the traditional site of the Transfiguration of Jesus (Luke 9.28–36). Four miles (7 km) along the road from Afula to Mount Tabor is **Nain**, where Jesus raised the widow's son from the dead (Luke 7.11). In 1880 the Franciscans built a chapel there on the foundations of an ancient church.

At the foot of Mount Tabor is the village of Daburiya. Coaches are not allowed up the mountain, and passengers must go up in taxis. It is a steep, narrow ascent, with hairpin bends. The top is 1,929 feet (588 m) above sea level. A 'sugar-loaf' mountain, with a flat top, which can be seen from great distances, from both Umm Qais (Gadara) and Mount Nebo (Siyagha) in Jordan, it is of majestic appearance. The road up should not be attempted by inexperienced drivers.

HISTORY Mount Tabor was already inhabited in Palaeolithic times. The prophetess Deborah destroyed Sisera's army here. Pagan gods were worshipped here, for which the prophet Hosea rebuked the people. The Gospel account does not name the mountain on which the Transfiguration took place. Origen, the most distinguished biblical scholar of the fourth century, believed that the tradition went back to apostolic times. In the fourth century a basilica was built here; in 570 the Piacenza Pilgrim saw three basilicas where Peter, James and John had wished to build three tabernacles. A contemporary Armenian monk said that one was larger than the others, and called the Church of the Lord. When Arculf saw it c.700 there were 'three large and renowned church buildings... All these, the monastery, the three churches, and the little cells of the monks, are enclosed in a stone wall...'

By the ninth century there were four churches, a bishop and eighteen monks. At the beginning of the twelfth century Tancred, prince of Galilee, gave the monastery and churches to the Benedictines, with endowments. The church was enlarged, and the abbey fortified with walls. After the Battle of Hattin in 1187 the monks had to withdraw, and in 1211–1212 Saladin's successor al-Malik al-Adil destroyed the church. He built a fortress, but dismantled it in 1217–1218. The monks returned in 1229–1239, but could only afford to build a small chapel. Finally, in 1263, the Mamluk sultan Baybars, after destroying the basilica at Nazareth, destroyed all the religious buildings on the mountain.

In the fourteenth century, Franciscans from Nazareth visited the site on the feast day, 6 August, and celebrated it there. At length, in 1631, Fakhr al-Din, prince of Sidon, who had gained possession of the area, gave the friars formal permission to settle there. They have been undisturbed ever since. The present monastery and pilgrim hospice, as well as the Latin basilica, were built in 1921–1924.

VISIT After the last hairpin bend we reach the top of the mountain quite suddenly. We enter the grounds through a gateway, the Bab al-Hawa, the Gate of the Winds, which leads to the remains of the thirteenth century Mamluk fortress. We proceed up a long avenue to the car park in front of the Latin monastery. The Greek monastery and church are visible on the left.

THE BASILICA Consecrated in 1924, the basilica is the work of the architect Antonio Barluzzi, who also worked on the Church of All Nations in Gethsemane. There is a memorial bust in his honour outside the entrance. By any standards it is a masterpiece, enhancing its surroundings, and enhanced by them. It is modelled on Syrian architecture of the Roman period. There is a nave and two aisles, and a wide stairway descends from the middle of the basilica to an open crypt, which preserves both an ancient altar and an apse (*synthronon*) with seating for clergy. These are most probably Byzantine, and may even be what Arculf saw c.670 and told of to Abbot Adomnan of Iona.

RUINS On both sides in front of the basilica are the ruins of the Benedictine monastery. On the north the walls of the refectory and chapter house are still standing, as is a small oratory. On the south there are further ruins and part of a mosaic pavement. There is a museum, with objects recovered from the site. Visitors can enter the main hall of the hospice, where there are some stalls. At the south end is a balcony, with splendid views which should not be missed on a clear day. Lunch can be ordered for groups of pilgrims (Tel: 06-767489).

THE GREEK CHURCH The plateau is divided by a wall running east to west. The Franciscans have the south side, the Greeks the north. The Greek Orthodox Church of St Elias (Elijah) is built among the ruins of a former Crusader church and monastery. On the west side of the church a cave is shown which is said to have been the dwelling of Melchizedek, king and priest, who brought bread and wine, and blessed Abraham (Gen. 14.18–19).

NAZARETH

The evangelists do not agree on where Mary and Joseph lived before Jesus' birth. Matthew 2 implies that it was Bethlehem, but Luke 2.4–5 says it was Nazareth. A strong tradition places the birth of Our Lady in Jerusalem, where she was related to Zacharias, a priest whose service in the Temple necessitated his residence in the Holy City. Luke 1.39–40 relates her visit to his wife Elizabeth when she was reported to be with child, a journey she appears to have made alone. Traditionally this is to Ein Kerem, but it is not plausible that she would have travelled alone, a young Jewish girl in child, the three-day journey from Nazareth to Ein Kerem.

When the Holy Family returned from Egypt, it was to Nazareth they went for fear of Herod Archelaus (4 BC to AD 6). Thenceforward it was Jesus' home town (Matt. 13.54; Luke 4.16), where they had relatives (Matt. 13.54). As late as AD 249 St Conon, at his trial before his martyrdom, declared that he was born at Nazareth and that he belonged to the family of the Lord.

MODERN NAZARETH The town has a population of about 40,000, half Muslim and half Christian. Alongside the town is the Jewish town of Natzrat Illit. There are many churches and chapels, but only five buildings of any antiquity. Nazareth was not an early pilgrimage centre, nor did Constantine erect a basilica here when he had those of the Holy Sepulchre and the Nativity built. He only gave permission to one Joseph of Tiberias to build a church here. Nazareth had a bishop by 460, but it is not until 570 that a pilgrim from Piacenza speaks of a basilica of 'the house of the Blessed Virgin Mary'. Arculf (670) is the first to connect the site with the Annunciation, which he and other pilgrims place in a stone house, not a grotto.

EARLIER CHURCHES There is no trace of Joseph of Tiberias' church. Excavations begun in 1955 disclosed a Byzantine church, which did not include the Grotto of the Annunciation. Al-Mas'udi saw it in 943, but it appears to have been demolished in the eleventh century, perhaps by Caliph al-Hakim in 1009, or one of the Seljuq Turks. The Crusaders found it in ruins in 1102, and built a cathedral, which was complete by 1106. This incorporated the ruined Byzantine church, and was 81 yards by 32½ yards (74 x 30 m), with three apses at the east end. The Grotto of the Annunciation lay under its north aisle. The basilica was destroyed by the Mamluk sultan Baybars in 1263, but the grotto was unharmed.

The buildings lay in ruins until 1730, when the Franciscans obtained a *firman* (decree) from the Ottoman sultan, which allowed them only six months in which to construct a new church. This, a comparatively small building, was built in the manner of the *martyria* in the churches in Rome, the principal altar being raised on a balcony built across the top of the grotto, leaving it exposed to view. This

The upper church of the Basilica of the Annunciation at Nazareth

church was only 23 yards long and 16 yards wide (21 x 14.7 m), and incapable of serving the needs of the thousands of pilgrims who come to Nazareth.

THE NEW CHURCH Accordingly demolition began in 1955, enabling the whole site to be investigated archaeologically. The new church was then built, with a pilgrimage shrine at ground level, incorporating the remains of earlier buildings, and a large church in the upper storey to accommodate large pilgrimages.

In the centre of the underground church is the apse of the Byzantine church. In front is a basin about 2½ yards (2 m) square, believed to be a pre-Constantine baptistery because of its shape and the graffiti on its plastered walls. It was found sealed under a mosaic. Other remains of this period lie outside the north wall of the Crusader church: stores, granaries, oil presses and the foundations of dwellings. On the left of the basin stairs lead to a mosaic floor inscribed: 'Gift of Conon, a deacon of Jerusalem'. Behind the Byzantine apse is the triple twelfth century apse and a staircase. The Altar of the Annunciation is a seventeenth century one, inscribed: '*Verbum Caro Hic Factum Est*' (Here the Word was made flesh). Below it is a marble plaque venerated by pilgrims as the place on which Our Lady stood. Roman columns stand in front of this altar, brought from Caesarea or Sepphoris.

THE UPPER CHURCH The upper church is reached by stairs in the north-west corner. Its doors, windows, walls and lantern are elaborately decorated. A huge mosaic behind the high altar celebrates the doctrines of the Second Vatican Council as set forth in the dogmatic constitution *Lumen Gentium*. Other themes are the holy places cared for by the Franciscans, the Fathers of the Church and St Francis and

One of the 'Nazareth capitals', found in 1908

his followers through the ages. The dome is designed to express Jewish and Christian mystical numerical symbolism. On either side of the massive nave are pictures of Our Lady from twenty countries, all mosaics except for that of Portugal, which uses *azulejo* tiles. In the centre of the nave an *oculus* looks down to the Grotto of the Annunciation. Outside the upper church is a separate baptistery because this church also serves as a parish church for the Latin faithful in Nazareth.

THE MUSEUM Nearby is a portico, sheltering part of the excavations of first century Nazareth and a small museum. Although this is visible to some extent through a grille, visitors are admitted under the supervision of a curator. The exhibits are clearly identified. Most of the sculpture is twelfth century. The principal exhibit is the assemblage known as the 'Nazareth capitals', which were found buried in 1908. The capitals are of local stone, but are clearly paralleled by examples found in France at Vézelay, Plaimpied, Autun and Chartres. They are of such excellence that an eminent scholar has described them as 'the culmination of Crusader art in the twelfth century'. Four of the capitals are polygonal in shape, and one is rectangular, arranged as follows: St Thomas; St Peter; Our Lady; St James the Great; and St Matthew. The central, rectangular capital, which depicts Our Lady, has never been satisfactorily explained. It may refer to her Assumption.

Not one of these capitals has ever been used. It is believed that they were buried hastily in 1187, after the Battle of Hattin. Possibly they were intended to decorate an elaborate porch, a scheme which would have had to be abandoned following Saladin's victory. Alternatively, they could have been intended for the decoration of a shrine in the form of an edicule, similar to the Tomb of Our Lord in the Holy Sepulchre, which was widely imitated at this period.

THE 'HOLY HOUSE' OF LORETO The Santa Casa, or Holy House, in Loreto, Italy, was popularly believed to be the House of the Holy Family in Nazareth. According to traditions which do not antedate the sixteenth century, it is reported to have been carried by angels from Nazareth to Italy, reaching Loreto in 1291. Until 1921 when it was burnt by accident, a statue of Our Lady, of Lebanese cedar-wood, was venerated there; it has been replaced by a replica. A Bull of Pope Paul II refers to this statue in 1464 as having been brought by angels, without any mention of a Holy House. The first mention of a house is in a Bull of Pope Julius II in 1511, by which time a shrine had been erected which had come to be called the Holy House. Pope Julius spoke with prudent caution of 'pious rumour'.

The house bears no resemblance to any known house in the Middle East of the first century AD, nor indeed at any other time. The rumour can, however, be explained. The landowner in 1291 was Guy II de la Roche, duke of Athens, whose mother was a member of the Byzantine Imperial family, Angelos. Her full name was Helena Angelina: in both Latin and Italian *angeli* means angels. She was married to Count Hugh de Brienne, of a family closely connected with the kings of Jerusalem and Cyprus. Thus the sending of a statue from Nazareth at the time of the fall of Acre in 1291 would not have been surprising, and it is this simple family transaction that could have been transmuted in popular legend.

ST JOSEPH'S CHURCH Leaving the museum, to the north one reaches a courtyard, with the Church of St Joseph on the north side. It was rebuilt in 1914 on foundations that are seen outside for most of the lower courses of masonry. In medieval French romanesque style, it is of a refreshing simplicity. The first mention of it occurs in the work of the Franciscan Quaresmius (1616–1626) as 'the house and workshop of Joseph'. Matthew 13.55 refers to Jesus as the son of a *tekton*, and Mark 6.3 calls Jesus a *tekton*. Although usually translated carpenter, the Greek word *tekton* can mean one who works in wood, stone or metal. In a treeless country Joseph could not have been a carpenter in our sense of the word. Wood was imported only for ploughs and yokes, and wooden tables have been found in Jerusalem alone. There is no mention of a workshop before c.1620, when it would appear to have arisen from popular sentiment. Since 1914 the church has been known also as the Church of the Nutrition, as the place where Jesus grew up.

Excavations under the church have revealed a cave system, including four silos, three cisterns for storing water, and what has been identified as a baptismal font with seven steps leading down into it. It seems to have been built out of an earlier silo. There are carefully planned air ducts to keep the place fresh. There are also the remains of a mosaic from a building no longer in existence. The excavators interpret the system as a baptismal complex belonging to the Judaeo-Christians.

THE SYNAGOGUE CHURCH Up the street almost due east of St Joseph's Church is the Greek Catholic church known as the Synagogue Church. It is believed to be on the site of the synagogue where Jesus preached (Luke 4.28–29).

ST MARY'S WELL AND ST GABRIEL'S CHURCH To the north of the town is the Greek Orthodox Church of St Gabriel, and adjacent to it Mary's Well. The latter is filled from a spring 162 yards (148 m) away by a conduit. It is venerated because this water source would have been used by the Holy Family, and it is led into the church by a stone duct. The church in its present state is a seventeenth century construction over the remains of three former churches. By the north wall of the crypt is the well, with an Arabic inscription: 'Annunciation of the Virgin and Well of Water', thus locating the Annunciation here. Certainly there was a Byzantine church here in the sixth century, and one of considerable size in Crusader times. The church first received the name of St Gabriel in 1187; it was only after 1600 that the name Mary's Well was attributed to it.

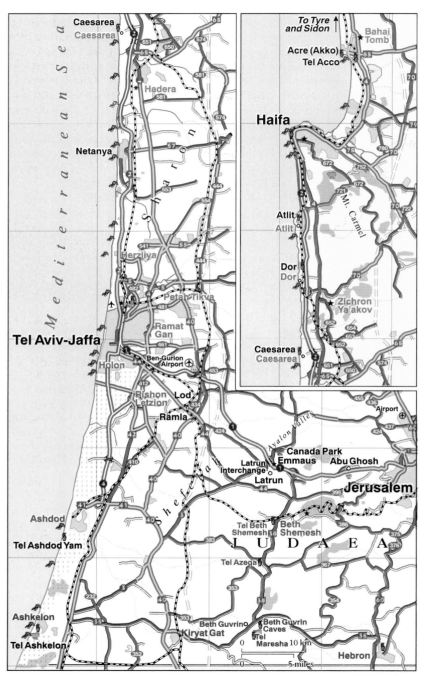

Caesarea
Caesarea

To Tyre
and Sidon
Acre (Akko)
Tel Acco
Bahai
Tomb

Hadera

Haifa

Netanya

Atlit
Atlit

Herzliya

Dor
Dor

Petah Tikva

Mt. Carmel

Ramat
Gan

Zichron
Ya'akov

Tel Aviv-Jaffa

Holon
Ben-Gurion
Airport

Caesarea
Caesarea

Rishon
Letzion
Lod

Ramla

Airport

Ayalon Valley

Canada Park
Emmaus
Abu Ghosh

Latrun
Interchange
Latrun

Jerusalem

Ashdod

Tel Ashdod Yam

Tel Beth
Shemesh
Beth
Shemesh

J U D A E A

Tel Azega

Ashkelon

Tel Ashkelon

Beth Guvrin
Kiryat Gat

Beth Guvrin
Caves
Tel
Maresha

0   10 km

0   5 miles

Hebron

Mediterranean Sea

Sharon

Shefela

© Carta, Jerusalem

6. Jerusalem to Tel Aviv and the Coast

From Jerusalem the road descends towards Jaffa and Tel Aviv. Half a century ago this was a rough metalled track, which today has been replaced by a modern dual carriageway.

ABU GHOSH

About 6 miles (10½ km) west of Jerusalem is Abu Ghosh, named after a powerful village sheikh in the sixteenth century. For years he was the terror of the neighbourhood. Here Eusebius placed Kirjath-Jearim, where all the tribes met to receive the Ark of the Covenant back from the Philistines, and renounced pagan gods (I Sam. 6.21–7.4). Here Samuel received his appointment as judge over Israel.

There are the remains of a Crusader church in the village below, with wall paintings in a poor state of preservation, which have been studied by Gustav Kühnel in *Wall Paintings in the Latin Kingdom of Jerusalem*, Berlin, 1988, with abundant coloured illustrations. The church is known as the Church of the Hospital of St John at Emmaus, an identification disputed elsewhere. It appears to have been founded either shortly before 1137, or shortly after 1141. However, the dates are so close that the dispute is largely academic.

The church has three naves of equal length, and three apses closed by a wall so that they are not visible from outside. The central nave is higher than its sisters. The plain exterior of the church gives it the aspect of a fortress (a crypt repeats the ground plan). The decoration of the church was never completed; only the three apses and two eastern bays were painted. It is thought that it was halted when the Latin Kingdom collapsed in 1187, but of this there is no historical evidence. A century ago Karl Baedeker found the paintings in a better state, and in 1901 the Comte de Piéllat made twenty-four water-colour drawings of them. The paintings were frescoes, that is, executed on fresh plaster. Iconoclasm and vandalism have contributed to their deterioration, but, after the pillar paintings of Bethlehem, they are the second most important assemblage of Crusader painting in the country.

In the central apse little remains of the principal figure of Christ. Four figures are on his right, and three on his left. Adam on the right and David on the left have almost completely deteriorated. Eve is behind Adam, with Abel and the prophet Isaiah. On the left, with David, are Solomon and John the Baptist. Below them is a representation of the Resurrection, which has almost completely disappeared. In the south apse there are two levels. Abraham, Isaac and Jacob occupy the upper level, with the souls of the just being brought to them in allusion to the words of the burial service in the Roman rite. In the north apse Christ is enthroned in glory, with Our Lady and John the Baptist as intercessors for mankind. This fresco is extremely ill-preserved.

In the aisles one panel represents the Koimesis (Falling Asleep) of Our Lady, with the Apostles journeying on the clouds. This is perhaps based on some lost apocryphal source. In addition there are two bishops on either side holding books in their hands, and distinguishable by their liturgical vestments. The other panel, on the south wall of the nave, represents the Crucifixion, and includes Our Lady, John the Beloved Disciple, and the three Holy Maries. Another figure, with a

The Cistercian Abbey of Latrun was founded in 1890 by monks of the Trappist Order

sponge-bearer behind him, is the centurion, in an attitude that suggests witness and confession of faith. A spearman is also identifiable. Either side are the two thieves, one with his head bowed, the other, the good thief Dismas, looking towards Christ. There are angels beside the cross, and figures representing the Church and the Synagogue. Piéllat also saw icons of saints which have now completely vanished.

The dedication of the church refers to the Knights Hospitaller, who had the church from 1142 until 1187. From about 1392 the Franciscans had a church and a hostel for pilgrims here, but in 1490 they were massacred and the place deserted. Later it was used as a mosque. In 1583 Prince Nicholas Christopher Radziwill stopped here on 9 July. The Marquis de Vogüé visited it in 1853, and twenty years later the French ambassador in Istanbul obtained it for France, in compensation for the loss of the Franciscan rights in the Church of St George of Lydda, which had been seized by the Greek Orthodox. In 1899 the French Benedictines gained possession of the church and restored it. In 1958 it was transferred to the Society of St Vincent de Paul, or Lazarists.

EMMAUS

In Canada Park, just over 1 mile (2 km) north of Latrun Junction, are the ruins of the village of Amwas, or Emmaus, which was wiped out in the 1967 war. It was an historic centre for the Maccabees (1 Macc. 3.40; 4.3; 9.50); the Fifth Macedonian Legion was stationed there by Vespasian. In 70 Titus gave it the title of Nicopolis, the Victorious City. Origen, Eusebius and St Jerome all believed it to be the Emmaus of the Gospels (Luke 24.13), but this has not been accepted by Fr Bagatti who prefers El-Qubeibeh (see Itinerary 5), a view not generally approved.

LATRUN

Near to the Latrun Interchange is the Cistercian Abbey of Latrun, founded in 1890. The name Latrun derives from that of a Crusader castle, on the site of which the abbey now stands, called Toron des Chevaliers, or Turo Militum, the Knights' Tower. This became corrupted to el-Atrum, whence into Latin, Castrum Boni Latronis, the Castle of the Good Thief. It is a fine example of the growth of pious myth. The monks here, commonly known as Trappists, are bound by a vow to silence. The guest master is permitted to converse with visitors. Most excellent wines and cheeses are produced for sale.

RAMLA

From Latrun a road leads 10 miles (16 km) to Ramla. It was founded as a military camp and headquarters for Palestine by the Umayyad caliph Sulayman ibn Abd al-Malik, brother of al-Walid I, in about 712–15. It is the only city founded in Palestine by the Arabs. According to the Arab geographers it was built from the ruins of the nearby Lod (Lydda), from which the population migrated. It became the principal city of Palestine (Filastin) until Crusader times. It retained its importance under all the Arab dynasties and under the Ottoman Turks, and for a time Napoleon used it as his headquarters. Traditionally it was the birthplace of St Joseph of Arimathaea, to whom the Franciscan church is dedicated. The Franciscans settled there in 1296, and in 1403 they made an agreement with the Mamluk sultan for a dragoman (guide and interpreter) and six friars to reside there for the service of pilgrims. The convent contains a room in which Napoleon slept in 1799 — with the result that the convent was sacked and the friars massacred.

MEDIEVAL PILGRIMS Having landed at Jaffa, at the end of the fifteenth century pilgrims were often accommodated in a hospice there for several days. It had a large and beautiful court with many chambers, and a fountain 'full of good and wholesome water'. There was no furniture, but mats could be bought or hired. In 1480 Fr Felix Faber recounts how an altar was set up in an inner courtyard, and that, after Mass, there was a sermon and instructions given by the father guardian of the Holy Land on the conduct to be observed on the pilgrimage. They were reminded that a papal dispensation or the father guardian's absolution was required for anyone entering the profaned Holy Land. He warned them to be wary in dealings with Muslims, against the bad habits displayed by some tourists, such as the carving of names and other graffiti, and chipping fragments off monuments, and advised them to pay cheerfully whatever was demanded of them, 'not forgetting the poor convent of the brethren of Mount Zion in Jerusalem'. There were also exhortations to greater devotion. The pilgrims found the wait tedious as they longed to reach Jerusalem, a wait necessitated by hostile Bedouin on the way.

THE WHITE MOSQUE OF RAMLA The monument is known as the White Mosque of which little is left; the most outstanding feature is the minaret. For Christians this is the 'Tower of the Forty Martyrs', for Muslims the 'Tower of the Forty Companions of the Prophet'. Only part of the structure, the porticos, were roofed: a double-aisled portico with a *mihrab* (a niche to indicate the direction of Mecca to be assumed in prayer), and single porticos on the other sides. The southern wall facing Mecca is not straight, indicating that at some time it was rebuilt after having been found to be incorrectly orientated towards Mecca, a fault found elsewhere. Below ground there are numerous cisterns, and there is a small building for ablutions in the centre of the unroofed area.

An inscription on the base of the minaret alleges that it was built by Sultan al-Nasir Muhammad b. Qala'un in 1318, although it is known that it was repaired under Sultan Baybars (1260–1269). Its appearance bears a distinct resemblance to North African minarets, of which the prototype is the Great Mosque of Kairouan, of the eighth century.

THE GREAT MOSQUE This mosque was formerly the twelfth century Crusader Cathedral of St John the Baptist, and to them are due the entrance arch and certain features of the interior. The elaborate Corinthian capitals attached to some of the piers were doubtless robbed from elsewhere. An inscription dates its conversion to a mosque in 1268.

LOD

North-east of Ramla is Lod, the ancient Lydda, important enough to have been taken as spoils of war by Thutmose III. The Maccabees made it the capital of a toparchy. Christianity was established early here, and St Peter visited the place and cured Aeneas of paralysis (Acts 9.33).

A church in honour of St George is recorded here in the fifth century, and it is general opinion that he was the George of Cappadocia who intruded, as an extreme Arian bishop, into the see of Alexandria in 357, and was murdered there in 361. Another view is that a saint of that name was martyred in or near Lydda in the early fourth century. Many stories have grown up round his name, but the legend that he slew a dragon is not recorded before the twelfth century. As a soldier saint he became popular in Crusader times. His rank as patron saint of England probably dates from the reign of Edward III (1327–1377), who founded the Order of the Garter under his patronage in 1347. The tomb of St George is in the crypt of the present church, and was opened by Australian troops in 1917, when they removed some bones with a view to forwarding them to the archbishop of Canterbury as relics. They were ordered to replace them forthwith.

JAFFA

From Ramla, Route 44 leads to Jaffa and Tel Aviv. The old town of Jaffa, partly destroyed during the mandatory period, has now disappeared. It existed in Egyptian times, and was the port for Jerusalem from the time of Solomon: it was to here that the wood for the Temple was brought down from Lebanon by sea (2 Chron. 2.16), and later for the building of the Second Temple (Esdras 7.3). It lost importance when Herod built Caesarea. Here St Peter raised Tabitha from the dead (Acts 9.36).

Under the Crusaders it regained importance. The walls were repaired in 1100. Throughout Crusader times and under the Ayyubids and Mamluks it was the principal port for pilgrims, whose transport vessels from the west were monopolies in the hands of wealthy Venetian families. St Louis rebuilt the city wall in 1251; it was captured by Baybars in 1267. It had no importance until it was revived under the British Mandate. There is a small mosque near the lighthouse, the reputed site of the house of Simon the Tanner, and the Mahmudiyyeh Mosque, with Roman pillars robbed from Caesarea and Ashkelon. It is a very picturesque place.

The picturesque port town of Jaffa on the Mediterranean coast

TEL AVIV

It is a wholly modern town, important commercially, and also the residence of many of the diplomatic corps. Before the Jewish settlement began in 1909 it was nothing but sand-dunes. There are no ancient monuments. The seat of a university, it is also remarkable for the number of its museums. These are important because they cover all periods from pre-Israelite times to the present day.

The Ha'aretz Museum Complex (in Ramat Aviv) includes museums of ceramics, glass, the history of writing, science, ethnology and folklore, ethnography, and a planetarium; there is also the Archaeological Museum, the Israel Defence Forces Museum and the Diaspora Museum (Bet Hatfutzot), as well as the Helena Rubinstein Pavilion of Modern Art.

ASHKELON

Two sites south of Tel Aviv merit attention, Ashkelon and Ashdod, respectively 32 miles (52 km) and 21 miles (34 km) away.

South of the new city is the ancient town of Ashkelon, which was situated above an underground river, the remains of a prehistoric salt lake. The ruins are now contained in a national park to which there is a small entry fee. The site was continuously inhabited from the Bronze Age until Mamluk times. In the Late Bronze Age it was under Egyptian control, but by the twelfth century BC had fallen to the Philistine invaders. With its rich agricultural potential it was an obvious attraction to the incoming Israelites, but, according to Judges 1.19, never conquered. It is famous for Samson's exploits (Judg. 13–16).

For the Philistines its importance was as a seaport, and it was this that attracted the attentions of the Assyrians in the eighth century BC. Herodotus records its destruction by the Babylonians in 604 BC. Later it was an autonomous city under the Seleucids and the Ptolemies. According to Josephus, Herod the Great was born here. Although Jews lived in the city, it was never a Jewish city. Under the Romans and Byzantines Ashkelon, together with Gaza, was famous for agriculture and the wine trade, a tradition that continued into the middle ages.

EXCAVATIONS Albeit of a crude nature, the first excavations by any Westerner were carried out here by Lady Hester Stanhope, in 1815; she uncovered a huge basilica and a statue that she had smashed, lest it be thought that she was seeking treasure. She was the niece and political hostess of the British prime minister, William Pitt. Some statues survive among the ruins, as well as a wall, and a public building of Herodian Ascalon from the city that Herod the Great built in honour of Augustus. Half a mile (c.1 km) away is the Philistine harbour. Much of the site has been robbed for building, and the Roman theatre has altogether disappeared.

TEL ASHDOD

North of Ashkelon is Tel Ashdod Yam (south of the modern city of Ashdod). Another of the Philistine cities, it was where the god Dagon, half man and half fish, was venerated. There is little to see here, although there are some remains of a Crusader fortress.

It was a merchant city where textiles were manufactured from Late Bronze times, and traded far inland to Ugarit. By the time of Joshua it was in Philistine hands, and it seems to have remained so. When the Philistines captured the Ark of the Covenant, it was brought to the temple of Dagon (1 Sam. 5.1) in the ancient city of Ashdod. Later it fell to Babylon and to Persia. As a Hellenistic city it was known as Azotus. Count Hugh of Ibelin erected a castle here, which was called after his name; there are also the remains of a Crusader church, which was later converted into a mosque, now deserted.

NORTH OF TEL AVIV

Driving northwards to Tel Aviv and beyond, one travels up the ancient Way of the Sea through the most densely inhabited area in modern Israel. Shortly after Tel Aviv one reaches the Plain of Sharon, famous for its fertility (Isa. 36.2), where the popular seaside resort of Netanya is to be found. At Umm Khalid, to the north of Netanya and yet still within the city limits, are the remains of a Crusader castle, of Roger the Lombard, and a necropolis of the Herodian period.

CAESAREA

Further on along the coast is Caesarea (in Arabic Qaisariya, in rabbinic Hebrew Qisri or Qisrin). The name Caesarea Maritima was unknown in ancient times; more common than others was Caesarea of Palestine. It was named Caesarea by Herod the Great, in honour of his patron, Caesar Augustus, but an earlier town of Phoenician origin, Straton's Tower, had already existed as a port town on the site. Its earlier history is obscure. Herod built Caesarea between 22 and 10/9 BC. It had a theatre and amphitheatre, a market, a palace, and streets on a grid plan in the Roman fashion. A long narrow point was enlarged to make a harbour, where a promontory gave shelter. This Herod called Sebastos, whence Sebaste, the Greek name for Augustus. The harbour walls were elaborately constructed.

The Romans annexed Judaea in 6 BC, and made Caesarea the headquarters of the provincial governor and his administration. Of these governors Pontius Pilate was one. At first the province was known as Judaea, later Palestina. In AD 66, when the Jews revolted, the pagans massacred most of the Jewish population. Vespasian wintered here, and gave the city the status of a Roman colony, making its citizens full Roman citizens. Derisively, the rabbis called it 'the daughter of Rome'.

EARLY CHRISTIANITY Christianity was brought early to Caesarea. It was evangelised by St Philip (Acts 8.40) and visited by St Peter (Acts 10.1 ff.), when he was sent for by the centurion Cornelius after St Peter had had a vision that nothing was to be called unclean and that the Jewish sumptuary laws were abrogated. Here there took place the dramatic trial of St Paul before the governor, Festus, King Herod Agrippa and his wife Bernice (Acts 23.26 ff.), after which he embarked for trial in Rome.

In 195 a council was held here, which ordered Easter to be kept on a Sunday. The theologian Origen and St Alexander were ordained priests here; and Origen taught here until his death in 254. His pupil Pamphilus succeeded to his library, which later was inherited by his pupil Eusebius, who, out of reverence for his master, took the name of Eusebius Pamphili. He is celebrated as the father of church history, and to him we owe most of what we can know of the early church. Later Eusebius became archbishop, and as such consecrated Constantine's Basilica of the Holy Sepulchre.

EXCAVATIONS There are extensive remains: the site covers 235 acres. In addition, since 1971 the port area has been explored, with underwater excavations as well as work on land. Caesarea continued to be of commercial importance until after the Crusades, and it was from here that the Polos set out in the thirteenth century for their travels to the court of the Great Khan of the Mongols in far-off Peking (Beijing).

The earliest excavations in the 1950s disclosed sewers and walls of the Hellenistic period, and storehouses for the port. In 1959–1964 an Italian expedition uncovered the theatre, demonstrating that it had undergone several stages of development. Under the Israel Government Department of Antiquities there followed excavations of the elaborate water supply system, some of it leading from the southern slopes of Mount Carmel. Further excavations within the medieval city disclosed somewhat unclear information about the Byzantine and medieval periods. Remains of the Early Arab period have been found all over Caesarea.

The Crusaders, however, only occupied 22 acres, or scarcely one-tenth of Roman and Byzantine occupation. This was a walled city with paved streets. The Crusader church was never completed. A fortress was constructed overlooking the harbour. To the north of the Crusader city is a synagogue, used from Hellenistic

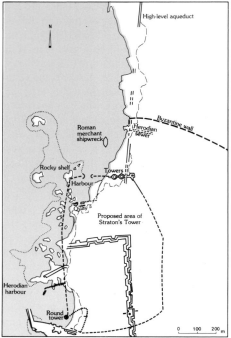

Above: General plan of Caesarea's harbours

Below: Aerial photograph of the Herodian harbour

times until the fifth century AD, and perhaps into the Arab period. There are no signs of use after the eighth century.

Excavations in the 1970s in the western part of the medieval city disclosed a city of the Byzantine period, with a palace on the promontory with a pool, and a reception room 27½ x 39 feet (8.4 x 12 m), flanked by two rooms 16¼ x 24 feet (5 x 7.3 m), all at one end of a great portico with columns on three sides. Much of this is exposed to rough seas, and is slowly being eroded. The reception room has a carpet-like mosaic similar to one found in Herod's palace in Jericho. The mosaic floors in the other rooms are first or second century. The building is certainly Herodian, and was possibly intended as a residence for him.

There were further excavations in the 1980s and 1990s. It has been possible to identify the site of an amphitheatre, north-east of the old city and accommodating about 4,000, using aerial photography. A temple platform dominating the inner harbour was found, along with further warehouses (*horrea*), and a *circus*, or running track. A *mithraeum*, a temple and sanctuary of the god Mithras, with frescoes showing the god slaying a bull, was also found, a rarity in the Near East and the only one known in Israel. Extensions to the water supply were built c.130, perhaps to accommodate a larger military presence.

From the Byzantine period, quantities of houses have been found and yet more defences. A fortress was built by robbing the stone from the theatre, out of fashion because it was so derided and hated by the Church Fathers. Luxurious villas and baths were also found in the neighbourhood. In the sixth century an octagonal church was built, recalling to mind those of Capernaum and Gerizim. A church of St Lawrence survived into the nineteenth century, but no trace so far has been found of Caesarea's renowned Great Mosque. Within the old city a small walled city still survives, with the evocative name of the 'English City'. It was presumably a merchant quarter. This, and very much else, remains for future excavation and research, which is as well, for archaeological techniques continue to develop and become refined.

HARBOURS The extent of the remains of the Herodian harbour was identified only in 1960. With some intermissions, surveys both on land and below water have continued to the present time, and an annual expedition of the Department of Maritime Civilisation is undertaken by the University of Haifa.

North of the Crusader city was a Phoenician harbour close to Straton's Tower. A quay of ashlar blocks was exposed, of the third to second centuries BC. To the south Herod constructed a far larger harbour which Josephus describes in great detail. Here great ships could lie at anchor completely protected from the rough south winds, 'and this he effected by letting down vast stones of fifty feet in length, not less than eighteen in breadth, and nine in depth, into twenty fathoms deep... This mole that he built by the seaside was two hundred feet wide', one side as a breakwater against the waves, the other having a protective wall with towers.

The harbour was adorned with two statues, one of Rome, the other of Caesar. The whole complex took twelve years to build. Nor was it crudely done, for there is evidence that the engineers took pains to prevent the accumulation of sand from the action of the waves and currents by a system of breakwaters. What they could not prevent was subsidence, and, as the breakwaters ceased to be visible, there is evidence that ships were wrecked and broke their backs.

The Crusader harbour was c.3 feet (1 m) lower than at present, and occupied part of the Herodian harbour. It is strange to reflect that here have stood characters so disparate as Herod, Pontius Pilate, St Paul, Crusaders and the Polo brothers, not to mention countless pilgrims.

DOR
Farther north the road leads to Dor, which was long contested between the Philistines and the Phoenicians (the site of ancient Dor is north of the present-day settlement). Before them it was inhabited by a mysterious people known as the Sikil, of whom we as yet know virtually nothing. An Egyptian record of c.1100

BC records the name of its king, Beder, among an account of a journey to Byblos, as one of the Sea Peoples. Systematic excavations have taken place since 1980; as yet the two lowest strata have not been penetrated. It seems likely that these may resolve part of the problem of the Sikil.

EARLY HISTORY OF DOR A twelfth century BC foundation for the maritime city-state of Dor would coincide with the arrival of other powerful groups in Syro-Palestine, the Israelites and Aramaeans, the Phoenicians (who were to found a great trading empire which stretched from Tyre and Sidon to beyond the straits of Gibraltar, and perhaps to Britain), and the Philistines, whose resistance to the incoming Israelites is a principal theme in their migration. It was a period of great unrest in the Semitic world, which only slowly unfolded as a new system of states and settled culture. It is too simplistic to see it as a contest between Israel and Philistia only; it was an upheaval that opened a new era in which some peoples emerged as new powers, while others were absorbed or disappeared. This is the importance of Dor, as a palimpsest from the Sikil people to the Early Arab period, when Dor still had bishops. Shortly afterwards it became desolate, and remained that way until the Crusaders built a castle here called Merle.

EXCAVATIONS Accounts of the excavations are available up to 1991, and time must be allowed for further study and reflection, and for publication.

Dor already had a maritime connection in the Middle and Late Bronze Ages, for pottery of Cypriot origin has been found, as well as some Mycenaean wares. It seems clear that the Sikil and the Philistines formed part of the Sea Peoples, and that soon after there arrived another people from the same group, the Phoenicians. By then it appears that a substantial town had been established, and the Phoenicians soon became paramount. In the eleventh century the connection with Cyprus persisted, but also with connections inland to Samaria, and farther afield to Assyria. Of particular interest is a Negroid head used as the knob on the lid of an ivory box.

By the sixth century BC, in the Persian period, a residential quarter had been laid out like a grid on principles that are closest paralleled at Olynthus in Greece and Mount Sirai in Sardinia. It is not surprising that there was evidence of an extensive industrial area, in bronze and iron slag, and perhaps glass waste. There were the remains of murex snail shells, from which the famous purple Tyrian dye was made. Connections with eastern Greece and with Corinth are very clear from what so far has been the largest assemblage of Greek pottery in Israel. And there are cult objects from Greek, Cypriot, Egyptian, Persian, and even Western sources, demonstrating the wide embrace of the Phoenician popular religion.

After the conquest of Alexander the Great and his Seleucid successors there was little change in building or other local techniques, or in imports. There is evidence of systematic medical practice, and of an official system of weights and measures. Throughout this period Dor was a pagan city; the first Jewish evidence belongs to the period of the Herodian kings under the Romans. The fortifications of the city continued to show Phoenician influence even into the Roman period.

BYZANTINE DOR There are few remains from the Byzantine period, but a large church has been found built upon what may have been a pagan cultic place on which a Greek temple was built. By the fourth or fifth century this had become a

A pottery figurine head in Greek Archaic style, of the Persian period

large church on a basilican plan, with three, and eventually five naves. The north aisle was divided into four rooms, of which one contained a pool, reminiscent of the large Epiphany tank at the Baramous Monastery in Wadi el-Natrun, Egypt. At the eastern end of the south aisle was the tomb of a saint, of unknown identity. The stone covering had a hole into which oil could be poured so that it came into contact with the relics of the saints, after which it drained into a plastered basin adjacent to the tomb. The oil was then taken away by pilgrims as a relic. Al-Mas'udi records a similar practice at Nazareth in the Church of the Annunciation as late as the tenth century. All the floors were richly decorated with mosaics.

THE PORT The sophisticated commercial and cultural life was dependent on a no less sophisticated port. According to Greek legend, Dor was founded by Doros, the son of the sea god Poseidon. It is protected by a series of small islands, which not only break the force of the waves but also enable ships to be loaded in

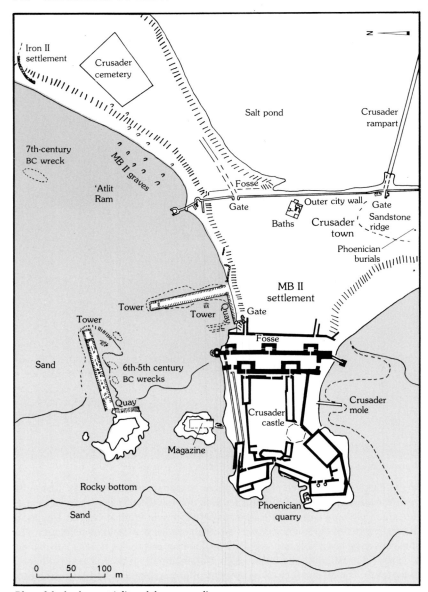

Plan of the harbour at Atlit and the surrounding area

comparative safety, a rare advantage on the coast of Israel. Sand, arriving from the mouth of the Nile Delta, has preserved the evidence of thousands of years of use, recoveries having been made by underwater surveys. As the level of the Mediterranean rose in the eleventh century BC, so new quays were constructed on top of the old ones. In the Persian period there was a dockyard for the building and repair of ships, with both wet and dry docks. An aqueduct brought fresh water and there were also fish ponds.

FROM THE CRUSADERS TO NAPOLEON   Dor declined sharply after the Arab period. The Crusaders built the castle of Merle on the top of Tel Dor, occupying it briefly. In 1664 a ship from Greece was wrecked, carrying a French consul, and Cypriot wine and cheese. The harbour was still known in the eighteenth century, when Napoleon used it as a supply base. It is a monument to the failure of his Syrian campaign, for, on 21 May 1799, after his defeat at Acre, as the French army retreated to Egypt they jettisoned cannons, rifles, daggers and other equipment, which can still be found on the seabed.

ATLIT

About 9 miles (14 km) before Haifa on the coast are the remains of the Crusader fortress and the originally Phoenician town of Atlit (north of Atlit today). It is possibly the Kartah mentioned in Joshua 21.34; and the name seems to have persisted, for a Mutatio Certhae, the changing-post of Kartha, is mentioned by the Bordeaux pilgrim who left an account of his journey of AD 333. The promontory on which the fortress is built was cut off by a man-made defile (or gorge) in Phoenician times, for it still bears Phoenician lettering cut in the hewn rock.

When the Crusaders arrived in 1099, it was a haunt of highway robbers. In or about 1118 the Knights Templar established a police post, of which the ruins can still be seen. The castle was not constructed until the Fifth Crusade, in 1218, in order to control the coastal road, and with a view to the recovery of Jerusalem from the Ayyubids. These knights were assisted by Teutonic Knights and other Crusaders, who named it Castrum Peregrini, Pilgrim Castle. The Knights Templar were able to hold it until the Latin Kingdom finally collapsed in 1291. It stood siege in 1220, when 4,000 persons daily were fed in its hall. It was virtually impregnable because it could always be provisioned from the sea. In 1265, when the Mamluk sultan Baybars sacked the town, he left the castle alone.

ATLIT CASTLE   The castle was largely demolished after the Mamluks evicted the Crusaders from Acre in 1291. The Ottoman Turks robbed it to build the sea-walls of Acre. Further ruin was caused by an earthquake in 1837. It is still possible, however, to form some idea of it. On the east there was a triple line of defences, with five towers. A second line of defence of roughly rectangular form, following the outline of the promontory, surrounded an inner quadrangle. Broadly, it was similar to the triple defences of Damietta. Bridges and passages connected its walls. There was an octagonal church with five eastern apses.

Excavation has not made clear where the refectory and kitchens were, but the refectory was probably the large hall on the lower level, with a rose decoration in the roof. Outside the perimeter were stables, and, to the north, a cemetery in which the dead were buried without names in accordance with Templar custom elsewhere, in all some 1,700. Many of the flat tombstones bore an emblem of the man's trade flanking a cross: a mason had a hammer and set square. The masonry was of the same high standard as that of contemporary Syria and Egypt, and it is possible that Arab masons were employed.

EARLY ATLIT In addition to the Crusader remains there are those dating from Phoenician until Hellenistic times. Coins and jewellery have been found of Greek, Phoenician, Egyptian, and Mesopotamian origin. Of the Crusader period, a small church survives outside the walls, perhaps for the grooms and servants attending the stables that held 300 horses, and also a bath-house.

Off an island in the harbour are further remains of harbour works dating back to Phoenician times, with some wrecks under water. There are quays and break-waters. A Neolithic site has also been located north of the harbour under the present sea level, submerged when the Mediterranean rose during the eleventh century BC.

HAIFA

Haifa is the principal port in Israel, and its third largest city. It takes its name from a Semitic root meaning shelter, but never developed as a port of any consequence until 1905, when it became the terminus of the Hejaz railway to Damascus and to Medina in what is now Saudi Arabia. It has no ancient remains of significance.

THE CARMELITES The older part of the town lies at the foot of Mount Carmel. At the head of the promontory is the Carmelite Monastery of Stella Maris, Our Lady Star of the Sea. A path nearby leads to a cave, venerated by Jews, Muslims and Christians, where Elijah is said to have meditated when he fled from the wrath of Ahab (1 Kings 19) on his way to Beersheba. His halt is not mentioned in the Bible. An uninterrupted succession of hermits on Mount Carmel until the founda-tion of the Carmelite Order, one of extreme asceticism founded by St Berthold in c.1154, is claimed, but lacks historicity. The order has produced great mystics, including St Teresa of Avila and St John of the Cross. The Carmelites have had a chapel at Haifa since 1767, but the monastic buildings date from 1890 only.

THE BAHAI GARDENS The most spectacular sight in Haifa is the Bahai Gardens, with beautiful cypress trees, the seedlings of which were brought from Shiraz, in Persia. A white marble building contains the tombs of founders of the Bahai faith, a syncretism of Islamic, Jewish and Christian doctrines. On the opposite side of the road which bisects the gardens, a Grecian style building houses the Bahai museum, archives and library. The best view is from the town below.

MOUNT CARMEL Behind Haifa, the Carmel range stretches along the side of the Plain of Esdraelon for 15 miles (24 km), with a width of 3 to 5 miles (5 to 8 km). One of the peaks at the south-east end is the traditional site of the contest between the priests of Baal and the prophet Elijah: when the former failed to call down fire from heaven, Elijah rebuilt the altar and offered a sacrifice upon which fire fell immediately (1 Kings 18). At one time there were some small monasteries on top. Some earlier monastic buildings of the Carmelites were used by Napoleon in 1799; when he withdrew in the May, the monks and wounded were massacred.

ACRE

Visible from Haifa across the bay is the town of Acre (in Arabic, Akka; in Hebrew, Akko); in Crusader times it was known as St Jean d'Acre. Its importance derived from a natural promontory which is occupied by the old city; modern Acre has developed on the mainland to the east of the promontory. After the Old City of Jerusalem, the old city of Acre is the best preserved in all the Middle East outside the Arabian peninsula.

The Bahai Gardens in Haifa

EARLY ACRE Its name occurs in the Egyptian Execration Texts, and it appears at first to have resisted the Israelite immigration (Judg. 1.31); nevertheless in the reign of Solomon it is believed to have been one of the twenty cities in Galilee granted to Hiram, the king of Tyre (1 Kings 9.11–13). Under the Persians it was an important administrative and military centre. After Alexander the Great's conquest it fell to the Ptolemies. It became an important commercial city, and resisted the Maccabean revolt because it could result in commercial loss. In 63 BC

The harbour at Acre

under Pompey it became autonomous, and subject to the Roman proconsul for Syria. Julius Caesar visited it in 47 BC; under Nero it became a Roman colony as a settlement for veterans. In AD 66 it served Vespasian as a base to suppress the first Jewish Revolt (AD 66–70).

St Paul spent a day here on his third journey, but no bishop is recorded before 190. Although it served as the harbour for Galilee, it was regarded as outside the boundaries of the Holy Land. After the Arab conquest in 636 it continued as a port and shipbuilding centre. Under the Umayyad Mu'awiya I (661–680) fleets were built here for expeditions against Cyprus and to North Africa. In 1104 the Crusaders took Acre with the help of a Genoese fleet; in 1187 Saladin took it, but in 1191 it was retaken by Richard I of England and Philip Augustus of France. On 26 March 1217 St Francis of Assisi landed here: although the Crusaders and their kingdom have now long perished, there then began a spiritual conquest which, in different ways, has endured to the present day.

Together with Caesarea, Acre was a principal centre for trade with the West and the capital of the revived Latin Kingdom. The Orders of St John (Hospitallers), the Knights Templar, the Teutonic Knights and St Lazarus all had headquarters here, with colonies of Venetians, Genoese and Pisans near the harbour. The English had a tower north-east of the city.

TEL ACCO East of Acre is Tel Acco, a mound which was first inhabited in the Early Bronze Age. The pattern of settlement up to the Arab period is very similar to Caesarea. Similar results have been obtained from excavations in the city proper as far as is possible. In 1292 the Mamluk sultan al-Malik al-Ashraf took the city and razed it. It did not revive until the beginning of the seventeenth century, when the Druze emir, Fakhr al-Din, rebuilt part of it. In the eighteenth century under Dhaher al-Amr (1750–1775) and Ahmed al-Jazzar (1775–1804) much rebuilding

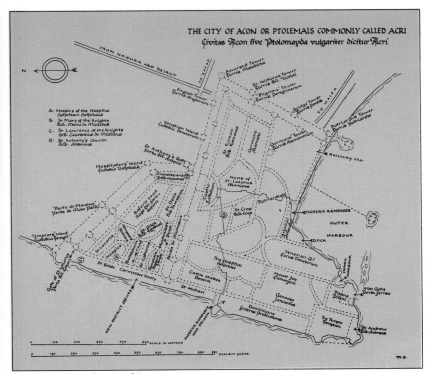

THE CITY OF ACON OR PTOLEMAIS COMMONLY CALLED ACRI
Civitas Acon sive Ptolomayda vulgariter dicitur Acri

Plan of the Crusader city of Acre

took place. A Great Mosque was built in 1781; baths and a citadel followed, partly re-using earlier constructions. Some Hellenistic remains and part of the city wall, a glass furnace and a temple survive from that period. From the Crusader period there remains the refectory of the Order of St John (wrongly called the crypt) and the El-Bosta Halls, which served as an infirmary. The new jetty of the harbour covers the walls of earlier times, in which Roman, Tulunid (Arab), Crusader and Ottoman periods intermingle. Most of what is to be seen is eighteenth and nineteenth century.

PAPAL VISIT Pope Paul visited Acre in 1964, but he was not the first pope to do so since St Peter's time. In 1271 Gregory X (Tebaldo Visconti) (1271–1276) was elected while on a pilgrimage to the Holy Land; he was a layman at the time. His pontificate was marked by the introduction of the conclave (assembly of cardinals) for the election of a pope, and by the Constitution of 1274 which has lasted, with only some minor changes, until the present day.

TYRE AND SIDON

Over the Lebanese border lie the towns of Tyre and Sidon, which were visited by Jesus (Mark 7.24) and became Christian in the first century (Acts 21.3–4). Tyre is on a long promontory, and Sidon by a headland, gaining protection from the sea.

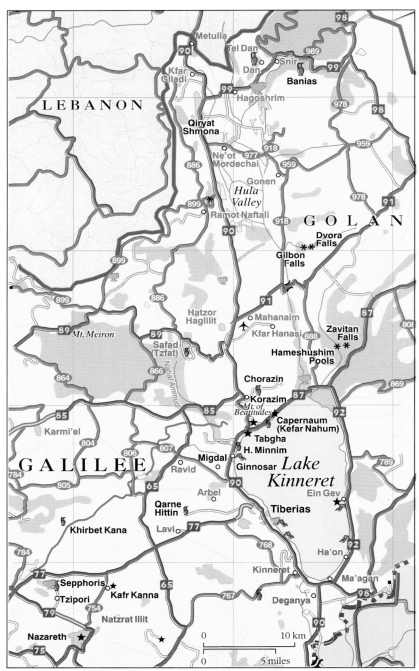

© Carta, Jerusalem

7. Nazareth to Tiberias, Capernaum and the North

SEPPHORIS

Follow Route 79 from Natzrat Illit and then turn right to the settlement of Tzipori, which lies up a by-road to the north, about 4 miles (6½ km) in all. Beyond it lies the site of the ancient Tzipori (Sepphoris). Called Diocaesarea in Roman times, the city of Zeus and Caesar, it was the capital of Galilee in the time of Jesus. The Gospels do not record that Jesus ever went there, but it is the traditional home of his grandmother, St Anne, and it might be supposed that he may have visited it for that reason, or to pay taxes.

Its first mention in literature is in Josephus, but the site is older than that, for Iron Age deposits have been found here. It was the administrative centre in Hasmonean times for all Galilee; Herod took it in 37 BC, and on his death it passed to his son, Herod Antipas, who resided here until he founded Tiberias. Herod Antipas fortified Sepphoris and changed its name to Autocratoris, meaning the All-powerful. During the first Jewish Revolt Sepphoris sided with Vespasian; after AD 70, Rabbi Judah HaNasi and the Sanhedrin established themselves here and made it an important centre of Jewish learning. The Mishnah (the first authoritative compilation of the Oral Law that accompanies the Written Law, that is, the Five Books of Moses) was redacted here. Only later did the Sanhedrin move to Tiberias. In the time of the emperor Constantine a certain Count Joseph, who built the church at Nazareth, and who was a convert from Judaism, tried in vain to build a church here. By the sixth century there was a bishop.

THE TEL A Crusader fortress was erected on top of the tel, on top of an earlier Roman building, itself perhaps a fort or administrative building. Near it was a piazza and a theatre with a capacity of 4,500 seats. Most of it rested on rock, and was paved, but the paving has been mostly robbed. It was of the usual Roman plan. Nearby was a palace or large mansion, with a central hall surrounded by rooms on three sides. It had elegant mosaics. On the western side of the tel was a residential area, with elaborate water supplies, with some houses having *mikva'ot*, Jewish ritual baths. There were also subterranean cisterns.

On the summit of the tel there were a number of sumptuous houses of the Byzantine period, with mosaics of exceptional workmanship. One showed the annual pagan festival of the Nile flood, and the Nilometer, a graduated pillar for measuring the depth to which the Nile flooded from year to year. An attempt was made to identify one building as a church, but there was no conclusive reason for it. Presumably the church or churches have simply not been located. The Talmud mentions eighteen synagogues in Sepphoris, but again not one has been located. There are extensive cemeteries of all periods. As things stand there is still much to be learnt from this site.

CANA IN GALILEE

Returning to Nazareth, the road to Tiberias (Route 754 and then Route 77) passes Kafr Kanna, usually identified with Cana in Galilee. In Christian tradition this is where Jesus performed the miracle of changing water into wine at the wedding feast (John 2.1–11). Today it is a town of about 11,500 inhabitants, most of whom

The Franciscan and Greek Orthodox churches at Kafr Kanna

are Muslim, and the rest Christian. The lower levels of the Franciscan church here have Roman remains thought to date from before the fourth century, in addition to Byzantine and Crusader remains. It is thought to be on the site of a third century synagogue. The site was acquired by the Franciscans in 1641, and the present church built in 1879.

In the adjacent Greek Orthodox church is shown an earthenware jar that is said to have been used on the occasion of the miracle of turning the water into wine; similar jars were shown in the middle ages.

Eight miles (13 km) north of Nazareth is **Khirbet Kana**, an uninhabited mound of ruins, where there is also a Franciscan church, formerly a mosque. Apparently a synagogue stood here c.AD 500. The present church was built in 1883, and an inscription records the place in which stood six water pots: *'Hic erant sex hydriae positae'* (Here were placed the six water jars). Be this as it may, it seems very unlikely that a synagogue could have been constructed on a site known at an early period to be sacred to Christians. Nevertheless this site of Khirbet Kana has been preferred to that of Kafr Kanna by many pilgrims.

THE HORNS OF HITTIN

Almost 4 miles (6 km) west of Tiberias is Qarne Hittin, or the Horns of Hittin, so called from the shapely hill which resembles an Arab saddle, and rises to two peaks resembling horns, *qurun*. It has been mistakenly identified by some with the Mount of the Beatitudes, but this cannot be so, for it is too far from the lake. The site was a strategic strong point along the ancient Via Maris, the Way of the Sea from Damascus to the coast.

It was here that Saladin defeated the Crusaders on 4 July 1187, leaving the Latin Kingdom of Jerusalem in ruins. Twenty thousand Christians were killed, and

30,000 taken prisoner. The Knights Templar and Hospitallers made a last desperate stand round the king, Guy de Lusignan, and the Wood of the Cross was captured and taken to Damascus.

TIBERIAS

The town of Tiberias, now a flourishing commercialized resort with hotels and restaurants along the lakeside, was founded by Herod Antipas between AD 18 and 20. It was named after the emperor Tiberius, and located south of the present inhabited area. According to Josephus, it was populated by the king attracting residents, 'by equipping houses at his own expense and adding new gifts of land'. In a rich agricultural area, it quickly became prosperous. Here Herod Antipas built a magnificent palace with ceilings 'partly of gold', and a synagogue, a huge building capable of accommodating a large crowd, together with royal treasure houses and archives. During the reign of Emperor Elagabalus (218–222) Tiberias became a Roman colony.

The Sanhedrin moved here from Sepphoris, and it was the seat of a major academy of Jewish learning which contributed to the compilation of the Jerusalem Talmud, a monument of biblical criticism, tradition and exegesis still powerful in influence after a millennium. There was a municipal council, some thirteen synagogues and the other appurtenances of a cultivated Roman city. South of the city medicinal springs drew visitors to therapeutic baths. It was in Tiberias that the Masoretes vocalised the Hebrew texts of the Scriptures, using a system that endures to this day. Preachers, poets, scholars and rabbis abounded. In the ninth century there were some signs of decline. The end came in 1033 when an earthquake destroyed the whole city.

THE ANCIENT CITY Little of the ancient city remains today: part of the *cardo* or main street, baths, a market, an exedra or assembly hall, a reservoir, a tower and

Looking out over the Sea of Galilee

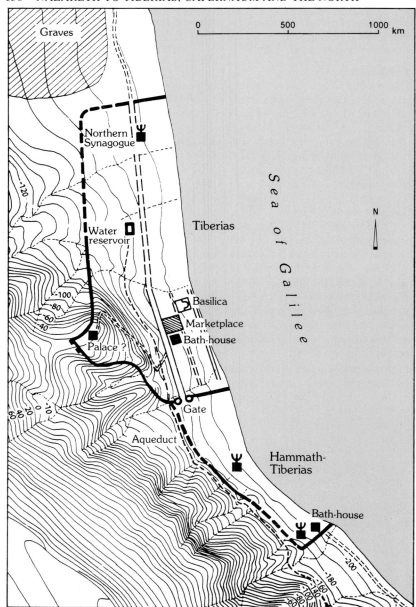

Plan of the ancient city of Tiberias

the south gate. Of the thirteen synagogues mentioned in the Talmud only one has actually been identified. Since so much of Tiberias has been built over, excavation can only be random and adventitious.

ST PETER'S FISH A particular pleasure in Tiberias is the flat fish *chromis Simonis*, otherwise known as St Peter's Fish. It is so called because the mouth is extremely narrow, just sufficient to hold the tribute-money of the stater (gold or silver coin of the Greek city-states) which St Peter drew from the water (Matt. 17.27). The miracle, however, is more likely to have taken place farther north near Capernaum, than off Tiberias. The peculiarity of this fish is that it carries in its mouth the eggs laid by the female, and, for a short while, the immature young. St Peter's fish, however, had somehow acquired a gold coin. This fish is obtainable in most of the lakeside restaurants.

CHURCHES In the fourth century Count Joseph built a church here. However, it has never been located. Willibald and other pilgrims saw a church here dedicated to St Peter, which perhaps stood where the Great Mosque is. It was a round church, like that on Mount Gerizim. From the sixteenth century on the Franciscans have visited Tiberias to celebrate St Peter's feast day on 29 June, but their present property was acquired only in 1847, and rebuilt in 1870. It rests on Crusader foundations, and the church has an apse resembling the keel of a boat; it has no connection with the church of the fourth century.

Polish troops occupied the Casa Nova hospice of the Franciscans during the Second World War, and built a monument in honour of Our Lady of Czestochowa, their national patron.

MAIMONIDES About a mile (1.6 km) north of the old town is a Jewish cemetery in which, among many poor people, a number of distinguished rabbis are buried. Chief among these is one commonly known as Maimonides, who has been referred to as 'the Moses of his time'. His Hebrew name was Moses ben Maimon, in Arabic Abu Imran Musa ibn Maymun. He was the most famous of all the Hebrew philosophers and physicians of the Arab period.

He was born at Córdova in Spain in 1135, but following persecution the family migrated, reaching Cairo c.1165. The claim that he professed Islam in public and Judaism in private has been sharply rebutted. In Cairo he became the court physician and friend of Saladin, and of his son Malik al-Aziz. From 1177 until his death in 1204 he was the *nagid* (leader) of the Jewish community in Cairo. He was equally distinguished as an astronomer, theologian, physician, and, above all, as a philosopher. His leading philosophical work, *Dalalat al-Ha'irin* (*The Guide of the Perplexed*), was for those who were firm in their religious beliefs and practices, but, having studied philosophy, were perplexed by the literal meaning of biblical anthropomorphic and anthropopathic terms.

He aroused the anger of orthodox theologians by championing scientific thought against 'fundamentalism', whether biblical or koranic. Written in Arabic, his works were translated into Hebrew; some were later translated into Latin. In this way his teachings percolated to Christians as well as to Jews, and traces of his influence have been found in the works of the Dominicans Albertus Magnus and St Thomas Aquinas, the Franciscan Duns Scotus, the Jewish philosopher Baruch Spinoza, and the philosopher Immanuel Kant.

In accord with his last will and testament, his body was carried overland from Cairo, following the route that it was believed Moses and the People of Israel had taken to reach the Promised Land, for burial in Tiberias. He occupies an eminent place in the debate between faith and reason. His tomb is still visited by pilgrims.

THE SEA OF GALILEE Motor boats leave the quay at Tiberias at frequent intervals for trips on the lake. Although the town is mentioned in the Gospels, it is not associated with any incident in the life of Jesus. The surface of the lake is 685 feet (209 m) below sea level, but this varies at different times of the year according to the melting of the snow on the mountains of Lebanon. It is 13 miles (21 km) long and 7.4 miles (12 km) across at its widest. The lake is known in Hebrew as the Kinneret, from the Hebrew *kinnor* (harp), for that is its shape. Other names are Lake Gennesaret, the Sea of

Traditional portrait of Maimonides

Galilee, and Lake Tiberias. It is fished in two ways, by line, as St Peter did in the Miracle of the Stater (see p. 151); and by casting a seine net, as described in the miraculous draught of fishes (Luke 5).

The lake is subject to sudden violent storms, as described in Matthew 8.23–26. They are caused by the funnel effect of winds in the *wadi*s (watercourses in the time of rains, but dry at other times), and can reach such fury that one can scarcely stand upright. Allusion is made to a similar scene when Jesus walked on the water, and bade Peter to come to him in order to test his faith.

Looking south-east from Tiberias, on a clear day the Jordanian town of Umm Qais, the ancient Gadara, can be seen. It was there, when Jesus healed the man possessed of devils, that the evil spirits passed into a herd of swine — still plentiful in the region today.

MAGDALA

A road runs northward along the western side of the lake to Capernaum (Kefar Nahum), and beyond to Banias. Off this road to the west is Migdal, the site of ancient Migdal (also known as Magdala Terikheai or Magdala Nunaya), the city that gave Mary Magdalen her name (Luke 8.2). According to rabbinical tradition she had aroused public indignation by divorcing a Jew, Pappus ben Juda, whom she deserted to marry a pagan officer of Herod Antipas, named Panther. A somewhat different portrait of her is found in the Gospels (Luke 8.2; Mark 16). Hers was the principal part in the recognition of the Risen Christ.

Josephus describes a town of importance. Fishing, weaving and dyeing were principal industries. In AD 70 it had 4,000 inhabitants; Josephus himself made it his headquarters. Shortly after it was destroyed by the Romans. Later, pilgrims speak of a church on the reputed site of Mary Magdalen's house, but of this only

The Sea of Galilee at sunset

a wall and two towers remain. The Via Maris passed through here, and some sections of the stone-paved road remain.

GINNOSAR

On the shore of the lake is Ginnosar, a kibbutz with an excellent restaurant. It also houses a first century AD boat, such as the apostles would have used. It was found on the lakeside when the water fell to an exceptionally low level in 1986. It is kept in water under cover, as part of the process of conservation; the specially constructed pool is situated in the Yigal Allon Museum on the kibbutz. A small charge is made for admission to view it. It is a flat-bottomed, very shallow boat, 27 x 7½ feet (8.2 x 2.3 m). The fright of the apostles when waves were breaking over their boat in a storm (Matt. 8.23–26) is easily imaginable after seeing this frail vessel.

There are a number of caves in **Nahal Ammud**. It was in this area that, in 1923, F. Turville-Petre excavated, finding a Neanderthal skull (*Palaeoanthropus Palestinensis*). The Japanese also found the Ammud Man in the same area in 1961, belonging to the Upper Palaeolithic.

BETHSAIDA

The native village of Peter, Andrew and Philip (Matt. 11.21; and numerous other references) is generally placed at Hurbat Minnim (Khirbet Minya), north of Migdal. Jesus performed many miracles here, and finally cursed it (Matt. 11.20) for failing to do penance in spite of them.

TABGHA

After about 1 mile (1.6 km) Tabgha (Tabkha) is reached, the modern Arabic name a distortion of the Greek name Heptapegon, the Place of Seven Springs, which is

The Church of the Beatitudes

also the meaning of the Hebrew name Ein Sheva. Three churches commemorate the Beatitudes, the Multiplication of the Loaves and Fishes and the Apparition of the Risen Christ to the Apostles (the latter is known also as the Church of the Primacy of St Peter).

THE CHURCH OF THE BEATITUDES   This is reached by a track from the north side of Route 87, and is taken care of by Franciscan sisters, who maintain an adjacent hospice. It was built in 1938 to commemorate the Sermon on the Mount (Matt. 5.1–12), and is a building of exquisite beauty and proportions. The view of the lake from it is superb. Not far away were found the remains of the fourth century Chapel of the Sermon on the Mount, with part of a mosaic surviving. The remains of the building can now be seen in Capernaum. The building was of rough-hewn basalt, the most common material available in the locality. There was also a small monastery here.

THE CHURCH OF THE MULTIPLICATION OF THE LOAVES AND FISHES This is located on the side of the road closest to the lake. There was already a church here in 384, which was replaced in the fifth century by a basilica and a convent. The basilica had a large open courtyard decorated with mosaics. A narthex led into a cruciform church, with three aisles. The apse and presbytery contained an altar with a stone on which Jesus placed one of the loaves (Mark 6.30–44; Matt. 14.13–21; John 6.1–14). The whole church and its sacristies were covered with mosaics, which included birds and animals represented with great elegance. There were seven mills in the vicinity and a number of cisterns. On the main site a large church has been built by German Benedictines, following a visit by Pope Paul VI on 5 January 1964, when he expressed a wish for a more worthy monument. There is a car and coach park, a café and a gift shop.

Mosaic symbolizing the Multiplication of the Loaves and Fishes at Tabgha

THE CHURCH OF THE APPARITION OF THE RISEN CHRIST On the lake shore itself is the church in which the Primacy of Peter is commemorated. The small chapel, built by the Franciscans in 1933, lies beside the lake shore. Here Christ conferred the Primacy upon Peter. The rocky steps referred to by Egeria in 384 were once visible on the south of the old church; here, she says, Our Lord stood. She does not speak of a church, but it is claimed that one was built here by the empress Helena. In the ninth century twelve thrones (Luke 22.8–30) were shown, and the bases of six pairs of columns can be seen when the lake is low. The church was destroyed c.1187, repaired about 1260, and razed to the ground in 1263. The steps were bull-dozed in 1970.

CAPERNAUM

Further on round the lake from Tabgha is Capernaum (Kefar Nahum in Hebrew). There is parking outside the Franciscan property. The site of the ancient village is occupied partly by the Franciscans, who have owned it since 1894. A further part, the property of the Greek Orthodox church, was a 'no-man's-land' until 1967 (before that time the church would not allow anyone to excavate there). The principal Franciscan excavations took place in 1968–1984 under the patronage of the Italian government; the Greek Othodox site was excavated between 1978–1982 by Vassilios Tzaferis on behalf of the Israel Department of Antiquities and Museums. As might be expected on a site which extends for 325 yards (297 m) along the shore, the two excavations showed differing results, the Greek excavation adding materially to the stratigraphical history of the site.

The Franciscan site is entered through a parking lot; the convent is on the right after the entrance. There is a small entry fee. There is an Italian garden with carved masonry from the ruins of the ancient synagogue, an oil press, and grindstones.

Capernaum has no mention in Sacred Scripture before the Gospels. It was the centre of Jesus' Galilaean ministry: Matthew 9.1 speaks of it as Jesus' 'own city'. Here five of the apostles, Peter, Andrew, James, John and Matthew, received their calling; Jesus stayed many times in Peter's house, and preached in a synagogue which had been built by a Roman centurion (Luke 7.5). There is no doubt that there was a synagogue here in Jesus' time.

Until the fourth century Capernaum was inhabited only by Jews, who were cursed by Rabbi Issi of Caesarea for unorthodoxy. (It is not necessary to assume that these persons were Judaeo-Christians.) By 381 and 384 the pilgrim Egeria was able to note that 'the house of the prince of the apostles has been made into a church, with its original walls still standing... There is also the synagogue where the Lord cured a man possessed by the devil'. Remains of both edifices can still be seen, but almost all of the synagogue is a construction built over an earlier one in the late fourth or early fifth century. In 571 a pilgrim from Piacenza noted that 'the house of St Peter is now a basilica'. Probably both edifices were destroyed in the Persian invasion of 614, together with much else. An earthquake did further damage in 746; by the thirteenth century there were only the houses of seven poor fishermen to be found here.

Capernaum had an up and down history from the Middle Bronze Age onward, with remains of habitations of all ages from then until Byzantine times. It was never fortified. On the other hand it was important enough to have a customs post, over which St Matthew had presided (9.9), and a military detachment under a centurion. The whole village was never greater than about 10 to 12 acres in

Plan of the fifth century octagonal church at Capernaum, after Fr Corbo

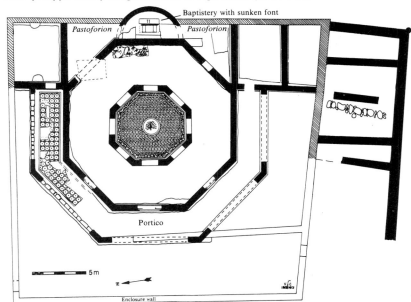

Baptistery with sunken font

Pastoforion

Pastoforion

Portico

5 m

Enclosure wall

dimension. A paved imperial road crossed it. The orderly arrangement of the houses suggests careful planning, the main street passing the synagogue and the octagonal church. It was divided by lanes into blocks. The houses were built of local basalt and roofed with dried mud and straw.

There was no organised water supply nor sanitary facilities; the lake served in both cases. Other than the government official and soldiery, the inhabitants made their living by fishing, farming and trade. There was no industry, and the masons responsible for the synagogue would have come from outside.

THE BASILICA The most striking construction is the modern basilica over the House of St Peter (to be found in the Franciscan area), built so that one can look down on the remains, on what looks like a tangle of walls. On display is a plan which uses different colours to differentiate between the original house, the two stages of the 'house-church' as mentioned by Egeria, and the final stage in which an octagonal church was superimposed above, respectively of the first, fourth and fifth centuries. Thus, the original building consisted of rooms round a central courtyard, or atrium. It is to be remembered that the courtyard in oriental houses is a centre for activities rather than a decorative feature. Eventually this seems to have been covered over, the church consisting of two concentric octagons, and one external part-octagon, or portico.

The plan of the fifth century octagonal church shows an arrangement which is reminiscent of the Dome of the Rock and of the rotunda of the Holy Sepulchre, enabling worshippers to circumambulate in a ceremonial manner, as is still done in the Holy Sepulchre. On the east side of the octagonal church is a small apse containing a baptistery. Its position is interesting in that it has been placed in so prominent a position, where one might expect an altar. On either side of the apse are *pastoforia*, sacristies and stores, with further rooms on either side. The Byzantine rite normally requires a *prosthesis*, a table for the preparation of the sacred elements before they are carried to the altar, and a bakery in the vicinity for baking hosts. Inscriptions on the former walls, in Aramaic, Greek, Latin and Syriac, all graffiti, confirm that this is indeed the House of St Peter and mention Jesus as Lord and Christ. There is no occasion for doubt that the fourth century stage was the house-church described by the pilgrim Egeria, and it is not impossible that its construction is owed to Count Joseph, who sought permission to build churches in Tiberias, Nazareth and elsewhere.

All the earlier buildings were reduced to ground level for the construction of the octagonal church. The peacock mosaic centrepiece on the floor is surrounded by a geometric design identical with one surviving in the Church of the Loaves and Fishes in Tabgha. The proportions of the octagon are similar to those of other octagonal churches in Italy and Syria, and that on Mount Gerizim. Here in Capernaum pilgrims came to implore the pity and mercy of Christ.

THE SYNAGOGUE Two blocks away from the House of St Peter is the syna- gogue, the most splendid of buildings to be found in Capernaum. It has a main prayer hall, a portico on the east side, accessible from the prayer hall, and, on the south, an independent porch, on the side that faces Jerusalem. The prayer hall has a broad nave and two narrow aisles, separated by elegant columns. The interior was plastered and coloured, and ornamented with reliefs. The carved stone capitals of the pillars, the gables and the cornices are of a richness unexampled among surviving synagogues in Israel. Depictions of animals are common, but a Medusa and even a Roman eagle have been found among the carvings. There are also typical Jewish emblems: a *shofar* (ram's horn), an incense shovel, and a *menorah* (seven-branched candelabrum); there is also a representation of the Ark of the Covenant, depicted as a Hellenistic temple on four wheels. (A coin of Hasmonean times also has an ark carried on four wheels.)

It is generally accepted that this synagogue was built in the fourth century AD, and only completed in the fifth. Accordingly, it could not have been the synagogue in which Jesus taught (Luke 7.5), which had been built by a Roman centurion. Excavations beneath

Ruins of the synagogue at Capernaum

the floor of the fourth or fifth century synagogue have disclosed the remains of domestic buildings, and a large floor of basalt stones of the first century AD, which V.C. Corbo believed to be that of the Roman centurion's synagogue. In the area of the prayer hall was also a basalt wall, therefore of materials different from the imported white limestone of which the later Roman synagogue is built. S. Loffreda considers that this wall is an intermediate stage between the first and fourth century synagogues. Whatever the truth may be, this second synagogue was likely to have been built on the site of a former synagogue if one was available, in accordance with common practice both for synagogues and churches. The sumptuous elegance of the second synagogue, on which no expense was spared for ornamentation, suggests an element of competition, against Christian pilgrimages to the House of St Peter such as Egeria recorded.

In the view of Loffreda and of Corbo, the area of the Franciscan excavations was deserted altogether by the ninth century AD.

GREEK EXCAVATIONS Only some small areas have been excavated within the Greek Orthodox property, but with results that give a different chronological picture for that site. Four areas have been excavated. In area D a massive building of undetermined date has been found, with two fish pools that drained into the lake. Presumably they were used for storing fish. In area C a public building was found, used later privately, with strata from the Byzantine period until the end of the tenth century. In area B were strata dating from the seventh century under the Byzantines to the mid-thirteenth century under the Ayyubids. An interesting feature was the

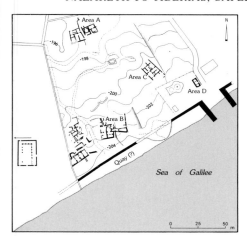

Plan of the excavations in the Greek Orthodox area

thick plastering of many floors, to prevent water seeping in. In area A a variety of occupation sites was found, dating from the seventh to the tenth centuries AD, with evidence also of Roman occupation. Beneath one floor evidence was found of Early Bronze Age residence. The buildings were all built of black basalt, with dry-stone walling, with the courtyards and streets paved either with beaten earth or stone.

There was evidence that the earthquake of AD 746 wrought havoc in the town. After the earthquake the new houses had smaller dimensions, and the quality of building, hitherto high, declined.

Some scholars have held that Capernaum ceased to exist after the Arab conquest, or at least at the beginning of the Abbasid caliphate in 750. However, the excavations carried out in the Greek site have shown that occupation continued into the tenth century. The whole village would appear to have contracted, but the presence of a gold hoard of 282 dinars would suggest that the community enjoyed a certain measure of wealth. When the Russian Abbot Daniel visited Capernaum in 1106 he said it

> was a very great city and many people lived in it but now it is deserted... the prophet says, 'Woe unto thee, Capernaum.' Thou shalt be exalted to heaven and thou shalt be brought down to the depths of hell. It is from this city that the Antichrist will come and it is for this reason that the Franks [Crusaders] have now abandoned all the city of Capernaum.

On the north side of the village is an old cemetery some 216 yards (198 m) from the synagogue. It was excavated by the Franciscans in 1976–1977. It had an open-air monument (*nephesh*) and an underground burial place (*hypogeum*). The first was of highly polished limestone; the second, of basalt, contained three limestone sarcophagi, and had been robbed in ancient times. It probably belongs to the first two centuries of the Christian era.

It is often asked what good archaeology can do. At Capernaum at any rate it enables us to tread in the very footsteps of Jesus.

CHORAZIN

Returning westward from Capernaum down the road to Tiberias after about 1 mile (1.6 km) turn right, and shortly right again, to the Gospel place of Chorazin, which is near to the modern settlement of Korazim. It was cursed by Jesus (Matt. 11.21), and there is nothing remaining but ruins, including those of a black basalt synagogue, which is probably of the third century AD. The main road passes through many modern settlements in what is a rich agricultural area, settled by early Zionists in the 1880s.

Caves and niches in the rock cliff overlooking the spring at Banias

BANIAS

A source of the Jordan River (running through lush woodlands and now part of a nature reserve 7½ miles [12 km] north-east of Qiryat Shemona) is Banias, the Caesarea Philippi of Matthew 16.13–19, which relates how Jesus 'came to the territory of Caesarea Philippi' and asked his disciples, 'Who do people say the Son of Man is?' Simon Peter replied, 'You are the Messiah, the Son of the living God.'

Jesus replied, '... And I say to you: you are Peter, the Rock; and on this rock I will build my church, and the powers of death shall never conquer it. I will give you the keys of the kingdom of Heaven...'

Where precisely this event took place cannot be determined from the Gospels, nor is there any reason given that Jesus should have entered the 'territory' of Caesarea Philippi.

HISTORY OF BANIAS The ancient name of Banias (spelt Panias, Paneas and Paneias in Greek and Latin) refers to a grotto sacred to the god Pan, from which a spring that is one of the sources of the Jordan River rises. The place was already sacred to Pan in the third century BC. In 2 BC Herod the Great's son Philip named it Caesarea in honour of Augustus, and, to differentiate it from Caesarea Maritima, it became known as Caesarea Philippi. When Herod donated the territory to his son Philip, it was as an independent kingdom, which included the Golan, Trachon, Hauran and Batanea, situated in present-day Israel, Syria and Jordan. It was primarily Iturean and Phoenician.

The Jewish community was massacred in AD 66; in 70 many Jews were killed either by gladiators or by wild beasts in the circus. By the early second century Jews were beginning to return. Christianity was established here at an early date, and the first bishop is said to have been a contemporary of St Paul. One bishop attended the Council of Nicaea in 325. At this time Eusebius reports that he saw here two statues of a woman kneeling to Jesus with her hands outstretched; he believed it to be a representation of the woman who was healed of a twelve-year issue of blood (Matt. 9.20). The Gospel account, however, speaks of the woman simply touching the hem of Jesus' garment; more likely they were statues of Isis and Serapis, popular pagan deities. Several more bishops are known before the Arab period.

Since 1967 there has been considerable excavation here, which is still continuing. The shrine or sanctuary of Pan has been cleared, along with the Herodian palace, and a town centre and suburbs, indicating occupation into the late Roman period. The town was perhaps destroyed by earthquake in 363. Later, there are buildings of the Fatimid era. In part of the town centre, a basilica has been identified, with mosaic floors, which perhaps was used as a church. There is no conclusive evidence for this, and perhaps it was a civil basilica, or law court. There is also some possibility of Crusader constructions, but as yet the dating is unconfirmed. The constructions may be Fatimid, with Crusader repairs. There is no evidence that it was a pilgrimage centre at any time. Abbot Daniel and John Phocas both located the Gospel incident at Caesarea Maritima on the coast. It is very unlikely, therefore, that there was ever any commemoration here.

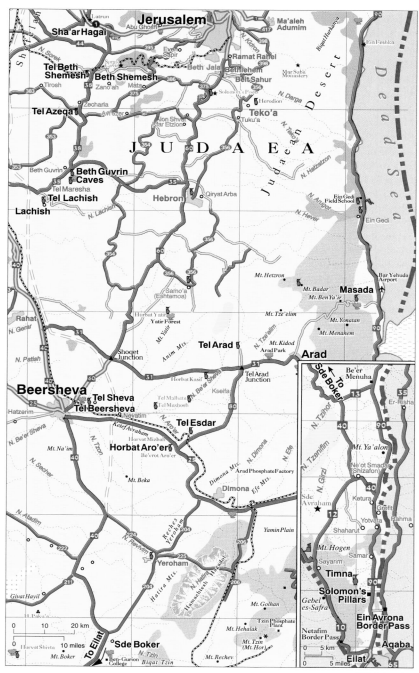

© Carta, Jerusalem

8. From Jerusalem to Beersheba and the South

Beersheba (Be'er Sheva) can be reached by two routes from Jerusalem: directly via Bethlehem and by-passing Hebron; or by following the Jerusalem-Tel Aviv road as far as Sha'ar Hagai, and then turning left on to Route 38.

TEL BETH SHEMESH

Taking this latter route, 20 miles (32 km) from Jerusalem, on the northern edge of the Shefelah (coastal plain of Israel), is Tel Beth Shemesh, near to the town of Beth Shemesh (the House of the Sun), originally a Canaanite cultic name. It was already occupied in the Middle Bronze Age. When it was taken by the Israelites, it was allotted to Dan (Josh. 19.41). After the battle of Eben-ezer and the capture of the Ark of the Covenant by the Philistines, it was returned to the Israelites here (1 Sam. 6.9 ff.). By this time the Ark was mounted on a wagon, as depicted on a stone carving at Capernaum; originally it was carried by Levitical priests (Josh. 3.3), ahead of the people. The site, which has been extensively excavated, was surrounded by a wall of coarse boulders of the Late Bronze Age until the Hellenistic and medieval periods. Of particular interest is a series of Iron Age II *shekel, neshef* and *pym* weights, carefully graduated and numbered. This region was the scene of many of Samson's exploits against the Philistines (Judg. 13.24 ff.).

TEL AZEQA

Continuing south, off the Beth Shemesh-Beth Guvrin road is Tel Azeqa (Khirbet Tell Zakariyya), at the east end of the Valley of Elah, where David fought and killed Goliath (1 Sam. 17.1).

BETH GUVRIN

The emperor Septimius Severus made Beth Guvrin (Beit Jibrin) a Roman city in AD 200. He named it Eleutheropolis, the City of Freemen. The Crusaders called it Bet Giblin or Gibelin. The Roman-Byzantine city was about 110 acres in extent, the Crusader city about 7½ acres. There are the remains of a Roman theatre, a Roman inn with magnificent carvings, a church of basilican type with a single apse, and a number of tombs of the fifth century.

On a hill south-east of Beth Guvrin is a site called El-Maqerqesh. There are remains of mosaic floors, with geometrical, animal and bird designs, that were laid from the fourth to the sixth centuries.

The cemeteries include cave burials and tombs with distinctive Christian and Jewish symbols, showing that in Roman and Byzantine times there was no difference in design between Christian and Jewish tombs. They too belong to the fourth to sixth centuries. There were also man-made caves which were cuttings for the extraction of chalk. Bell-shaped to secure stability, they were cut from the seventh to tenth centuries in order to provide raw material to make lime and cement for building in neighbouring cities. Later on the caves may have been used for other purposes. Beth Guvrin itself had no wells or springs: water was brought to the city via two aqueducts.

CRUSADER REMAINS There are also the remains of a triapsidal Crusader church, built in the late 1130s, and probably destroyed at the end of the century.

The interior of a bell-shaped cave at Beth Guvrin

The northern aisle was repaired, and probably re-used as a chapel in 1240–1244. South of the church are the remains of houses and stores. Some of the moats that surrounded the Crusader city have survived.

Near the chapel wall is a tomb, quaintly attributed locally to Nebi Jibrin or Jibril, the archangel Gabriel.

Isometric reconstruction of the Fosse Temple, Lachish

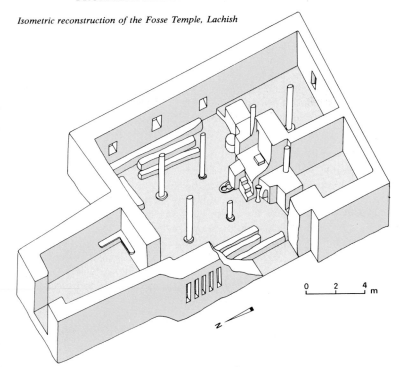

0   2   4
m

z

LACHISH

South-west of Beth Guvrin is Tel Lachish, an Amorite town taken by Joshua (10.3, 31). It was excavated by J.L. Starkey from 1931 until 1938, when he was murdered. He and his team excavated according to the methods taught by Sir Flinders Petrie, later to be developed by Sir Mortimer Wheeler. So accurate were Starkey's methods that his findings have not been set aside by subsequent excavation.

HISTORY OF LACHISH Settled first in Neolithic times, and thereafter continuously occupied until the Middle Bronze Age, a fortified city, with a palace, cultic site and cemetery developed. About 1500 BC it was destroyed by fire. Rebuilt in the Late Bronze Age, Lachish entered documentary history: it is subsequently mentioned in papyri, cuneiform tablets, and in the Tell el-Amarna Letters of the fourteenth century BC. Lachish became an open city, with no wall. A new temple, the Fosse Temple, was built: it was a very modest structure. More elaborate was the Acropolis Temple, which was roofed with cedar-wood from Lebanon, but on an Egyptian plan. Situated relatively close to Egypt, it was with this country that Lachish had its closest connections. The Fosse Temple was destroyed by fire c.1200 BC, and the Acropolis Temple c.1150 BC, along with the rest of the city.

Lachish was abandoned until the tenth century BC, when it was again resettled. There has been no trace of resettlement until the period of the United Monarchy. It was destroyed by fire again c.925 BC, and re-emerged as a fortified city, as related in 2 Chronicles 11.5–12 and 11.23. It now had strong walls and gates, a palace, and apparently the beginnings of a planned water system, all of which were again destroyed. This has been ascribed to both Sennacherib's campaign from Assyria in 701 BC and to the Babylonian campaign of 597 BC. The latter may be considered the less likely, for the siege ramp of the Assyrians still survives, together with Assyrian arms and military equipment. The city seems to have been abandoned until it was rebuilt and refortified under Josiah (639–609 BC). However, once again it was destroyed by fire in 598 BC, this time by Nebuchadnezzar. In the Persian period Lachish was reoccupied, and a palace and a solar shrine built. There have been further finds from the Hellenistic, Roman and Arab periods.

THE NEGEV

The road now enters the region known as the Negev, the 'dry land' par excellence. Little was known of its archaeological history until 1959, when Nelson Glueck published no less than 400 sites, many of them hitherto unknown. They were already inhabited in the Chalcolithic period (c.4500–3200 BC). Thereafter there was a hiatus until what may be called the Abrahamic period, twenty-first to nineteenth centuries BC. Whereas in the north the rainfall could be between 10 to 16 inches (25–40 cm) a year, in the south as little as 1 inch (2½ cm) could fall.

Throughout the Negev are the ruins of Judaean villages and fortresses from the time of Solomon on until the captivity into Babylon. It is Solomon who is recorded as the first to trade from the port of Ezion-geber, somewhere near modern-day Eilat. From the second century BC to the seventh century AD the area was in the Arab trading state of Nabataea, allies of the Romans. There was intensive agriculture and careful conservation of water. Nabataean trade extended throughout Arabia to the shores of the Indian Ocean, directly controlling the northern parts of the route. Other Arab kingdoms held the southern routes, bringing luxury goods, including gold, frankincense and myrrh (the latter two items grew in torrid southern Yemen). All these Arab tribes (such as the Ammonites, Moabites, Edomites and Nabataeans) and the Israelites were related to an extent, as described in Genesis of Abraham's two sons, Isaac and Ishmael (in Arabic, Isma'il), his sons by Rebecca and Hagar the bondwoman respectively. The Qur'an relates the same tradition, and it is substantiated by the common origins of the Semitic languages.

BEERSHEBA

Ancient Beersheba is a group of sites surrounding the modern town, including Chalcolithic cave settlements, on both banks of the Beersheba valley, and Tel Beersheba (Tell es-Saba'), east of the modern town.

The first group, belonging to the Middle Chalcolithic period, had rectangular rooms 23 x 10 feet (7 x 3 m), entered by a sloping tunnel. There were fireplaces, basins and silos in the courtyards, and similar arrangements in the rooms, sometimes with large bell-shaped silos closed by flagstones. Nearby, at Hurbat Matar, there were similar arrangements, and evidence of a small copper industry: anvils to crush ore, fireplaces with slag, and fragments of crucibles. There were axes, chisels and awls, as well as mace heads, ornamented handles and various articles, which were probably imported. There were also basalt and haematite objects imported from Jordan, probably in finished form. Pottery was made locally.

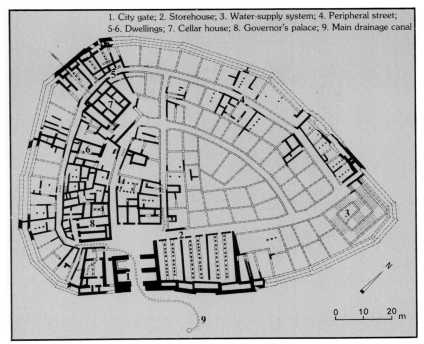

1. City gate; 2. Storehouse; 3. Water-supply system; 4. Peripheral street; 5-6. Dwellings; 7. Cellar house; 8. Governor's palace; 9. Main drainage canal

A plan of the city at Tel Beersheba

Pendants were common, made of bone, mother-of-pearl, turquoise and other stones. Other objects were made of bone and ivory. There were figurines which differ stylistically from any found elsewhere. In one house an ivory workshop was found, with a bench and tools, a hippopotamus tusk, and figurines.

Some of the floors were decorated with pebbles, painted with red ochre after they had been arranged in groups of 7, 14, 21 and 37. The people were dependent on subsistence agriculture, both cereal and vegetable, as well as on their sheep and goats. Cattle were rare, and there were no pigs. Neveh Noy also had a 'treasure chamber', like the Cave of the Treasure at Nahal Mishmar; it contained two standards, two axes and a fragment of a crown, all made of copper.

Beersheba is situated in a *wadi*, with rich alluvial soil, which offsets the scarcity of rain. It is at a crossroads: with Hebron to the north, the Judaean Desert and the Dead Sea to the east, the coastal plain to the west, and Negev towns to the south.

In biblical times it was populated by different peoples: Philistines in the west, the tribe of Judah in the north, Amalekites and Kenites in the south, and Edomites in the south-west. The valley was occupied from the Iron Age to the Arab conquest; after c.700 it was unoccupied for a millennium. In Sacred Scripture it was seen as the southern boundary of Israel, the northern boundary being Dan and the Golan Heights: the saying 'from Dan to Beersheba' is to be found in Judges 20.1.

Some random remains of the Chalcolithic period have been found, but they do not seem to amount to continuous occupation, which begins in Iron Age I. At first

An excavated well at Tel Beersheba

it was a village settlement, perhaps for semi-nomadic herdsmen. Initially pits were used as houses, but permanent settlement and stone houses existed, it seemed, by the appointment of Joel and Abijah, sons of Samuel as 'judges over Israel... in Beersheba'. Fragments of figurines suggest a not too rigid view of orthodoxy.

There were extensive drainage and water systems. In the centre of the site was a large pillared structure which was apparently a storehouse. Incorporated into one of the walls were the remains of a horned altar. It suggests that, perhaps during the religious reforms and centralization of Hezekiah, a temple and its altar had been demolished. It may have stood near the main gate, but this is not certain. The excavations have made it clear that this was a carefully planned and laid-out city with a regular pattern of streets in relation to public buildings.

BEERSHEBA: 19TH TO 20TH CENTURIES In 1900 a Turkish garrison was installed here, along with a governor, as a centre for administration of the Bedouin in the Negev. During World War I the Germans built a narrow-gauge railway from Beersheba to Sinai. It was taken by Allenby on 31 October 1917. The police station and British war cemetery also belong to this period, and the municipal museum is housed in a mosque built in 1915. The public garden, with a monument to Allenby, has an archaeological zone to the east, in which there are Byzantine wells. A casemate wall may belong to the reign of Hezekiah, or to his predecessor Uzziah.

TEL ARAD

From Beersheba, take the road towards Hebron but turn right at Shoqet Junction to reach the site of Tel Arad; the modern town of Arad is approximately 6 miles (10 km) farther on. Tel Arad has been extensively excavated, and was occupied first as a Canaanite city, then as an Israelite, Roman, Byzantine, and finally Arab settlement. Scripture mentions Arad as a Canaanite city, and it is mentioned in a list of cities made for Pharaoh Shishak in the fifth year of Rehoboam's reign as 'the citadels of greater Arad'.

It was already settled in the Chalcolithic period, as a series of small villages. By the Early Bronze Age caves were still inhabited but houses were also being built. The presence of Egyptian pottery indicates that trade with Egypt had begun. Shortly afterwards there were public buildings, a reservoir, a palace and a sacred precinct. By the middle of the third millennium BC the city had been destroyed and abandoned, for reasons that are not clear. There were twin temples, one with a stone altar, the other with a stone stela. There were numerous figurines, indicating a worship of natural forces. Arad's prosperity was based on its commercial contacts with Egypt and the copper mines of Sinai, when copper was in world-wide demand.

After a gap of some 1,500 years the site was occupied again, in the late twelfth to early eleventh centuries BC. By the time of King Solomon there was a citadel area with storerooms and industrial installations as well as houses. A hoard of silver ingots suggests some primitive form of exchange. Some refinement is suggested by the existence of a scent industry. A temple with a sanctuary and altar faced eastward, as did Solomon's Temple. There were two stone incense altars and a large stone altar with a channel to drain off the blood of sacrifices. This was the first Israelite altar that has been identified in an archaeological context.

Significant also were epigraphic finds in Hebrew and in Aramaic, of the late eighth century to the sixth century BC. There were also Greek ostraca (inscribed potsherds) of the third to second centuries BC. The Aramaic ostraca belong to the Persian period during which Aramaic became the official language, gradually ousting Hebrew as the spoken tongue of common speech. From modern-day Arad

Plan of the citadel at Tel Arad

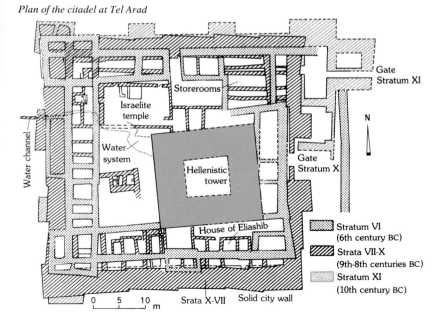

a road leads to Masada, 13 miles (21 km) away, and the Roman ramp up the mountain. There is a path up the mountain. However, if you prefer to take the cable car up, approach Masada from the Dead Sea side (see Itinerary 4).

HORBAT ARO'ER

At Tel Arad Junction take the road towards Dimona. South-west of Beersheba just off the Beersheba-Dimona road, the site of Horbat Aro'er is tentatively identified with the 'Ararah of 1 Samuel 30.28, and in the Septuagint version of Joshua 15.22. Excavation of the site has so far not exposed anything earlier than the seventh century BC. About the middle of the century a natural hill-top was surrounded by a strong wall, and the summit flattened before the

The Holy of Holies in the sanctuary at Tel Arad

erection of buildings. Only part of the site has been excavated. Some Chalcolithic sherds have been found and also the handle of a jar from Rhodes. The greatest part of the pottery and of cultic objects show Assyrian and Edomite influences. Occupation ceased at the time of the Babylonian Exile, and was not resumed until the Herodian period.

The town of this period was within the Iron Age walls, but was not otherwise fortified, except for a small fortress built at the south-east end of the mound. It was built with drafted ashlar blocks with prominent bosses. An ostracon was found, apparently listing the wages of farm workers. A coin of the Roman procurator Antonius Felix, dated AD 59, gives a rough approximation of the date of what was a short-lived settlement that ended after AD 67, the date of the latest coin finds.

TEL ESDAR

About 1 mile (1.6 km) north-east is Tel Esdar, initially occupied in Chalcolithic times and in the Early Bronze Age. It was again settled in the Iron Age, after having been abandoned for 1,500 years. It is one of the earliest Israelite sites in the Negev. Its houses were arranged in a circle on the top of the hill. It was occupied in Roman and Byzantine times.

SDE BOKER

Continuing southwards, Sde Boker is the kibbutz where David Ben-Gurion lived in retirement after resigning from being the first prime minister of the State of Israel. He and his wife are buried here. The Jacob Blaustein Institute of the Ben-Gurion University of the Negev is also situated here. Some prehistoric graffiti have been found.

An example of the unusual rock formations at Timna

TIMNA

Eighteen-and-a-half miles (30 km) north of Eilat is Timna, important as the site of ancient copper mines, on which the prosperity of the region was based for long periods in ancient times. Mines were opened here in 1955, and closed in 1976 because of a fall in the world price of copper; they were re-opened in 1980. The ancient mines, known as Timna Park, and popularly called King Solomon's Mines, lie west of the modern mines.

The Timna Valley lies alongside Wadi Araba, covering some 44 square miles (70 sq km), and contains two types of copper, carbonates and silicates. There are numerous mine workings, shafts and galleries, and mining tools from various periods, as well as slag heaps. Eleven ancient camps have been located in the centre of the valley. There are remains from the Late Bronze Age and Iron Ages I and II. Only one smelting site has been identified in the valley, but a number have been found outside. Roman and Early Arab copper smelting was located farther south, at Be'er Ora. The period of exploitation was from the fourth millennium BC until Early Arab times.

Mining techniques varied at different times. Deep shafts, descending as much as 114 feet (35 m), were sunk vertically to discover the layers of copper deposit. From these, narrow galleries were driven laterally. In all of these were found abandoned tools and pottery sherds. Smelting furnaces were found in the camps from different times, and there is evidence of smelting techniques throughout the whole period.

Many thousands of small objects have been recovered, including votive figurines. A small temple has been excavated, with an altar and a stone bowl, presumably for libations. Animal bones and ash remain from sacrifices. Charcoal was manufactured from acacia trees for use in the furnaces; these gradually developed from a hole in the ground fired by bellows to purpose-built stone furnaces. There were also storage pits for ore. There was a sanctuary in honour of the Egyptian goddess Hathor, with huge Nubian sandstone pillars, evidence of the place of origin of at least some of the miners. It can be dated from c.1320 BC.

Egyptian votive offerings, alabaster, pottery and stone vessels, beads, wands, ring stands, amulets, glass, gold ornaments, decorated earthenware and porcelain animal figurines, seals and scarabs, and one small sphinx, are paralleled by non-Egyptian objects, probably Midianite. Cartouches of the pharaohs have been found from 1318 until 1156 BC. The attribution of the mines to King Solomon in the tenth century BC is manifestly impossible to sustain.

In Wadi Amran exploitation began in Chalcolithic times. At one of the sites explored, exploitation extended from Roman times until the eighth and ninth centuries under the caliphate. In the Arab period the miners, by contrast with earlier methods, worked in large chambers in an irregular pillar-and-stall system.

There are the remains of a major town and a small fort. Genesis 36.40 mentions Timna as a chief descended from Esau, brother of the patriarch Jacob. Verse 42 mentions that Esau was the father of the Edomites; earlier he had moved to Edom because he and Jacob could not continue to live together on account of the size of their respective families, flocks and herds.

EILAT

Eilat, which became part of Israel in 1949, is the most southerly settlement in the country, and it is here that the frontiers of four countries meet: Egypt, Israel, Jordan and Saudi Arabia. It is reputedly near the site of Ezion-geber, where Solomon built a fleet and manned it with the aid of Hiram, the king of Tyre (1 Kings 9.26–28), although the precise site has not yet been located. Ophir, to which Solomon's and

The aquarium at Eilat

Hiram's fleets journeyed, has also never been identified. This narrative is intertwined with the narrative of the visit of the Queen of Sheba, that is, of the kingdom of Saba in southern Yemen from which the present-day Shabwa takes its name.

Modern-day Eilat is situated at the tip of the Gulf of Aqaba. It has a military base, an airfield, a deep water port, hotels, a museum, and an international bird-watching centre; 5 miles (8 km) south of the town is an underwater aquarium, the Eilat Coral Reserve.

In the Gulf is Coral Island, called in Arabic Jazirat Fara'un, Pharaoh's Island. It is formed by two hills joined by an isthmus (neck of land). The remains on the north hill seem to be post-Crusader. The Crusaders occupied it in 1116, and called it Ile de Graye. They held it until 1170, when Saladin took it. There is no evidence of Crusader occupation on the surface, but there are Byzantine remains.

From Eilat one can drive back north along the western coast of the Dead Sea, and so to Jerusalem. It is a beautiful drive.

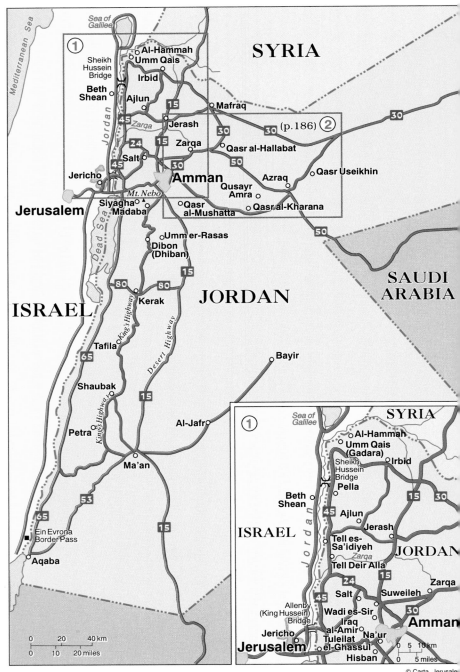

© Carta, Jerusalem

9. Excursion to Jordan

There are three border crossings to Jordan, one at Ein Evrona (north of Eilat), one at Allenby Bridge (north-east of Jericho), and one near Beth She'an. No cars, private or hired, may be driven across in either direction; however, there are buses to shuttle people between the border posts. Once past the border control, you can take a bus or a taxi to Amman. However, you may find it easier to make such arrangements in advance, through a travel agent.

AMMAN

Amman is the capital of Jordan. In about 1900 it had a population of 2,000. By c.1945, under the British Mandate, it had grown to about 5,000 inhabitants. Today, as a result of emigration from what was Palestine and a natural increase of population, it numbers about 1.2 million people out of a total population estimated at about 4 million.

For all this, the Rabbath-Ammon of the Bible existed as the Ammonite capital as long ago as the exodus from Egypt: in the time of the Judges, Gileadites to the north, Ammonites in the centre, and Moabites to the south fought the Israelites, until a composition was reached during the reigns of David and Solomon. The tribes of Reuben, Gad and half of Manasseh settled on the east of the Jordan River, but seem to have become absorbed in the earlier populations. All suffered similar fates under Assyria, Babylon and Persia, but were spared the deportation to which the Israelites were subjected.

After the conquest of Alexander the Great the whole area was under the Ptolemies of Egypt until it was taken by the Seleucid Antiochus III c.218 BC. In 63 BC Amman was one of the ten cities of the Decapolis. In AD 106 it was absorbed into the Roman Province of Arabia, and it is to this period that the visible ancient buildings in the city belong.

THE CITY OF AMMAN Because of its quite meteoric development Amman is a very confusing city, the more so because many of the streets lack street name signs, as well as owing to a lack of systematic planning. The city is situated on rolling hills (known locally as *jebel*). From the Roman and Byzantine periods the sites of four churches are known, one on the acropolis with two on its sides, and the fourth on the site of the mosque known as the Husseini Mosque. Built in 1923, it replaced a mosque of the Umayyad period just west of the nymphaeum, known only from plans and drawings made in the nineteenth century. Similarly an Umayyad castle on the acropolis, which had its own mint, has also disappeared.

ROMAN PHILADELPHIA Under the Romans Amman was known as Philadelphia. Little remains of it. The centre of the present city is the Roman theatre, which was capable of seating 6,000, with a colonnaded garden in front, part of which survives. At its eastern end was an odeum, a small theatre for musical performances. To the south-west was the nymphaeum, a temple of the nymphs.

Beside this is the Traditional Jewels and Costumes Museum, also containing magnificent mosaics from Madaba, Jerash, Hisban and elsewhere, which it has been necessary to remove from their sites because of vandalism. At the eastern end of the front of the theatre is the Folklore Museum, housing a collection of

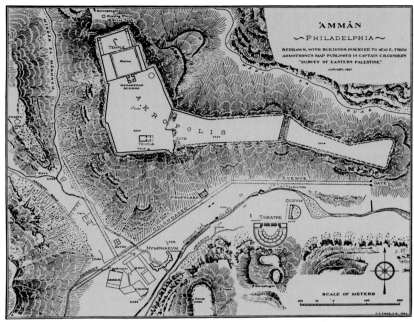

A plan of the acropolis and lower city, based on a late nineteenth century drawing

miscellaneous items of the life of the people, including a Bedouin goat-hair tent complete with domestic utensils and tools, musical instruments, a camel-saddle and handwoven rugs.

To the north, opposite the theatre, is the acropolis, or Citadel Hill, on which remains of the Bronze Age have been excavated; these constitute the earliest inhabited part of Amman. Imitations of Mycenaean and Egyptian stone vessels demonstrate its commercial connections. There are the remains of several city walls, and of Roman, Byzantine and Umayyad periods. At the south-west corner stood a Roman temple dedicated to Hercules, the successor it seems of earlier temples. There is a small museum, built in 1950, that spans prehistoric times until 1700; it houses one of the Dead Sea Scrolls, found in the hills of the Judaean Desert, when the western bank of the Jordan River was in Jordanian possession, 1948–1967.

AMMAN TO JERUSALEM

This route passes through Na'ur, a settlement of Circassians founded in 1778, at which point the road to Petra branches off to the left, passing Hisban and Madaba on the way. Along the way, dolmens can be seen on the left, and a panorama of the mountains of Moab, including Siyagha and Mount Nebo (Jebel Naba).

TULEILAT EL-GHASSUL Further on, but before the road reaches the border, a path leads to Tuleilat el-Ghassul, an important Neolithic and Chalcolithic site which was excavated in the 1930s, with further excavations by the British School of Archaeology in Jerusalem in the 1960s and 1970s, during which radio-carbon techniques established an absolute chronology. More than 10,500 square metres of settlement have been exposed, in a series of mounds. It is the largest Chalcolithic site in the country, but very few copper objects have been recovered. Stone predominates. Seven wall paintings have been found, including a spectacular geometrical Star of Ghassul, which suggests a culture which had a developed knowledge of mathematics. Other houses were decorated in bright colours, portraying geometrical motifs, people, animals and stars. The men seem to have been bearded and tattooed; the women wore beads of shell and stone.

King Hussein Bridge (also known as Allenby Bridge) is the crossing point into Israel. Jericho is further on and the road then continues to Jerusalem.

TO THE JORDAN RIVER, AND UP THE JORDAN VALLEY

Leaving Amman to the north-west, and passing the remains of an Ammonite fort along the way, one comes to Suweileh, a Circassian village settlement founded by Sultan Abdul Hamid in 1878. It is now heavily populated, and virtually a suburb of Amman.

SALT Situated in the administrative district of Balqa, Salt was the provincial capital in Ottoman times. The seat of a bishop in Byzantine times, in 1220 a fort was built here by the Ayyubid sultan of Damascus al-Malik al-Mu'azzam Sharaf al-Din, on earlier foundations. The Mongols destroyed it in 1260; the Mamluk sultan of Egypt, Baybars, rebuilt it in 1261. Ibrahim Pasha, son of Muhammad Ali the Great of Egypt, razed it in 1840; the barracks were rebuilt by the Ottoman Turks in 1870.

The road continues into the Jordan Valley, and the summit of Jebel Yusha shortly comes into sight, the reputed burial place of the prophet Hosea. His tomb is shown in the mosque (Nabi Yusha). Soon after sea level is reached one nears the royal winter palace. There are numerous remains in the vicinity.

ALLENBY BRIDGE The bridge, built in 1946 and named after General Allenby, replaces an earlier pontoon bridge; the Jordanians now call it King Hussein Bridge, after King Abdallah's father.

The site of **Bethany beyond Jordan**, where John the Baptist was baptizing (John 1.28), has been much disputed. It was possibly in this vicinity, where Joshua and the Israelites are believed to have crossed the Jordan. Shrines commemorating the baptism of Jesus by John are on the opposite side of the river.

In this region Jebel Mar Elyas, a hill 1 mile (1.6 km) north-east of the river in Wadi el-Kharrar, commemorates the place from which Elijah was taken up into heaven (the commemoration is based on Matt. 11.14, Mark 9.12 and John 1.21). Across the border, near Jericho, is the Greek Orthodox Monastery of St John the Baptist, rebuilt in 1882, and repaired in 1937 and 1955 (see p. 104).

WADI ZARQA Proceeding up the valley, the road crosses Wadi Zarqa, the biblical brook Jabbok (Gen. 32.22), which flows into the Jordan River. It was in this vicinity that Jacob wrestled with an angel and became reconciled to his brother Esau (Gen. 32, 33).

TELL DEIR ALLA About half a mile (1 km) further on, Tell Deir Alla is visible, the site of the ancient Succoth (Gen. 33.17), where Jacob rested, building for himself a house and booths for his cattle. There were excavations in the 1960s, but there is nothing to be seen.

TELL ES-SA'IDIYEH Further on one comes to the important site of Tell es-Sa'idiyeh, which was most recently excavated by the British Museum in association with the Palestine Excavation Fund. Its identification either as Zaphon (Jg. 12.1) or as Zarethan (Josh. 3.16; 1 Kings 7.46) is disputed. Excavations by the University of Pennsylvania revealed an acropolis and houses, with occupation going as far back as the ninth century BC. More recent excavations show destruction of occupation in the twelfth century BC, with more interruptions in the eleventh and tenth centuries BC. Occupation continued into the Roman period. A lower mound was occupied in

Wadi Zarqa, the biblical brook Jabbok

the Early Bronze Age. The excavations were filled in to render them safe.

PELLA At Tabaqat Fahl are the scattered remains of ancient Pella, one of the cities of the Decapolis, already settled in Lower and Middle Old Stone Age times. At that time Pella was on the shore of a large lake in the Jordan Valley, and enjoyed a cooler and damper climate. It is mentioned in Egyptian lists of conquests in the second millennium BC, and was a Canaanite town. It seems to have been abandoned in the Persian and Hellenistic periods; its claim to have been refounded by Alexander the Great cannot be sustained. In the second century BC it revived as a trading city, and a commercial centre for import and export between the coast and Syria. It was resistant to Jewish practices, and was destroyed on the orders of Alexander Jannaeus in 83 BC. In 63 BC Pompey found it in ruins. Towards the end of the century it revived again, and to this period many of the visible remains of buildings belong. They include public baths, an odeum and a nymphaeum, and a large temple known only from its depiction on a coin. In the fourth century several churches, a monastery and a cathedral were constructed. As paganism became extinct, so artifacts show its replacement by statuettes of the Blessed Virgin and holy amulets. In 636, following the Arab invasion, and the new directions of caravan routes, the city slowly declined, until an earthquake virtually destroyed it in 747. There was some limited occupation in Abbasid and Mamluk times.

Pella as a Christian refuge Pella has a certain importance in the history of the Church, in that it was to Pella that Jerusalem Christians fled during the Bar Kokhba

Remains of a fifth century church at Pella

Revolt of AD 132. Here lived Ariston of Pella, a Christian apologist, who wrote a disputation in which Jason, a baptized Jew, converted a fellow Jew, Papiscus, by proving to him that the Messianic prophecies had been fulfilled in Jesus Christ.

AMMAN TO IRAQ AL-AMIR

Iraq al-Amir (the Caves of the Prince) is about 10 miles (16 km) to the west of Amman. It can be reached via Wadi es-Sir, or from the Amman-Jerusalem road. Although there is quite a small monument here, it is approached through spectacular scenery, and is itself an object of beauty.

Iraq al-Amir is generally accepted as being the Ramath-Mizpeh of the Bible (Josh. 13.26), and the Tyros fortress built by Hyrcanus in the first quarter of the second century BC. The Tyros fortress is described in some detail by Josephus (*Antiq.* XII), and there seems no reasonable doubt about this identification. A plastered building, excavated in 1962, also fits into this context.

The site consists of a partly inhabited mound, on which fragments of ancient masonry are incorporated in the dwellings. South-west of the mound at about 547 yards (500 m) is the Qasr al-Abd (Castle of the Servant). It is surrounded by the remains of walls and gates. The Qasr itself is remarkable in being built of megalithic stones. The interpretation of what survives of it has been greatly disputed: whether it was a fort, a manor, a pleasance, a mausoleum, a palace or a temple. There is no precise evidence of what it was used for; nevertheless, careful modelling identifies it with a two-storey château, the lower storey for accommodation and stores, the upper for dwelling. It cannot have been a temple, for none of the characteristics of a Syrian temple are present: there is no triple division lengthwise, no cell for the god, no trace of an altar, nor *favissa* for the disposal of waste from offerings.

North of the Castle of the Servant are the remains of what is known as the Square Building, which was built with re-used masonry of Hellenistic date. The earliest

A stone lion carved in relief at the Castle of the Servant, Iraq al-Amir

occupation of the site was in the Early Bronze Age.

North of the Square Building is an aqueduct, still in use by the villagers, and, in a cliff side, caves which afford them storage places and room for stalled animals. Josephus called attention to the carved animals visible in his day. There remains a feline carved in relief on the east wall, somewhat eroded, but still of elegance.

The existing village inhibits much large-scale excavation. Comparison with the so-called 'desert castles' (see p. 185), which in reality are chiefly what remains of the better buildings of Umayyad country houses and estates, suggests that this was such a one, but of an earlier period.

AMMAN TO THE NORTH

Having reached Suweileh, one turns right for Jerash, passing through Safut, a village with Roman and Byzantine remains. Continuing northwards the road crosses Wadi Zarqa. Jerash is 32 miles (51 km) north of Amman. Together with Petra, it is one of Jordan's major attractions. It is a large and well-preserved site, with excellent facilities for visitors, including a rest house with a pleasant restaurant and bar, and small shops on the site itself.

Wadi Jerash divides Jerash into two halves. It is the ancient river Chrysorrhoas (the Golden River), whose water provided an origin for a Bronze Age settlement. It flows through the centre of the site, the east side of which is entirely built over with houses, shops and workshops. Half a century ago it was a small Circassian village; today its population may be 20,000.

JERASH The original settlement seems to have been Garshu, hellenized as Gerasa, whence Jerash (Jarash). It came into being as a town in the second century

BC, and was developed as one of the Graeco-Roman cities of the Decapolis, including Philadelphia (Amman), Gadara (Umm Qais), Pella, Scythopolis (Beth She'an), Damascus, Hippos, Canatha, Dium and Raphana. It was laid out on a conventional Roman town plan in AD 50–60, and expanded after 106 when the Romans annexed the Nabataean kingdom and formed the Province of Arabia. The town was culturally mixed, with Aramaic-speaking Arabs, and a Hellenized élite that knew and used both Greek and Latin. Among them, in the first century AD, was the neo-Pythagorean philosopher, Nicomachus, expert in music and the mystical theory of numbers.

Jerash was prosperous until the third century, when it shared in the troubles throughout the Roman Empire. Under Constantine the Great it adopted Christianity, and had a bishop who attended the Council of Seleucia in 359. Churches continued to be built into the sixth century. It was over-run by the Persians in 614, and then by the Arabs from the peninsula at the Battle of Yarmouk in 636. Under the Umayyads of Damascus its agriculture prospered along with its caravan trade; the creation of the Abbasid caliphate in Baghdad in 750, which made it a backwater, coincided with a series of earthquakes which devastated the town. It was a squatter town until Circassians were settled here in 1878, and more recently expanded due to Palestinian immigration and the tourist trade.

Visit As one approaches by road the triumphal arch (21; see plan, p. 182), erected by Hadrian in 130, comes into sight. Immediately on the left is the hippodrome or circus (20), 267 yards (244 m) long, for horse and chariot races, and athletics. At the southern gate (19) is the Visitors Centre, where entrance tickets are sold. There is a car park, and, unofficially, an officious small boy who demands *baksheesh* for looking after the cars. He can safely be ignored.

Near the hippodrome is a vast cemetery, with the funeral chapel of Bishop Marianos. The city wall, begun in 60–70, after numerous expansions is now some 2.2 miles (3½ km) long, and a yard (c.1 m) thick, enclosing about 201 acres. There were some hundred towers and at least four gates. The southern gate through which one enters was probably built c.130. On the left is the temple of Zeus (16), patiently undergoing restoration, with an elliptical plaza (the forum) in front of it, with an elegant colonnade (15). Behind the temple is the southern theatre (17), of the first century, once capable of holding 6,000 persons. From the forum starts the great colonnaded street of the *cardo maximus*, interrupted only by two tetrapylons (14, 5). The two tetrapylons are set at the beginning of the south and north *decumanus* respectively, colonnaded streets that intersect the west side of the surviving city. From the south tetrapylon a street runs east to a bridge over the river, via which one can reach the eastern baths (12).

Proceeding down the *cardo*, there is a church assumed to be the cathedral (11), and a nymphaeum (10), with a fountain in honour of the nymphs. Behind the cathedral is the Church of St Theodore (23), of 496.

Beyond the nymphaeum, steps lead to the sanctuary of Artemis (9), Jerash's principal monument, built in the second century. It was reached originally by a sacred processional way which began at the northern bridge of the town, and had a propylaeum (a grand entrance). Seven flights of stairs reached the temple terrace and a precinct 175 x 131 yards (161 x 121 m), with double rows of Corinthian

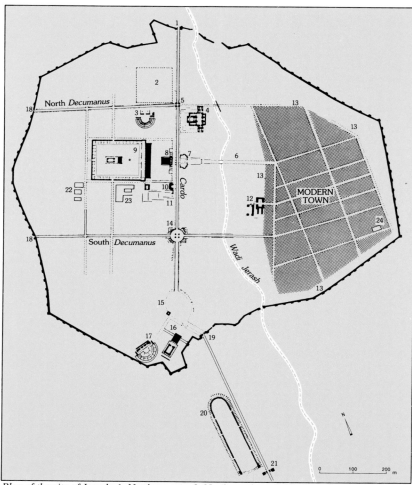

Plan of the city of Jerash: 1. Northern gate; 2. Northern plaza; 3. Northern theatre; 4. Western baths; 5. Northern tetrapylon; 6. Processional road; 7. The gates in the precinct of Artemis, east of the *cardo*; 8. The gates in the precinct of Artemis, west of the cardo; 9. Sanctuary of Artemis; 10. Nymphaeum; 11. Cathedral; 12. Eastern baths; 13. Residential quarter; 14. Southern tetrapylon and the round plaza; 15. Forum; 16. Temple of Zeus; 17. Southern theatre; 18. Western gates; 19. Southern gate; 20. Circus; 21. Hadrian's triumphal arch; 22. Churches of St Cosmas and St Damian, St George and St John the Baptist; 23. Church of St Theodore; 24. Church of Procopius

columns on all four sides. In front of the temple was an open-air altar. The temple itself was relatively small, with an internal *cella*, the dwelling place of the goddess and her statue. There is some evidence that this sophisticated and magnificent building was never finished. In Byzantine times it became a pottery factory, and later a small fort which was destroyed by King Baldwin II.

There are numerous Byzantine churches in Jerash, thirteen of which have been

The forum at Jerash

identified so far, but with more quite likely to be found. Apart from the cathedral, the most interesting are the three churches of St Cosmas and St Damian, of St George, and of St John the Baptist (22), all in the same building, and erected between 529 and 533. To the south-east of the town, but still within the walls, are the remains of a church built in 526–527 by a certain Procopius (24). The mosaics delight in geometrical patterns, some of them very elaborate, and include human forms, a priest carrying a censer, his wife, and trees, the latter dated AD 533, caught in the wind, like the palm tree in the Dome of the Rock in Jerusalem.

The cathedral, dated by an inscription to AD 400, has two main churches set in a single line, and two smaller churches. Few of the mosaics have been uncovered pending suitable methods of conservation. Many of the mosaics in the churches so far exposed have been published in M. Piccirillo, *The Mosaics of Jordan*, Amman, 1993; they have since been covered over to protect them from vandalism.

AJLUN North-west of Jerash a road leads 14 miles (22½ km) to Ajlun, among magnificent scenery. Ibn Battuta visited it when he journeyed through Syria in 1326, and found it 'a fine town, with a large number of bazaars, and an imposing castle, and traversed by a river with sweet water'. This castle is the Qal'at er-Rabad, which was built by Saladin's governor Izz al-Din Usama in 1184. Erected on the remains of a monastery, it was enlarged in 1214–1215, and later used by the Mamluks as a pigeon-post and fire-beacon station. The view from the top of the ruins is beyond imagination. On a clear day both the Dead Sea and the Sea of Galilee are visible, and all the Judaean hills between, as well as those of Samaria. In front is the Jordan Valley, and round about, the beautiful hills of Gilead.

IRBID Irbid is approximately 20 miles (32 km) away from Ajlun. A district headquarters with a modern university, it is partly built over an Early Bronze Age mound. In 1995 the university opened a special institute for the study of Islamic

The Arab castle at Ajlun

numismatics (coins and coinage). In recent times Irbid has become populous, but for the visitor the only place of interest is the Museum of Jordanian Heritage, reputed to be the best archaeological museum in the country. There is also a Natural History Museum.

UMM QAIS   Nineteen miles (30½ km) north-west of Irbid is Umm Qais, the biblical Gadara, one of the cities of the Decapolis. The site is outside a small village, with wonderful views overlooking the Golan Heights, the Sea of Galilee and Tiberias, and, to the south, the Jordan Valley. On a clear day, Mount Tabor (to the west) and Mount Hermon (to the north) are visible. Umm Qais is also accessible from the Jordan Valley, journeying up a winding escarpment on which the writer saw a dead swine, reminiscent of Matthew 8.28–34. Wild pig is said to be plentiful in the region today. Beside the entrance to the site is a restaurant and bar, with a terrace on which one can sit and enjoy the splendid view.

No evidence has been found so far of any occupation before the Hellenistic period. Antiochus the Great took it from the Ptolemies in 218 BC; his successors lost it to Alexander Jannaeus in 98 BC. It was rebuilt by Pompey after his capture of it in 63 BC, but had close connections with the Nabataean kingdom to the south. In 31 BC it was awarded to Herod after the Roman defeat of the Nabataeans; later, it was destroyed by Vespasian. Nevertheless, in the fourth century it had a bishop, and only fell into decline in the seventh century.

Gadarene culture   The wealth of the city of Gadara in the first century BC is attested by the Roman rumour that the theatre built in honour of Pompey on the Campus Martius in Rome in 61–54 BC was financed by Demetrius the Gadarene, wealth that could only have come from trade. In the same century Philodemus, Epicurean philosopher and epigrammatist, was born in Gadara; for Cicero the licentiousness of his matter ill-matched the elegance of his manner. The poet Meleager, who spoke Aramaic and Phoenician as well as Greek, was also born here; he looked back to Menippos, a third century BC freedman, a well-known satirist and cynic philosopher. There were other persons of distinction too, including Theodoros, the tutor of the emperor Tiberius.

The museum   There is a charming small museum in Bayt Rusan, the former

The ruins of one of the theatres at Umm Qais, the biblical Gadara

Ottoman governor's house, with a striking statue of a headless goddess in white marble. Scattered down the hill is the west theatre, a colonnaded street with shops, and baths. The acropolis is masked by a village of black basalt and limestone houses, of Ottoman times, of a distinctive character. There are very extensive cemeteries, and three mausoleums, with one underground, for multiple interments. As befits a merchant town, there have been quantities of coin finds.

About 5 miles (8 km) away are the remains of baths, at **al-Hammah**, where there is also a small hotel, and the remains of a theatre, a temple and a synagogue.

THE JORDANIAN 'DESERT CASTLES'

Apart from a string of forts of Ottoman Turkish times, Jordan also possesses a number of miscalled 'desert castles' — for some of them are not castles at all. Four of these go back to Roman times, and one is perhaps of Nabataean occupation; the rest belong to the eighth century, when the Umayyad caliphs ruled from Damascus. This dynasty gave way to the Abbasids, who ruled from Baghdad, in 750, and almost all these buildings seem to have been abandoned then. The most interesting and best preserved of them are situated within what is known as the 'desert castle loop', and they can easily be visited within a day from Amman. All these but one belong to the years between 700 and 750, and together give a picture of the Umayyad caliphate.

Various theories have been advanced for them. The Umayyad caliphs were still Bedouins at heart, and filled with nostalgia for the desert, rather than the town life of Damascus. There are several 'castles' north of Damascus as well as east of Amman. Hawking, hunting, horse-racing, poetry, wine and women filled the lives of these caliphs, not like the austere lives of the 'four Orthodox Caliphs', the immediate successors of the prophet Muhammad. There is evidence, however, that these 'castles' were more than country hunting lodges. They were agricultural

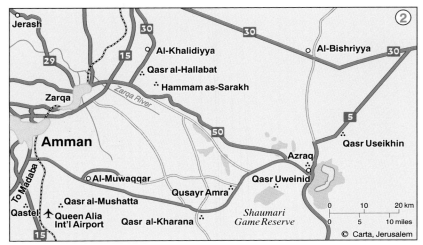

Map of the 'desert castle loop'

oases created by aqueducts bringing a water supply that enabled successful cultivation and gave prosperity to the region. They are also evidence of a sophisticated knowledge of building and decoration, including both carving and painting. They show too that the prejudice against representation of the human and even animal form did not exist in early Islam. They are comparable, rather, to the French châteaux of later times.

Almost all of them, including those in Syria, are described in K.A.C. Cresswell, *A Short Account of Early Muslim Architecture* (1958), revised and supplemented by J.W. Allan, Scolar Press, 1989, but here material has been drawn from other works and from personal observation.

Only two of the ones I describe here (Qastel and Qasr al-Mushatta) are outside the 'desert castle loop', but they are still easily accessible from Amman. For visitors who only have a limited amount of time at their disposal, Qasr al-Mushatta and Qusayr Amra should be given priority over all others.

QASTEL   This lies to the south of Amman. There are two buildings — a fort and a mosque — behind the modern-day village. The entrance to the fort is on the east side. Before it became ruined there were towers at each corner and three more on the north, west and south; there were four on the east. Excluding the towers, the building was 64 yards (59 m) square. Apart from the gatehouse there were six sets of rooms — each set comprising a central room and two smaller rooms on either side — placed round a courtyard. The tumbled pillars lying about show that the courtyard had a portico, and that the same pattern was repeated in an upper storey. Fragments of mosaic cubes and some painted plaster indicate that the interior was once elaborately decorated.

Qastel derives from the Latin *castellum*, a small castle. There is no evidence of Roman remains, and, by comparison with other Umayyad buildings, it can be dated to about 744. West of the northern part of the fort is a small mosque, of masonry

The walled enclosure at Qasr al-Mushatta

identical with that of the fort. It is roughly square, 69 x 59 feet (21 x 18 m), with a roofed sanctuary. There was a minaret at the north-west corner. The two buildings were probably erected about the same time. There is evidence of other buildings in the modern village, and it was possibly a much larger settlement than now.

QASR AL-MUSHATTA This is the most famous of all the Umayyad palaces. It lies to the south-east of Amman, but, for security reasons, one is required to drive round the periphery of the Queen Alia International Airport.

It is a great walled enclosure, with towers, five on the west, north and east, six on the south. Of these, four contain latrines. Within the square no buildings were ever begun on the west and east. Those on the south possibly never rose above ground level; only those on the north seem to have been completed.

It is possible to drive in through the gateway into the entrance hall and courtyard, flanked by other courtyards and rooms. Beyond is a great central courtyard, with, on the north side, the splendid triple-arched entry into a long basilican hall, which ends with a triple apse. Evidently this was a reception or throne room. The rest of this section was quartered, each quarter containing a main room with two smaller rooms on either side, allowing quarters for each of four wives. It was built of white limestone and of brick, decorated with elaborate carvings and friezes, vine-leaves and grapes being a principal theme, reminiscent of the decoration of a tie-beam in the Dome of the Rock.

For certain it would have been a building of wondrous beauty, before it was sadly wrecked by earthquake. Decorative features and methods of construction show that workmen from Egypt and Iraq as well as from Syria were employed to construct it. This, and the almost totally ruined palace of Qasr at-Tuba, were almost certainly built c.743–744, and left unfinished when Caliph al-Walid II died in 744. Another castle attributed to the same caliph is Qasr Bayir, north-east of Ma'an, now almost totally in ruins.

QASR AL-HALLABAT Qasr (more properly Qusayr, the little castle) al-Hallabat
lies north-east of Amman along Route 30, and is a large and imposing ruin. The
principal building is 48 yards (44 m) square, with four rectangular corner towers,
which once stood three storeys high. Within this courtyard is a keep, again with a
courtyard and a cistern. Outside the *enceinte* (enclosure) was a mosque, and, 1½
miles (2.4 km) away at Hammam as-Sarakh, a bath-house (see below). Excavation
has shown that there was an elaborate water system here which made this a centre
of intensive agriculture, with irrigated fields and gardens, and also olive orchards
and vines.

It originated as simply a small Roman fortress, in the form of the present inner
keep; it was part of a system of forts built by the emperor Trajan in 111–117. These
linked the trading city of Bostra, in Syria, with the Red Sea port of Ayla, now
Aqaba, guarding the trade route of Via Nova Traiana (Trajan's New Road). The
small fort was expanded under Caracalla in 212–215, when the larger structure
with corner towers was built round it. An inscription records its restoration in 529,
under Justinian.

It is thought to have been abandoned after the Persian invasion of 614, but,
under the Umayyads (661–750), was almost entirely rebuilt on the original plan.
It was decorated with elaborate mosaics and wall paintings. The mosque was also
built at this time.

Hammam as-Sarakh One-and-a-half miles (2.4 km) to the east a road leads to
Hammam as-Sarakh, its contemporary bath-house, comprised of an audience hall
flanked by two rooms, and a bath-house, with three rooms. All these were once
painted, but little more than traces remain.

AZRAQ Continuing eastward one reaches the oasis town of Azraq, to the east of
Amman. It is situated at an important junction, leading to as-Safawi in the north,

The fortress at Azraq

Iraq to the east, and Saudi Arabia to the south. It has thus long been an important caravan centre, and was also used by T.E. Lawrence (otherwise known as Lawrence of Arabia) as the headquarters for his journeys to Aqaba and in harassing the Ottoman Turks.

Ancient Azraq It has been inhabited for thousands of years, as the large scatter of flint tools of the Stone Age suggests. The fort was probably built by the Romans in 292–306. Its importance lay in its enormous water resources, now being exploited to supply the city of Amman, with the result that the water table is becoming dangerously low, and may dry up. The fort is built entirely of black basalt, and its site has never been excavated. Since the Romans and Byzantines, it has been continuously occupied into the present century. An inscription over the entrance records that it was rebuilt in 1237 by an Ayyubid governor.

The room above the gatehouse is the one Lawrence used. The whole building once had two storeys, and included stables on the ground floor on the north side. The mosque in the courtyard was almost certainly built during the Ayyubid period, in the early thirteenth century.

Azraq Shishan Two miles (3.2 km) south is the village of Azraq Shishan, where there are ancient water reservoirs, built with massive basalt blocks. Their date is not known. At the time of writing the fort caretaker was the son of one of Lawrence's former officers.

SHAUMARI GAME RESERVE Near Azraq is the Shaumari Game Reserve, with ostriches, gazelle and oryx. Only the ostriches are usually visible, for the animals tend to roam freely in the desert.

ROMAN FORTS Almost 10 miles (16 km) north-east of Azraq is **Qasr Useikhim**, a Roman fort which is accessible across a rough desert track suitable only for four-wheel-drive vehicles. About 10 miles (16 km) south-west of Azraq is **Qasr Uweinid**, another Roman fort, of c.AD 200. Both are very much ruined. North of Azraq is **Deir al-Khaf**, the Monastery of the Caves, yet another Roman fort. It is 66 yards (61 m) square, with corner and interval towers. These towers contained mangers, so presumably they were stables. There were two storeys of rooms along the walls. An apsidal structure, thought to be a church, was on the left side of the main courtyard; if this is correct, the fort was at some time occupied as a monastery. Outside are the remains of fields with furrows and walls, a reservoir and other traces of agriculture.

QUSAYR AMRA Now returning round the loop in the direction of Amman, west of Azraq, is Qasr (more correctly Qusayr) Amra — the (Little) Red Castle. This is no castle at all, but a bath-house, standing in a partly walled enclosure. It has been fairly accurately described as part of a hunting lodge. A short distance to the north-west are the remains of a small castle, with rooms round a courtyard. Between it and Qusayr Amra was a watch-tower, and the remains of a water system, with a view to irrigating a garden or orchard. Although the area has been surveyed, it would seem that it is not yet fully mapped.

The principal surviving building, the bath-house and hunting lodge, is the glory of Jordanian antiquities on account of its wall paintings. It is in two parts. There is a rectangular reception hall with an alcove, flanked by two rooms, windowless

Above: Qusayr Amra

Left: Detail from a fresco at Qusayr Amra

and apsidal in form. The apses have semi-domes; the alcove has a barrel-vault lower than the barrel-vault of the reception room. The bath-house part consists of three rooms, one barrel-vaulted, the second cross-vaulted, and the third with a dome. From this, now blocked up, a passage leads to an un-roofed enclosure, of uncertain purpose.

All the rooms have sockets on the lower parts of the internal walls, show-ing that formerly marble panels were fixed to them with dowels. Above the panels the walls were plastered and painted with frescoes in brilliant blues, browns, reds, bluish green, dull yellow, and yellow.

In the alcove the back wall shows a monarch with a halo. On the front edge of the arch was a Kufic inscription invoking a blessing on some person whose name has disappeared. Doubtless, this was a throne recess. On the left of where the throne would have stood a woman is waving a *flabellum*, or large fan.

In the audience hall there was the figure of a woman above whom appeared the Greek word '*Niké*' (Victory). This presumably refers to the six defeated rulers at the south end of the west wall, who could once be identified by inscriptions. The three front figures have their hands open in homage or submission. The remaining fragments of inscriptions identify four of the figures as the Byzantine emperor; the Visigothic king, Roderic of Spain; Chosroes, the emperor of Persia; and an unnamed negus of Ethiopia. The other two have lost their inscriptions, but may be the emperor of China and the *khaqan* of the Turks. If, as seems most plausible, they represent 'enemies of Islam' defeated in the reign of al-Walid I, then the painting must be from before his death in 715, and after the defeat of Roderic at the Battle of the Guadalete in 711. It thus provides a date for the whole construction.

On the right of this picture is a bathing scene, and then a group of men engaged in gymnastic exercises. Above is a spectacular scene of huntsmen herding onagers (a kind of wild ass) into a netted area. Onagers also appear on the east, north and south walls, suggesting that hunting them was a popular pastime. On the transverse arches are a musician and scantily dressed women; the side rooms beside the throne have vine-scrolls and geometrical mosaic floors.

In the first room, the *apodyterium* (the bath proper), a cupid flies above two figures lying on the ground. From one side of the window a woman gazes across at a man on the other side. There are numerous depictions of birds and animals. In the *tepidarium* (cool room) are several nude figures of women. In the *caldarium* (hot room) the splendid dome represents the vault of heaven, with stars and signs of the zodiac.

The artists, whose names are not known, were certainly Arab, for the Arabic script has been written by someone accustomed to writing it; the Greek inscriptions have been outlined in dark paint first, and then drawn in, making it unlikely that the individual even knew how to write Greek.

It is widely believed that Islam forbids the representation of the human form. Nowhere is there any such injunction in the Qur'an. Paintings existed in the Kaaba in 608; when Muhammad entered Mecca in 630, he ordered that a picture of Mary with Jesus in her lap should be preserved, and this remained until the Kaaba was destroyed in 683. When the great Iwan, the Arch of Ctesiphon, was used for Friday prayers in 637, it was decorated with paintings of humans, and these still existed in 897. St John of Damascus (699–754), a fierce opponent of the Iconoclast movement (which was against the use of images in religious worship in churches in the East), in his many writings never once accuses Muslims of association with iconoclasts. It was not until the end of the eighth century that a bishop of Harran includes Muslims as people opposed to painting the human form, saying that he who paints anything living will be compelled to breathe into it a soul on the Day of Resurrection. The Muslim objection to painting thus presumably became current only at the end of the eighth century.

QASR AL-KHARANA   Further west towards Amman is Qasr al-Kharana, which looks like a fortified castle. Most likely, because of its appearance, it gave the name to the 'desert castles'. It is 38 yards (35 m) square, with towers at each corner; there are towers on the west, north and east in the centre of each range of wall, and half towers at the entrance. It is two storeys high, and apparently was never completed. Identical sets of rooms are arranged at both levels, with shallow staircases on the west and east, surrounding a courtyard. The structure has numerous Persian features, including its brickwork, vaulting, squinches and stucco decoration. This

The 'desert castle' at Qasr al-Kharana

has given rise to a dispute over its date, some claiming that it is a Sassanian Persian building. Although some Byzantine wares have been found, Sassanian wares are absent, and Umayyad wares common. A graffito gives the date 710 (92 AH), and this in all probability is accurate.

FROM AMMAN TO THE SOUTH

South of Amman are two great roads which reach Aqaba, the Desert Highway and the King's Highway. The Desert Highway is a modern, fast route, with little of interest. The King's Highway (al-Tariq al-Sultan, the Sultan's Highway) passes through rich agricultural districts, which have not, however, attracted the heavy immigrant population of the north. It twists and turns its way through the Madaba district, with its heritage of mosaics, via the historic towns of Kerak, Tafila, and Shaubak, at which point the road continues to Petra, while another road branches left to Ma'an.

MADABA Madaba is a district headquarters, with an area roughly between Wadi Shu'aib and Wadi el-Mujib. Broadly, this area is that of the Byzantine diocese of the early centuries of Christianity. Its wealth derived not only from its agriculture but also from its position on a main caravan route. In conjunction with the availability of artists of genius, this enabled a flowering of excellence in mosaic art unsurpassed in the ancient Roman Province of Syria. It lasted approximately from the fourth to the eighth centuries, with some examples yet in the ninth century, after the shift from the Umayyad capital of Damascus to the Abbasid capital of Baghdad. It was this shift, combined with the expansion of conversion to Islam, that brought decay to the region.

A number of travellers from 1807 onwards reported ruins of interest in Madaba, and in 1868 the discovery of the Stela of Mesha, or Moabite Stone (see p. 198),

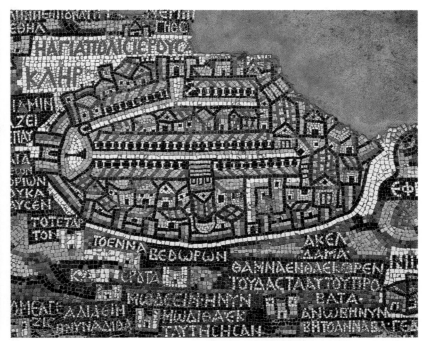

Above: *Section of the Madaba Map depicting the city of Jerusalem*

Right: *One of the mosaics at Madaba*

fuelled curiosity about the district. Mosaics were already reported, along with a map of the city, in 1891; the famous Madaba Map had been reported to the Greek Orthodox patriarch in Jerusalem in 1884. No action was taken until 1896, when the patriarch Gerasimos ordered the building of a new church in Madaba and the inclusion of the mosaic in its pavement.

The Madaba Map At that time the map, which extended from the Mediterranean to Amman, Kerak and Petra, with Jerusalem as its centre, measured about 81 x 16 feet (25 x 5 m). It depicts the Palestine of the Bible, neighbouring countries, and even a city plan of

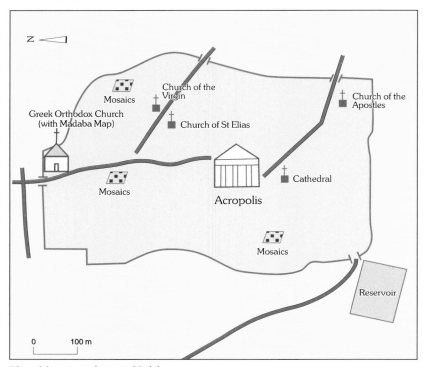

Plan of the principal sites in Madaba

Jerusalem that shows its principal buildings. Internal evidence has enabled it to be dated to between 560 and 565. It is entirely composed of stone cubes; no glass was used. It contained 2.3 million cubes — red, blue-green, brown, violet, black, white, yellow and grey — and it has been calculated that it would have taken 11,500 hours to lay. Unfortunately, during the building of the new church large portions were ripped up by workmen under ignorant supervision, thus destroying to a great extent the only existing map of ancient Palestine. In addition to the topographical information, local fauna and flora were also depicted. Lions, so frequently mentioned in the Bible, evidently still haunted the plains of Moab.

Madaba town The town plan shows the location of the cathedral and other churches in which mosaics are to be seen. The mosaics of the ancient church date its completion to 575/6. Of particular interest is its baptistery, on the north side of the atrium. A later baptistery formerly stood above it; excavation revealed the earlier baptistery below, complete with a *synthronon* (step-like seats for the clergy, with a throne for the bishop in the centre). The earlier baptistery was sunk below ground level, and intended for immersion; the later for infusion (the pouring of water on the person to be baptized, rather than immersion). A similar arrangement is to be found at Siyagha, and is probably the explanation for the shifting positions of the font in the Basilica of the Nativity at Bethlehem.

The Church of the Virgin was built above a private house, which already had a magnificent mosaic which gave its name to the Hall of Hippolytus. This church has a peculiar arrangement for its period, in that it has a circular nave and a long eastern apse. It is difficult to interpret. The greatest part of the nave is taken up by a square mosaic set in it, and it cannot therefore be taken as a model of the rotunda of the Holy Sepulchre. The mosaics show the church to be of the sixth century.

The Church of St Elias (the prophet Elijah) has a crypt below, in honour of St Aelianus, and can be dated to 608. The crypt has an elaborate geometrical mosaic, with birds and animals. The church of the Sunna family survives as a mosaic within a private house. The Church of el-Khadir is the property of the Greek Orthodox. The whole of the nave is covered by a single mosaic, in three parts with different designs. It is notable for its freely drawn representations of trees. The Church of the Salayta is so called after the family that once had a house here.

The Church of the Apostles has a full-length single mosaic in the nave, chiefly of birds, with, in the centre, a representation of a woman rising from the sea, with an inscription '*Thalassa*' (Sea) and the words:

O Lord God who has made
heaven and earth give life
to Anastasios and Thomas and Theodora
and to the mosaicist Salamanios.

It is probably to be dated to c.578–579. There are mosaics also in a number of private houses, in the Archaeological Museum, and in the Bruciati Palace, where the mosaic has been partly destroyed by a bulldozer.

MOUNT NEBO Some 5 miles (7 km) north-west of Madaba is Mount Nebo (Num. 32.3, 32.38, 33.47), from where Moses gazed upon the Promised Land that he was not permitted to enter. Its twin peaks, of Siyagha and el-Mukhayyat, are both Franciscan property.

Siyagha Its name means monastery, and there was already one here in 384, when the pilgrim Egeria visited it, and was hospitably received by the monks. Here, in the church, she was shown the place where the angels were said to have buried Moses, 'the man of God', denied entry to the Promised Land although he was permitted to see it.

Here, from a site which in 1933 was nothing but a tumbled mass of ruins, a church and other buildings have been recovered, and a small monastery constructed. The view westward is breath-taking, and in outline at any rate is what Moses himself would have seen. A brass plate has now been fixed overlooking the Jordan Valley, naming the principal towns that are dimly visible in the daytime, but clearly identifiable by their lights at night. The 'land flowing with milk and honey' is surely the rich agricultural land round Jericho and up the Jordan Valley. In a fan shape are Sodom, Masada and Qumran, Hebron, Bethlehem, Jerusalem (Mount of Olives), Ramallah, Nablus and Mount Tabor; the plate also points out the direction of the Dead Sea and of the Sea of Galilee.

The Memorial of Moses on Siyagha The church was built in two stages. What Egeria saw was a trefoil apse with a short nave, which did not stretch beyond the second arch of the present arcade. The floor was more than three feet (1 m) lower than the present one. There was a range of rooms on either side of what one may

The Springs of Moses, Ayun Musa

presume was an atrium. On the north-west side was a baptistery, with a font sunk into the floor into which the candidate could descend and then rise again on the opposite side. Space was provided in it for the officiating minister, and, opposite him, a small basin inset, presumably for infant baptism. On the south side of the church was a small mosaic cross, now regarded as a memorial of Moses.

In the second stage the floor was raised and an arcaded nave with side aisles added, with a clerestory of which traces exist. For the time being the whole has been covered with a temporary roof, to protect the mosaics and to make it usable as a church. The enlarged church had a range of buildings on either side. The old

Detail of the mosaic in the Church of the Lions, Umm er-Rasas

baptistery, with a mosaic dated 538, was filled in, and uncovered only in 1976. On the south side was a new baptistery, with a *synthronon* and a font above ground level in the chord of the apse. Evidently the ritual of baptism had been made more elaborate, and there had been a transition to infant baptism as the norm. The same, as has been seen above, was the case at Madaba.

The new baptistery has a mosaic dated 597, this providing a time bracket in which the transition took place. The reconstruction and enlargement of the church would seem to have followed an earthquake, but the need for a much larger church is explained by two brief inscriptions: one mentions an abbot (*higoumenos*), the other a bishop, and are placed on either side in front of the new font. On the same side as the new baptistery there was also a chapel of the *Theotokos*, of Our Lady Mother of God.

The nearby village of **el-Mukhayyat** had four churches, of St George, of the martyr saints Lot and Procopius, of Amos and Cassiseos, and a chapel of the priest John, of the fifth to sixth centuries. In Wadi Afrit is a small chapel known by the Bedouin as el-Keniseh (the Church), a small building which is almost square.

AYUN MUSA Below el-Mukhayyat is Ayun Musa, the Springs of Moses (Exod. 17.6; Num. 20.8), where Egeria records a great many monks, 'truly holy men known as ascetics'. She enthused over the spring 'which flowed from the rock, beautifully clear and with excellent taste'. There are the remains of other small monastic settlements in the neighbourhood, all with mosaics of the same period, testifying to the prosperity of the region in the fifth to sixth centuries.

OTHER MOSAICS South-west of Madaba are the villages of el-Teim, Ma'in, Ain Qattara, Ain Minya, and Hammamat Ma'in; to the south are Libb, Mekawir, Mishnaqa and Qurayat; and yet others to the east and south, all with fragmentary mosaics. Of these, those of Umm er-Rasas and Dibon are of special importance.

UMM ER-RASAS Umm er-Rasas (Mother of Lead) takes its name from lead mines. It is 19 miles (30½ km) south-east of Madaba. There are two groups of ruins, one within the fortifications, the other outside. The first group is undisturbed, but the second has been built over. There are Nabataean, Roman and Byzantine remains, the latter predominating. There are at least ten churches or chapels, both inside and outside the fortifications.

The most important building is the complex of St Stephen. The original church, dedicated to Bishop Sergius, was built in 586, to the north; to the east was built the Church of St Stephen, both with broad naves and narrow side aisles. South of St Sergius and west of St Stephen a tiled atrium was constructed, with an apse on the west side. From this a passage leads to a partly excavated polygonal building, an assemblage that might suggest that the whole complex had some connection with the Easter ceremonies.

Both churches are richly decorated with mosaics. Those of St Stephen include a carpet mosaic in the nave surrounded by vignettes of cities and towns in Palestine, Jordan and Egypt. Each of these places is labelled and represented by its most important building: Jerusalem — H Hagia Polis, The Holy City — is quite clearly marked out by the Holy Sepulchre. Its trapezoidal atrium, the *martyrion*, the *triportico*, and the domed rotunda above the Tomb of Christ can all be distinguished, and the complex is shown at a slightly oblique angle to the street, as it is in fact. The lay-out is as follows:

Jerusalem	Tamiathis	Panaou	Pelousion	Kastron Mefaa
Neapolis				Philadelphia
Sebastis				Midaba
Caesarea	Pseudostomon		Anti(n)aou	Belemunta
Diospolis				Areopolis
Eleutheropolis	Cynopolis		To Herakleion	Charach Louba
Askelon				Diblaton
Gaza	Theneseos	To Kasin	Alexandria	Limbon

Many of the names are obvious, and all but two can be identified. Kastron Mefaa is the ancient name of Umm er-Rasas, and Philadelphia of Roman Amman. Two dates are given in the inscriptions — 756 and 785, as are the names of clergy, benefactors and mosaicists. Out of fifty-six names, sixteen only are Greek names common among Christians; forty are of Semitic origin, giving some idea of the character of the population. These were no backwoodsmen, but city-dwellers with a high degree of artistic appreciation as demonstrated by the quality of the mosaics.

DIBON Twenty miles (32 km) south of Madaba is Dibon or Dhiban, a city first settled in the Bronze Age, and by the Moabites in the early Iron Age. The principal remains of the city are of the Nabataean and Byzantine periods. There is a Nabataean temple and the remains of two sixth century churches.

The Moabite Stone The most important evidence for the history of Dibon is the Stela of Mesha, or Moabite Stone, which for a long time was the earliest known example of Hebrew script, and which describes the wars of Moab against Omri, king of Israel. It was found at Dibon in 1868, by the Revd Frederick Klein. Most of the stone was fragmented by vandals, but Charles Clermont-Ganneau, of the French consulate in Jerusalem, had made a squeeze of it. From this was made the cast in the British Museum. The stone's remains are in the Louvre in Paris. Its accuracy as an historical record is confirmed by 2 Kings 3, dating it at c.835 BC.

The Stela of Mesha

It is the only written record of Jordan of such antiquity. It reads: 'I am Mesha, son of Chemosh, King of Moab, the Dibonite. My father reigned over Moab for thirty years, and I reigned after my father. I made the High Place for Chemosh in Qerkhah, a High Place of Salvation because he saved me from all my foes and let me see my pleasure on all those that hated me.

'Omri, King of Israel, afflicted Moab for many days, for Chemosh was angry with his land. His son succeeded him, and he also said: I will afflict Moab. In my days he said this, but I saw my pleasure on him and his house, and Israel perished in everlasting destruction.

'Omri seized the land of Madaba and dwelt there his own days and half his son's days, forty years, but Chemosh restored it in my days.

'I built Meon and made the reservoir there, and I built Keryathen. Now the men of Gad had lived in the land of Ataroth of old, and the King of Israel built Ataroth for himself. I fought against the city and took it, and I killed all the people of the city and made it a grazing ground for Chemosh and for Moab. Then I captured the shrine of Dudah and dragged it before Chemosh in Keriyoth, and I settled the men of Sharem and Mekhrath there.

'And Chemosh said to me: Go, take Nebo from Israel. I went by night and fought against it from dawn until noon, and I took it, and slew all the people, 7,000 men and women, for I had devoted it to Ashtar Chemosh. I took the vessels of Jehovah and dragged them before Chemosh.

'Now the King of Israel had built Yahas and lived in it while he fought against me, but Chemosh drove him out before me. I took two hundred men of Moab and all its chiefs, and brought them up against Yahas, and took them all into Dibon. I built Qerkhah, the wall of the forest and the wall of the mound, and its gates, towers and royal palace, and made two reservoirs in the middle of the city. Now there was no cistern in the city, so I said to all the people: Let every man make a cistern in his own house. I built the aqueduct for Qerkhah with the help of prisoners from Israel. I rebuilt Aroer and made the road through the Arnon, and I rebuilt Beth-Ramoth, for it was overthrown, and Bezor... and all Dibon was subject to me. I reigned over a hundred cities that I had added to the land.

'I rebuilt Madaba and Beth-Deblatein and the temple of Baal-Meon, and took the shepherd... the flocks of the land. Now Khernan the son of Dedan dwelt there, and Dedan said... Chemosh said to me: Go down against Khernan. So I went down and made war... and Chemosh dwelt in it all my days....'

KERAK AND SHAUBAK Just south of Dibon the road passes through the picturesque gorge of Wadi al-Mujib. Continuing south are al-Qasr and al-Rabba, between which there are the ruins of a Nabataean temple. Passing through a number of villages with Moabite remains, Kerak, the Kir-Moab of the Bible, is reached. There are numerous references to this place in the Bible, particularly in Judges and 1 Samuel. The Crusader fortress here was built in 1136 by Payen, the cup-bearer of King Fulk, and became the principal centre of Oultre-Jourdain (Transjordan). The last Crusader lord of Kerak, Renaud de Chatillon, was captured by Saladin at the Battle of Hattin in 1187. Ordered by Saladin to confess to Islam, he refused; whereon Saladin cut his head off with a single stroke of his sword.

Under the Mamluks of Egypt Kerak had a chequered history as a place of exile and consequent intrigue. After the Ottoman conquest it ceased to be important,

Panoramic view from the Crusader castle at Kerak

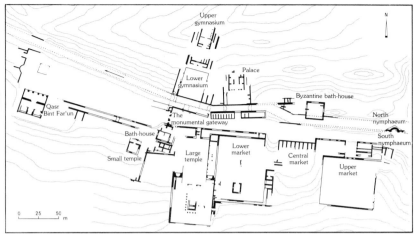

City plan of Petra

until it was made a provincial headquarters in 1894. From the castle there is a splendid view; on a clear day the Mount of Olives is visible. There is another Crusader fortress at **Tafila**, as well as one at Shaubak, founded in 1115 by Baldwin II as Mons Regalis (Mont Réale, the King's Mountain).

PETRA At 182 miles (292 km) from Amman by the King's Highway the descent begins to the great Nabataean city of Petra, 'A rose-red city — "half as old as Time!" ' as the Revd John William Burgon described it in his celebrated poem. By the Desert Highway it is 143 miles (230 km).

History Apparently Petra (whose name means rock) was not occupied before the fourth century BC. The first known ruler of the Nabataeans was Aretas (2 Macc. 5.8), with whom the high priest Jason sought asylum in 168 BC. A century later the kingdom had conquered most of southern Syria, Damascus included, and dominated the caravan trade. It was brought to an end by Roman annexation in AD 106. In 131 the emperor Hadrian diverted the caravan trade to Palmyra after his visit to Arabia, and Petra thereafter served largely as a religious centre.

In the fourth century the Province of Arabia was divided into two parts. Bostra became capital of the northern part which retained the old title; the south became Palaestina Tertia, with Petra as capital. By the fifth century Christianity had begun to penetrate, and the Nabataean temple was used as a church. Nothing is known of it during the earlier Arab period, nor until the Crusaders occupied it in 1127. They called it Li Vaux Moyse, the Valley of Moses.

The Mamluk sultan Baybars visited it briefly in 1276. Thereafter nothing is heard of it until it was visited by J.L. Burckhardt in 1812; he thought little of it. Although there was some exploration in the nineteenth century, it was not until 1929 that there was any excavation. All our knowledge is therefore very recent, and much remains to be done. Hardly any private dwellings have been encountered, and the greatest number of monuments consist of tombs. These have elaborate façades sculpted from living rock, with simple, undecorated tomb chambers

Above: Rock-cut caves at Petra

Left: One of the temples

behind, often of large size. It is these façades, of a pinkish sandstone of spectacular beauty, that have given Petra its name. Though a number of schemes have been worked out, there is as yet no more than the roughest chronology; nor is there agreement on the typological meaning of the various tombs. More than 650 monuments have been listed, and a visit of a few days cannot allow more than a glance at a small number. What follows is simply a guide to the most important or attractive.

Visit The main road from Amman reaches Wadi Musa, and turns west for Petra. Here is a government rest house, the Forum Hotel, and a Visitors Centre and gate at which entry tickets are purchased. Past the gate is the 'Horse-riding Point', at which Bedouin wait with horses for visitors. Petrol vehicles are not permitted inside. Each horse is accompanied by its master, who also acts as guide. A fixed charge is payable for both. Passing down the *wadi*, at the second bend there are the Sahri tombs on the right. Continuing round a broad bend, a narrow passage leads to a tunnel, to carry off rain-water if there is a flash flood. The es-Siq Gorge is now entered, a narrow passage never more than 16 feet (5 m) wide, and extending more than a mile (1.6 km) into the centre of the ancient city. At the first bend is a track to the left, which leads to the necropolis and High Place of al-Madras, with numerous tombs and the remains of an altar. The Siq now narrows, with walls towering up to 300 feet (91 m) on either side. Some of the ancient water-supply system is still visible.

Quite suddenly the Khazneh, or Treasury, Petra's most famous monument, appears at the end of the Siq, its façade carved from virgin rock, some 131 feet (40 m) high. Its name derives from Bedouin imagination, that the urn at the summit, some 11 feet (3½ m) high, contains treasure. It is pock-marked with rifle bullets, evidence of attempts to break it open. Behind the façade there is nothing but a plain room. The Khazneh is best seen in the morning between 9 am and 11 am, when the full sunlight falls on it, or in the late afternoon, when the rock itself seems to glow. The date of the tomb has been variously estimated, from 100 BC to AD 200.

The number of tombs and niches now increases, and shortly afterwards one reaches the Roman or Nabataean theatre, with seating for up to 8,000 spectators. From here the main area of the city is reached; it covers some 2 square miles (3 sq km). The construction of the theatre passed through and pierced many tombs and cave dwellings, and, like the rest, was carved out of solid rock. Above, on Jebel al-Madhbah (Altar Hill), is the High Place of Sacrifice with a carved altar, with further tombs in the vicinity.

Yet another necropolis lies north of the theatre, with the Urn Tomb, Corinthian Tomb, Palace Tomb and one dedicated to Sextus Florentinus, of the second century AD. The *wadi* now turns sharply, and discloses a nymphaeum, and a colonnaded street, of which some columns remain standing. It ends with the Temenos Gate, the entrance to the shrine known as Qasr al-Bint Far'un, the Castle of Pharaoh's Daughter. It is the Bedouin convention to ascribe any antiquity of unknown origin to the pharaohs, but the building rather is the temple of the god Dushara; near to the gateway is the temple of the Winged Lions, of al-'Uzza-Atargatis, the fertility goddess who was the partner of Dushara. The excavations, begun in 1975, and still continuing in 1993, show that these were but part of an extremely large sacred complex of great importance, of which much is yet to be learned. North-east of this temple is a Byzantine church with a mosaic.

West of the Qasr al-Bint is the Department of Antiquities Nazzal Camp, with a small museum, and a second, larger museum to the north. Another *wadi* now joins Wadi Musa from the north-east, with yet another necropolis. On the heights are the walls of the Byzantine city. After the junction of the *wadi*s their name becomes Wadi as-Siyagha, the Wadi of the Monastery; the remains of the monastery itself lie to the north-west. It is reached by a rock-cut path.

The monastery is similar in design to the Khazneh, but far larger. It is 162½ feet (50 m) wide, and 130 feet (40 m) high. The building is thought to have been built in the third century BC, and adapted later to Christian use. It would certainly have been intended as a temple in honour of Dushara.

From here the return journey to the entrance takes three hours. From Petra one can continue south to Aqaba.

AQABA

The town of Aqaba was a mere village in 1940; it is now a port town, constructed largely between 1958 and 1960. This is Jordan's only outlet to the sea, and its exports, of which phosphates constitute more than half, all pass through it.

Both at Eilat and Aqaba there is sweet water in plenty, only 6½ feet (2 m) below the surface even on the seashore. This would have been an additional attraction in ancient times, but as yet the site of the elusive Ezion-geber has not been found.

ANCIENT AYLA For the first descriptions of what the medieval Arab writers called Ayla one must turn to the Arab geographers. Ya'qubi wrote in the late ninth century that, 'The city of Ayla is a great city on the shore of the Salt Sea, and in it gather the pilgrims of Syria, Egypt and Morocco. There are numerous merchants and common people.'

In the tenth century Shams al-Din al-Muqaddasi visited Ayla from his native Jerusalem, saying, 'Wayla is a city on a branch of the China Sea. Great in prosperity with its palms and fish, it is the port of Palestine, the storehouse of the Hijaz.' By calling it Wayla he distinguishes it from 'the Ayla in ruins nearby', where a vast ruin contains Nabataean, Roman and Byzantine remains, but in which nothing has been found that could belong to the reign of Solomon in the tenth century BC.

By the tenth century AD it was a crossroads for the annual pilgrimage to Mecca for pilgrims from North Africa, Egypt, Palestine and Syria, with trade connections extending eastwards to China. Some fragments of its history remain. A Fatimid garrison was sent here from Egypt in 961. Local tribesmen sacked it in 1024. In 1072 it suffered an earthquake. The Crusaders seized it in 1116, losing it to Saladin in 1170. Ten years later Renaud de Chatillon held it briefly, but by the thirteenth century Abu al-Fida says there was nothing left but a fortification near the shore, when the settlement's name changed to Aqaba. There is still a castle standing about half a mile (1 km) south of the site of Ayla, the origin of the town of modern times.

Perhaps the answer to the problem of Ezion-geber is that it lies buried beneath the modern town, or that its site has been eroded by the sea. In either case there may yet be found some trace, underwater or under the sand.

In ancient Ayla distinct areas are evident: north of the port an area known as Ailana, a pre-Islamic town occupied between the second and seventh centuries AD; close to the present port the small settlement of Ayla of the seventh to twelfth centuries. The first area was a walled town, and a substantial section of it remains on the north-west side. There were four gates, and, in accordance with medieval Arab custom, we may assume that they were called after the directions to which their roads led: north-east, Bab al-Shams, the Syrian Gate; south-east, Bab al-Hijaz, the Hijaz Gate; north-west, Bab al-Misr, the Egyptian Gate; and Bab al-Bahr, the Sea Gate.

The north-west gate had twin towers of a round pattern that is repeated elsewhere in Jordan, and clearly of Umayyad times. Later, perhaps, shops were added. Houses of Umayyad, Abbasid and Fatimid times have been found, initially built of stone robbed from elsewhere, but by Fatimid times built of mud bricks. A larger building, known provisionally as the Pavilion Building from its central courtyard, is certainly Umayyad, for the levels sealed by its floors have disclosed nothing associated with later periods. On at least one wall was a painting, and also graffiti in a form of

Kufic script. The motifs of the painting were floral and geometrical. It is possible that this was the residence of a governor or other official.

Almost in the north-west corner is what is described as a Large Enclosure with a number of small rooms, a platform and drain. Its purpose is not known. Streets intersected the city from gate to gate, dividing it into four quarters. One might imagine that the lay-out, although visibly Umayyad, was that of a Roman camp. The Roman Xth Legion Fretensis was quartered here in the fourth century, and its remains could underlie the present site. Ceramic finds make this possible.

There are ceramic fragments from Byzantine times and for all the Arab periods; pottery has been identified from Baghdad and Basra, from Samarra, and from the Far East. They include celadon from the period of the Five Dynasties (907–960) and Northern Sung (960–1120), in northern China. Much came from Egypt. There is some evidence of the presence of Christians in this predominantly Islamic town. Apart from a large cross, there is also an ostracon inscribed with a cross and some lines of Hebrew poetry.

On the eastern shore is the fort of Aqaba, probably built by the Crusaders between 1116 and 1171. This is now used as a Visitors Centre, and also houses a small museum. It is mentioned by Abu al-Fida; it is claimed that his mention of the fort refers to a building by Sultan al-Nasir Muhammad c.1320. The only certain evidence is an ornate inscription that says it was built by Khayr Bey al-Ala'i during the reign of Sultan Qansaw al-Ghawri (1501–1516), the last but one of the Mamluk sultans of Egypt. The reading of the date is unclear, and can refer either to 1514/5 or 1504/5. Khayr Bey was well known as al-Mi'mar, the Builder.

Another inscription inside says the fort was partly rebuilt in the reign of the Ottoman sultan Murad III (1574–1595). The coat-of-arms over the entrance is that of the Hashemite royal family, and was placed there shortly after Hashemite forces liberated Aqaba in August 1917.

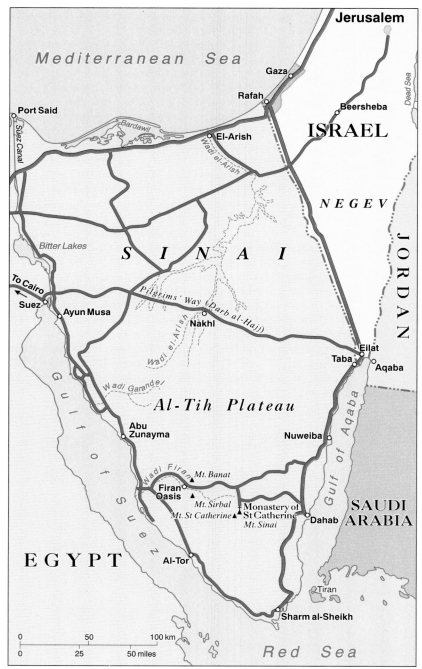

10. The Monastery of St Catherine and Mount Sinai

Sinai belongs to Egypt, and is a pear-shaped peninsula lying between Port Said and Rafah. Its Mediterranean shore has been the route of many conquerors for many thousands of years, including the pharaohs, Alexander the Great, Napoleon, and Allenby. Today, along its western and eastern shores, many holiday resorts have been developed. The mountainous centre, with its dramatic peaks and *wadis*, is scarcely inhabited, except for Arab nomads.

For pilgrims, certainly since the fourth century AD, the focus of interest has been the twin mountains of Gebel Musa, also called Mount Horeb or Sinai, where Moses received the Ten Commandments, and Gebel Katherina, the Mountain of St Catherine, martyred on 25 November 305, and whose body — according to pious legend — was mysteriously brought by angels in the ninth century.

By the end of the fourth century AD hermits and small groups of monks had spread here from Egypt and Palestine, and the fame of their holiness and austerity had already reached far-off Galicia in northern Spain. The first account of a pilgrim to Sinai is by a nun from Galicia (see below), who wrote an account of her four years of wanderings in the Middle East for her sisters. We still possess it in a truncated form.

There were already a scatter of little churches, bishops in some places, and what evidently were already organized pilgrimages to the sites connected with Moses. This was the beginning of the tradition still observed in the fifteenth century, when a Dominican, Fr Felix Faber, came in 1483, and then wrote a detailed account of his pilgrimage.

GETTING THERE

From Cairo, Air Sinai operates regular flights which take about 45 minutes. Flights from Cairo Airport are also organized by Zas Novotel. There are also daily services by coach organized by the East Delta Bus Service from the Abbasiya Terminal in Cairo. The journey takes between 6 and 9 hours. The distance is 275 miles (440 km) and can be completed by private car in less than 5 hours from Central Cairo. Petrol is available along the way, and the road surfaces are reported to be good.

From Israel, Arkia operates flights from Ben-Gurion International Airport to Sharm al-Sheikh, from where one must then take a taxi. It is also possible to drive to the Monastery of St Catherine from Eilat, via Taba, along the eastern coast of the Sinai.

There is a Tourist Village outside the monastery, and a hostel and guest house within the monastery's walls. It is advisable to book the trip through a travel agent, who can also advise on transport and opening times.

GENESIS AND EXODUS

A close examination of Genesis and Exodus will show that they are narratives of traditions gathered from different sources. The traditions that have gathered round Abraham are mainly Mesopotamian. With Jacob, Jordan enters the story, followed by Egypt. The underlying theme is that of theophany — the appearance of God to man: God reveals himself to Abraham in demanding the sacrifice of Isaac; God reveals himself to Abraham in the desert in the form of the three mysterious strangers; later he reveals himself in Egypt, plaguing the Egyptians and liberating Israel; in Sinai he reveals himself to Moses twice, and finally on Mount Nebo.

The triple revelation foreshadowed by the three mysterious strangers is taken up at the baptism of Jesus by St John the Baptist, when God the Father speaks from the cloud, recognizing the Son, over whom the Holy Spirit hovers in the form of a Dove. The final theophany is that of the Transfiguration, when Moses and Elijah, the Law and the prophets, appear in order to recognize the Godhead of Jesus transfigured before them. It is for this reason that the principal church at the Monastery of St Catherine is the Church of the Transfiguration, and not that of St Catherine, the patroness of the monastery.

THE REVELATION OF THE LAW

After the crossing of the Red Sea, the revelation of the Law to Moses at Sinai is the climax of the Book of Exodus. The versions we possess of the Five Books of Moses were not wholly brought together until after the return of the Israelites from exile in Babylon, c.530 BC. They recount narratives of events after Creation which commence with the start of the second millennium BC, more than a millennium and a half before. The earliest manuscripts that we possess may be the fragments found at Khirbet Qumran (see p. 105). Given so long a literary history, and taking into account the fact that for a long period this would have consisted of oral tradition, we cannot expect anything like modern scientific historical precision.

It need not be doubted that the Israelites did indeed cross the Red Sea or that the Ten Commandments were revealed to Moses at Mount Sinai, although it is impossible, save in the most arbitrary manner, to trace all the nomadic wanderings of Israel in the wilderness. They could not have travelled as in the Apocalypse — 12,000 of each tribe, numbering 144,000 in all (Rev. 7.4–8) — because in not one of the places enumerated was there a sufficient water supply for any large number of persons. Rather we must instead picture a long series of trickles of migration, which first began to coalesce east of the Jordan, and of which a coalition was led by Joshua across the river, to make a gradual conquest within the Promised Land itself. This they began where there was an abundant water supply, on the east bank of the river.

ANCIENT SINAI

From between 3000 and 1100 BC, inscriptions on stelae (upright slabs or pillars), which have been found in disused copper and turquoise mines in the area to which annual expeditions were sent, name almost every pharaoh. Ancient Sinai was thus well known to the Egyptians, and the Israelites in general could have been well informed as to the sources of water and of oases. The turquoise mines are to be found 15 miles (25 km) south of Abu Zunayma (Abu Zanima) in Wadi Maraghah; beyond it is Wadi Mukhattab (Valley of Inscriptions).

Farther on the road turns inland to reach the Firan Oasis, which by the fourth century AD was a Christian centre and had a bishop. In the surrounding mountains were caves inhabited by hermits, who had fled there initially to escape the persecution of Decius (249–251). At the Council of Chalcedon of 451 Pharan (Firan) was created an archbishopric subject to the patriarch of Jerusalem. Thus a Christian community existed solidly here before the institution of the monastery

The Firan Oasis

at Gebel Musa. The remains of the basilica and of the ancient city can still be seen. There are numerous ruined chapels and sanctuaries in the vicinity at Gebel Tahunah and a ruined church on the summit of Gebel Banat, the Mountain of the Virgins. To the south is Gebel Sirbal, with numerous hermits' caves.

In the Plain of Raha (Ease), where the Israelites are said to have rested, is to be found the Chapel of Aaron (Harun), where the Golden Calf (Exod. 32) is said to have been made.

MOUNT SINAI

Several routes lead to the summit of the mountain, but the most favoured is known as Sikka Sayyidna Musa (the Path of Our Lord Moses), which begins immediately behind the monastery. The ascent is commonly made before dawn, so that pilgrims can enjoy the beauty of the sunrise. The earliest part of the ascent is gentle, reaching Mayet Musa (the Water of Moses), believed to have been provided for a hermit, a cobbler, Sargarius, who lived there.

A further ascent reaches a small stone chapel of Our Lady, which commemorates a miracle. The caravan bringing food to the monastery had been delayed, and the monks determined to climb the mountain to implore divine aid. At this point Our Lady appeared to the monks, and told them to return to the monastery, where they found that the caravan bringing supplies had already arrived.

A staircase is soon reached. It is made up of some 3,400 steps, which are traditionally held to have been levelled by a monk called Moses, as a penance. Climbing 3,400 steps would be a penance in itself. At a gateway along the climb is a small plateau, where God is believed to have appeared to Elijah (1 Kings 19.8–9). A cave is shown in which he is said to have sheltered; beside it is shown a grotto in which he is said to have concealed himself. Further steps lead to the summit, below which there is a hollow in the granite that the Bedouin call Athar

Gebel Musa forms a majestic backdrop to the desert plain

Nagat al-Nabi (the Footprint of the Prophet's She-camel). This, they believe, is the true place from which Muhammad made his night-journey to heaven.

On the summit itself, there is a chapel on the site of one constructed in the time of Justinian, of which some traces remain, and a mosque. Here the Bedouin sacrifice a sheep once a year, on the *maulid* (festival, literally birthday) of Nabi Salih. The view from here is beyond all description.

THE MONASTERY OF ST CATHERINE

Fees are charged for entry, for residence and for visits to various chapels and peaks in the area. According to tradition, in 337 the empress Helena ordered the building of a chapel here in the valley, around the site of the Burning Bush (Exod. 3.2). Chronologically this is not possible, since she died in c.330.

EGERIA'S PILGRIMAGE The first pilgrim to describe the site was the Galician nun Egeria, c.384. She describes Wadi al-Raha 'in which the children of Israel waited while holy Moses went up into the Mount of God', where the Golden Calf was made, and where Moses took his father-in-law's cattle to pasture when God spoke to him 'twice' from the Burning Bush. Then she returned to Pharan, and came back to ascend Mount Sinai 'where the Law was given, and the place where God's glory came down when the mountain was smoking'. On top was a church and the cave of holy Moses. The pilgrims heard Mass, and were then shown 'all the different places... Egypt, and Palestine, the Red Sea and the Parthenian Sea

The ascent to the summit of Gebel Musa

(the part that takes you to Alexandria) as well as the vast lands of the Saracens'. They ascended Mount Horeb, heard Mass, and had 1 Kings 19 read to them, about how Elijah was sent to the Mount of the Lord, at the very stone altar that Elijah had erected. The Bush, 'still alive and sprouting', was situated within a very pretty garden, and there they stayed the night. They also saw many other small places to which memories of the children of Israel had been attached, all the way back to the land of Goshen in Egypt.

JUSTINIAN'S MONASTERY

At that time all seems to have been peaceful, but attacks on the hermits by ill-disposed tribesmen are recorded in 305, 370 and 400. No doubt such incidents provided good reason for the emperor Justinian to fortify an enclosure when a church in honour of the Virgin Mary was built in 537. Later, about 562, the Church of the Transfiguration was built, and the monastery garrisoned with 200 men — 100 Slavs and 100 Egyptians. Although it has been suggested, it is not likely that the present monastic servants are their descendants.

In the mid-ninth century the monastery became an independent bishopric; the first bishop, Constantius, attended the Fourth Council of Constantinople in 869. At first, relations with the local Muslims seem to have been good, but it was not long before the monastery was sacked, and the monks fled. Some returned, and, with the inspiration of the relics of St Catherine of Alexandria, whose body, so it was said, had been carried to Mount Sinai c.800, the monastery was revived. In the Crusader period relations between the Greeks of the monastery and the papacy were excellent — as at Bethlehem.

FR FELIX FABER'S PILGRIMAGE Fr Felix Faber, OP, gives a very detailed description of his visit of 1483, in a pilgrimage which followed much the same pattern as that of Egeria more than a millennium before.

The brethren received the pilgrims with every honour when they arrived about 9 am. After a short break they went to the Latin chapel, where Mass was celebrated in honour of St Catherine. They venerated her relics daily after Mass. They climbed Mount Horeb, to the chapel of Our Lady, where there was a Brother Nicodemus who knew Italian. The chapel honoured an appearance of Our Lady when the monastery had been troubled by snakes and other vermin. She came to tell them

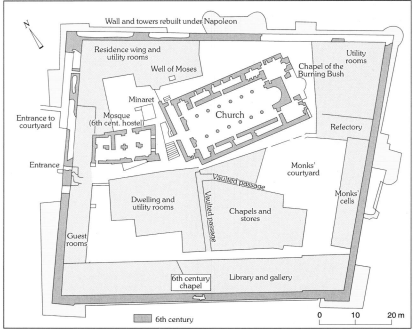

Plan of the Monastery of St Catherine

that henceforward she would protect the monastery. In token of good faith, for at first the monks were incredulous, she caused water to flow from a rock. Also on Mount Horeb was a chapel in honour of Elijah, a grotto where Moses saw God, and the Church of the Saviour, where he received the Ten Commandments from God. Here the pilgrims were entertained by some Arabs, and saw a large cistern for drinking water.

He said that two hours away was the Monastery of the Forty Saints, from where they ascended Mount Sinai, which they found to be a twin peak with Mount Horeb. There they saw where St Catherine's body had been brought by angels, and remained for 300 years. There were other sights too: a monastery which had no bells, but from which they sounded; a stream that was called after St Catherine; bushes from which they made walking-sticks as Moses had done; the place where manna was found; the rich garden of the monastery with 3,000 olive, orange, grenadine, fig and almond trees; the cave of St Onuphrius; the rock that Moses struck; the Monastery of the Saints Cosmas and Damian; and a spring that Moses had cursed.

In the church on 26 September they were shown the relics of St Catherine, after confession and holy communion. All the monks and their superior were present. They had some difficulty with the locks of the reliquary. They were taken into the Chapel of the Burning Bush, after having been required to take off their shoes as Moses had done. There lamps burned day and night. They visited other chapels with relics, some of Greek saints of whom they had never heard. Like Egeria, they saw where Aaron had set up the Golden Calf and the rock on which Moses had broken the first Tablets of the Law. Apart from the Church of the Transfiguration, there was a mosque — which still exists — and a little Latin chapel.

Fr Felix formed a poor opinion of the monks. They were not affable; the superior was proud and haughty. They hated the Roman Church, and did not allow Latin priests to celebrate at their altars. However, they were schismatics, not heretics. Living simply, nevertheless the monastery was itself rich from the gifts of kings, princes, sultans and nobles. They departed from the monastery with a Greek priest who was in charge of four camels, carrying boxes of pears and apples for the sultan, an annual gift that gave him pleasure.

REVIVAL In the years that followed the monastery was sometimes deserted, but managed to revive. In 1782 it was given full autonomy within the Orthodox Church. Napoleon had his engineers carry out some repairs, and so too did Muhammad Ali of Egypt. All through the ages the monastery has had rich benefactions. Pope Gregory the Great (590–604) sent furniture for a hostel. Other popes have followed his example. The twelve pillars of the church contain relics of the saints; prayers said at them have been granted indulgences on the usual conditions. It is perhaps the only church in the world where Latins may obtain indulgences in a Greek church. The richest benefactions have come from the tzars of Russia, who considered themselves successors of the Byzantine emperors. Russian rather than Greek taste is very evident in the churches.

VISIT The plan (see p. 212) shows the lay-out of the monastery. The modern entrance is on the west side; formerly visitors were winched up in a basket. The compound is a rough quadrilateral. The guest house is on the right of the entrance, with the monks' quarters on the far side. The museum and library occupy most of the south side, and there are service buildings on the north-east. The walls, repaired many times, rest on their sixth century foundations.

South-east of the church itself is an old refectory, similar to those in the Coptic monasteries in Wadi al-Natrun. The long narrow table behind which the monks sat, with their backs to the wall, was elaborately carved in wood. At the east end is a small apsidal niche with a wall painting of Christ. This niche is set in a large niche occupying the whole wall, with a painting depicting the Last Judgement, executed by a Cretan artist in 1573. There are other paintings on the lateral walls.

In the south-west wall of the monastery is a tunnel-vaulted chapel with sixth century wall paintings. The garden and orchard Egeria mentioned is still kept up. It must be one of the oldest existing gardens in the world. In this garden is the charnel-house, for lack of earth does not allow for graves. On the left of the door sits the skeleton of St Stephen the Porter, a sixth century monk, dressed in purple robes. On the right are the bones of martyrs and archbishops in open coffins. To the left is the ossuary, with separate piles of legs, hands, feet, ribs and skulls.

Besides the indulgences mentioned above, a number of popes have also issued bulls and proclamations in favour of the monastery. They include Honorius III (1217), Gregory X (1271–1276), John XXII (1316–1334), Benedict XII (1358) and Innocent VI (1360). However, no complete study is available on this interesting aspect of ecumenism.

The Monastery of St Catherine

THE CHURCH OF THE TRANSFIGURATION The church is 44 x 22 yards (40 x 20 m). It is on a basilican plan, with a domed *pastophorion* (small room) set back on either side of the main apse. Twelve pillars, inset with relics of the saints, one for each of the twelve months of the year, support a clerestory and roof. Originally there was an aisle on either side of the nave, equal in breadth to the *pastophoria*. These aisles have since been divided down the middle, thus creating a series of small rooms. On the north-west corner is a bell tower given by the Russians in 1871. This and the narthex are later additions. The roof is covered with lead, and inscriptions on the beams show it to be original. The architect was Stephen of Aila, modern-day Eilat. The main part of the church is known as the Katholikon. There is a superb iconostasis, dated 1612, painted by Cosmas of Crete, and numerous icons. Above the altar is a splendid mosaic of the Transfiguration of the sixth century. The floor is eighteenth century, as are the German chandeliers, made in Nuremburg. The gilded decoration is of unimaginable splendour.

THE CHAPEL OF THE BURNING BUSH The Chapel of the Burning Bush is behind the altar. It is earlier than Justinian's church. The bush, or its successor, is to be seen in the courtyard outside, transplanted from where today a silver plate marks the site under the small altar. The altar has alabaster legs and is enclosed by decorative mother-of-pearl miniature arcades on either side. The remainder is obscured by decorative cloths. It is possibly of great antiquity. The walls on either side are decorated with tiles of the Ottoman period, possibly Armenian in origin.

ICONS The monastery possesses what is probably the largest collection of icons in the world. There are over 2,000, large and small, from unique masterpieces to the most simple. They are to be found in the Katholikon, the Icon Gallery, various chapels, the sacristy, monks' cells and other parts of the monastery. The collection ranges from the sixth century to the nineteenth century. Those of the sixth century employed the so-called encaustic technique, whereby heated pigments were spread on to a prepared surface with a brush or hot iron. This enabled the pigments to penetrate deeply into the wood. This technique was replaced by *secco*, or painting in tempera, in the seventh century.

The icons of the seventh to ninth centuries came from local workshops, chiefly Egyptian, Palestinian, Syrian and Cappadocian. After the Arab conquest these sources dried up, and were replaced by icons from workshops in Byzantium. During the Comnenian Age (1080–1200) the collection reflects the classicism of that period. Of the eleventh and twelfth centuries are the so-called *menologia* (icons which relate to the day honouring the saint they depict), exhibited in the church on a special pulpit. They are of several types: twelve large icons, each showing the saints of one month; two diptychs (with two wings that can be closed like a book), that between them comprise all the saints of the ecclesiastical year; a four-winged icon and a twelve-winged icon, with saints and martyrs standing in rows.

Sinaitic icons, of the twelfth to fifteenth centuries, are portrait icons of personages associated with the life of the monastery, abbots, monks, patriarchs and saints, often with the painter prostrate before a subject of veneration, the Virgin of the Burning Bush, Moses, St Catherine, and St John Climacus. There are many icons of the thirteenth century also, and of the Palaeologan Age, chiefly of large subjects.

The monastery has houses also in Crete, the Sinaitic Church of St Catherine at Herakleion and that of St Matthew at Candia, with the result that there is a splendid collection of post-Byzantine icons.

THE MOSAIC OF THE TRANSFIGURATION The most important artistic feature in the monastery is the Mosaic of the Transfiguration in the sanctuary of the Katholikon. It is of an unusual character. Christ is shown in glory in a mandorla (an almond-shaped panel) of greys and blues, in a white mantle edged with gold.

The site of the Burning Bush

The iconostasis in the Church of the Transfiguration

His halo has a gold cross on a white and gold backing. The successive elliptical circles within the mandorla crossed by seven lighter rays suggest supernatural light. To the left of Jesus is Elijah, and Moses is to the right; in a kneeling position, John is to the left, and James to the right; between them, at the feet of Christ, is Peter, in a deeply reverential obeisance. The rays from the mandorla touch each of them.

The inside rim of the arch is decorated with medallions of the twelve apostles, Paul, Thaddaeus and Matthias replacing the three in the centre of the composition. The base of the apse has another series of medallions, of seventeen prophets. There are also two terminal medallions: on the left is Abbot Longinus (562–565/6), thus dating the mosaic — he later became patriarch of Antioch; on the right is one John, a monk of Sinai, who is possibly John IV, patriarch of Jerusalem (575–594).

There are two flying angels on the wall between the arch and its surrounding framework; to the south is a bust of the Virgin, with St John the Baptist to the north. On the upper part of the wall are two scenes, Moses before the Burning Bush, and Moses receiving the Tablets of the Law. It is thought that the mosaic was the work of craftsmen from Constantinople.

LIBRARY The library contains some 4,500 manuscripts, chiefly in Greek, but also in Arabic, Armenian, Coptic, Georgian, Slavonic, Syriac and one in Latin. Its most precious manuscript, known as the Codex Sinaiticus, was 'borrowed' in 1859 by the German scholar K. von Tischendorf for the tzar of Russia. It was not returned, and in 1933 the Soviet Russian government sold it to the British Museum for $100,000. It is of the fourth century. The most ancient Gospel manuscript now in Sinai is the fifth century Codex Syriacus. Many of the manuscripts are illuminated with miniatures. There are also some 5,000 old editions of printed books, some dating from the turn of the fifteenth to the sixteenth century.

The Mosaic of the Transfiguration

ST CATHERINE   The greater part of St Catherine's relics, traditionally brought to Sinai by angels, are in the church. Some were taken to Europe by Symeon Metaphrastes, who wrote her biography, to Rouen in France and Trier in Germany. His work is called *The Martyrdom of the Great Martyr and in the Name of Christ Victorious St Catherine.* Eminent as a woman of encyclopaedic learning, in every branch of letters and science, at the beginning of the fourth century St Catherine challenged Emperor Maximinus as an idolater. The emperor ordered fifty philosophers to dispute with her, but they failed to persuade her to forsake her faith. The emperor ordered her to be broken on a spiked wheel, but even this failed, and finally he had her beheaded. She had a widespread cult in the East, and, after the tenth century, likewise in the West. Perhaps no saint has been more frequently painted by the great Italian masters.

Her feast day is kept both by Greeks and Latins on 25 November, the day of her martyrdom. The remains of the relics of the saint are in a marble chest of ancient date in the sanctuary behind the iconostasis. In 1688 the tzar sent a silver casket for them, but it has never been used.

THE MOSQUE   To the west of the church is a mosque, originally built as a hospice for pilgrims in the sixth century. It was converted into a mosque in 1106 at the request of Amir Anushtakin al-Amiri for the use of the Gebeliyyah, as the local Bedouins are called, the 'Men of the Mountain'.

Bibliography

A full bibliography of the Holy Land would occupy very many volumes. Only a select number of the more important works, chiefly those in English, can be mentioned here. The Bible is indispensable, and biblical references have been given frequently in the text. Encyclopedias, such as the *New Catholic Encyclopedia*, the *Encyclopedia of Islam*, and the *Encyclopedia of Judaica*, contain ample bibliographies within their own spheres. Outstanding in excellence is the *New Encyclopedia of Archaeological Excavations in the Holy Land*, ed. E. Stern (Jerusalem and New York, 1993), both for its text and its illustrations.

Among atlases are D. Bahat, *The Illustrated Atlas of Jerusalem* (Carta, 1990); *The Atlas of the Crusades*, ed. J. Riley-Smith (1990); and, for an overview, G.S.P. Freeman-Grenville, *Historical Atlas of the Middle East* (Carta, 1993). Among the ample archaeological literature Kathleen Kenyon, *The Bible and Recent Archaeology* (1978), still provides an invaluable introduction. For history at different times, the following are all safe guides: J. Bright, *History of Israel* (1967); E.M. Smallwood, *The Jews Under Roman Rule: from Pompey to Diocletian* (1976); S. Runciman, *History of the Crusades*, 3 vols. (1951 ff.); and the magisterial works of P.K. Hitti, *History of the Arabs* (1961), and *History of Syria including Lebanon and Palestine* (1951).

On particular subjects Geza Vermes, *The Dead Sea Scrolls: Qumran in Perspective* (1977), provides an admirable introduction to what has become a vast and controversial literature.

For the Arabs, G. Le Strange, *Palestine Under the Moslems* (1890; reprinted 1965), contains the majority of relevant Arabic texts in translation, to which now must be added *Bayt al-Maqdis: Abd al-Malik's Jerusalem*, eds. J. Raby and J. Johns, Part I (1992) — Part II not being available at the time of going to press — with further texts from Georgian and Greek. An outstanding achievement of modern scholarship is J.W. Allan's updating of K.A.C. Cresswell, *A Short Account of Early Muslim Architecture* (1988), of which the original appeared in Penguin Books in 1958. It is as important for Jordanian buildings as it is for Israel.

For Jordan, useful essays are collected in *Treasures from an Ancient Land: The Art of Jordan*, ed. P. Bienkowski (1991), each essay with its own bibliography. In the past twenty years J. Wilkinson has greatly advanced our knowledge of pilgrim literature, with *Egeria's Travels*, 2nd ed. (1981), *Jerusalem Pilgrims Before the Crusades* (1977), and *Jerusalem Pilgrimage, 1099–1185* (Hakluyt Society, 1988). The Franciscan Printing Press, Jerusalem, publishes an annual catalogue free of charge, which covers much in this and related fields.

A critical study of the Holy Places, from Scripture, the Fathers, and from historical documents and archaeology, is Clemens Kopp, *The Holy Places of the Gospels* (1962), regrettably out of print and meriting being brought up to date.

On the Holy Sepulchre, V.C. Corbo, *Il Santo Sepolcro*, 3 vols. (1982), of which two are of plans and photographs, has greatly enhanced knowledge. It did not discuss the Tomb of Christ. Martin Biddle, 'The Tomb of Christ: Sources, Methods and a New Approach', in K. Painter, *Churches Built in Ancient Times: Recent Studies in Early Christian Archaeology* (Society of Antiquaries of London, 1994), is a major achievement of detailed scholarship, of which the technical results are still being studied under M.A.R. Cooper in the City University, London. Discussion of the Garden Tomb as the supposed Tomb of Christ has been brought to a conclusion by A. Kloner, 'The "Third Wall" in Jerusalem and the "Cave of the Kings" ', *Levant* (1986), pp. 121–130.

Little attention has been paid to the art treasures of the Jerusalem churches. B. Narkis, *Armenian Art Treasures of Jerusalem* (1979), is of especial interest, as is the study of the splendid display of tiles in the Armenian Cathedral of St James by J. Carswell and C.J.F. Dowsett, *Kutayha Tiles and Pottery from the Armenian Cathedral of St James*, 2 vols. (Jerusalem, 1972).

For the Greek Orthodox church, B. Tzaferis, *The Holy Places* (1987), has a splendid collection of coloured illustrations for the whole region. Not less splendid is the publication of the monks of Sinai themselves, Athanasios Paliouras, *The Monastery of St Catherine on Mount Sinai* (1985), available in various languages. The monastery is notable for its collection of icons not less than its manuscript collection. For the icons, K. Weitzmann, *The Monastery of St Catherine at Mount Sinai: the Icons from the Sixth to the Tenth Century* (Princeton, 1976, 1981), is the best account.

Among earlier guides, E. Hoade, *Guide to the Holy Land*, 10th ed. (1979), and that to Jordan (1982), both by Franciscan fathers, deserve mention. At a different level are two works by H.F.M. Prescott, *Jerusalem Journey: Pilgrimage to the Holy Land in the Fifteenth Century* (1954), and *Once to Sinai* (1957), recounting the adventures of Fr Felix Faber, OFM; and Stephen Graham's incomparable *With the Russian Pilgrims to Jerusalem* (1913); while H.V. Morton, *In the Steps of the Master* (1934), remains unequalled for its felicity of description.

Outside Europe no country other than Jordan has so remarkable a host of mosaics both religious and secular, as described in M. Piccirillo, OFM, *The Mosaics of Jordan* (1994). For the same country, R.G. Khouri, *The Jordan Valley: Life and Society between Sea Level* (1981), is a valuable discussion of the unique problems of the Jordan Valley. His ten small pamphlets, published at different times, on Jordanian historical sites, are models of their kind.

INDEX TO PLACE NAMES

Page numbers in italics refer to maps and illustrations or their captions.
The Arabic definite articles (el-, en-, et-, etc.) are disregarded in
the alphabetical listing.